# BIRDS OF INDIA

### Bangladesh, Nepal, Pakistan & Shri Lanka

*For*
**Nikhat** *and* **Samiha**
*who made all the difference*
*and for*
**Shobita**
*who made it possible*

# BIRDS OF INDIA

**Bangladesh, Nepal, Pakistan & Shri Lanka**
A photographic guide

## Bikram Grewal

Sunjoy Monga   Gillian Wright

Published by the Guidebook Company Limited, Hong Kong in conjunction with Gulmohur Press Pvt. Limited, New Delhi.

Project Editor: Toby Sinclair
Illustrations Editor: Caroline Robertson
Design: Gulmohur Press, New Delhi
Map Artwork: Bai Yilang

Produced by Twin Age Limited, Hong Kong


Printed in China


ISBN: 962-217-311-X

# ACKNOWLEDGEMENTS

The authors and the Publishers would like to thank the following people for their help in making this book possible.

Sumeela Rawat, Ashish Madan, Rattan Singh, Bittu Sahgal, Ayesha Billimoria, Kamal Sahai, Lt Gen. RK Gaur, Radhika Singh, Hashim Tyabji, Oliver Sinclair, Dr GS Monga, Prof. Ravin Monga, Jyoti Monga, Vinod Haritwal, Joslin Rodriques, Caroline Robertson, Celine Antony, Digant Desai, Reuben Israel, Krupakar Senani, MK Kuppuraj, Humayun Abdulali, Kavita Nagpal, Zafar Futehally, Premlata Punja, Surit Mitra, Narender Kumar, Dr. AG Urfi, Tania Sood, Manju Dubey, Kunal Nayyar, Joanna Van Gruisen, Ashok Dilwali, Ashish Chandola, Rajinder Bist, Ganga Grewal, Durgi Devi, KK Singh, S Deb Roy, Naomi Meadows, Nihar Barua, Anita Grewal, Baldev Singh, Ramesh Punja, Probal Barua, AS Rawat, RS Rawat, Mark Tully, Tim and Carol Inskipp, AS Negi, Harak Singh, Tara Sahgal, Geoff Cloke and Magnus Bartlett.

*Great Crested Grebe*

# Contents

# INTRODUCTION

The Indian region is incredibly rich in birdlife. Over 1200 of the world's 8650 species of birds are found in the region. This number rises to over 2000 with sub species included, which makes the Indian check-list twice the size of those of Europe and North America. This abundance is due to the variety of habitats and climate. Altitude ranges from sea level to the peaks of the Himalaya, the world's highest mountain range; rainfall from its lowest in the Rajasthan desert to its highest in the north-eastern town of Cherrapunji in Meghalaya, one of the wettest places in the world. Unlike more temperate zones, the climate of large areas of the Indian region encourages continuous plant growth and insect activity—abundant sources of avian nourishment throughout the year.

The peoples of the region have lived for thousands of years in close contact with its rich natural life. The earliest Hindu religious work, the *Rig Veda*, refers to some twenty species of birds, but its anonymous compilers must have been familiar with many more. Legends and myths grew around certain familiar species. The Brahminy Duck, for example, became the symbol of fidelity; the pairs mating for life, separating from one another at night to feed but keeping in contact by calls, and then reuniting at dawn. The *chataka*, either the Hawk Cuckoo or the Pied Crested Cuckoo, was said to drink only rainwater, no matter how thirsty it was. The Sanskrit poet Kalidasa, frequently uses bird imagery in his plays and poetry. His *Meghdoot* is a sensuous poem about a lover exiled from his beloved in the monsoon, traditionally the season for passion and romance among humans, and in fact the time when large water birds like storks, cormorants, egrets and cranes breed. Addressing a storm cloud the lover says,

> hen-cranes will know the time ripe for mating
> and rejoice when they note in the sky
> your eye-delighting presence; rest assured
> they will attend on you in patterned flight.

*Jewelled peacock, in the Golden Temple treasury, Amritsar*

*Blue-throated Barbet credited to*
*Mansur, c. 1615*

Not only poets, rulers too, expressed interest in ornithology. The great Mughals maintained royal menageries
and revelled in hunting on a grand scale. But they were
also meticulous in their observations of wildlife. In the
16th century, Babar, the first Mughal Emperor, observed
his first Pied Myna.

> When I threw a bridge over the Ganges and crossed it,
> driving the enemy before me, I saw in Lucknow, Oudh
> and these countries a species of *sharak* which has a white
> breast and a piebald head with a black back. I had never
> seen it before. This species probably does not learn to
> speak at all.

Babar's keen interest in nature was inherited by his son
Humayun, who even when fleeing India after being
defeated by an Afghan invader, stopped to have a painting
made of a bird of a type he had never seen before which
happened to fly into his tent. The Emperor Jehangir noted
with amazement the devotion of a Sarus Crane to its dead
mate. The bird refused to leave the bones of its spouse, and
when, weak and dying, it was lifted from the remains,
worms and maggots were found to have dug into its
breast.

The Mughal empire began to disintegrate at the beginning of the 18th century, and the spread of British power
gave enormous scope to officers in the police, civil, forest
and armed services to observe the region's plentiful bird
life. As British power grew, there were increasing numbers
of such officers, whose jobs required much less crippling
paperwork than those of their successors today. The result
was the pioneering work of Brian Hodgson, TC Jerdon and
Edward Blyth, often called the founders of Indian or_nitho-
logy. Jerdon's *Birds of India*, published in 1862, was based
on the work of all three men, assisted by a loyal group of
field workers.

The next major advance in ornithological knowledge
came with the arrival of Allan O Hume—perhaps more
widely known as a founder of the Indian National Con-
gress. For over a decade he and his team collected birds for
study over most of the Indian region. Hume also collected,
edited and published eleven volumes of bird observations
between 1872 and 1888. These volumes, collectively
known as *Stray Feathers*, are valuable reference works even
today.

A year after the last *Stray Feathers* was published, WT Blandford and Eugene W Oates produced the first volume of *Fauna of British India*. Three more volumes were published in the following nine years. These were the most significant reference works on Indian ornithology for at least twenty years. They included detailed observations from parts of the Indian region uncovered by previous work.

The next major work was by EC Stuart Baker, an Indian police officer for nearly twenty years, whose energetic enthusiasm for ornithology played an important role in popularising this branch of natural history study in India. In 1898 he joined the Bombay Natural History Society (BNHS), which had been gaining members and authority steadily since it was founded in 1883. Some of Baker's classic early work appeared first in the journal of the BNHS, including *Game Birds of India*. But Bakers's most notable works are the eight bird volumes of the second edition of *Fauna of British India*, published between 1922 and 1930, and the *Nidification of Birds of the Indian Empire*, published between 1932 and 1935.

*Brahminy Duck*

*Indian Postal Stamps, 1975*

The twentieth century saw an increasing number of talented and dedicated ornithologists in India—but the most celebrated and long lasting ornithological partnership was between Salim Ali and Dillon Ripley. Salim Ali's interest in birds resulted from a boyhood visit to the office of the Bombay Natural History Society with the corpse of a strange bird which he had shot. As he himself recalls,

> This must have been somewhere in 1908, and my first contact with the BNHS which was to become such an important element in the shaping of my life and career. All my nervousness vanished completely in the face of the charming kindliness...of Mr Millard [the Honorary Secretary]. I then realized that perhaps ALL white men were not the dogs our youthful fancy had painted them...I fumbled out my credentials and the little paper packet containing the mystery bird. He identified it at a glance as a Yellowthroated Sparrow, and bid me follow him to the reference cabinets...He patiently opened drawer after drawer for me to see the hundreds of different birds found in the Indian Empire, and I believe it was at this moment that my curiosity about birds really clicked.

The Yellowthroated Sparrow showed Salim Ali his way forward in life and in 1944 he met a young US army man in transit through Bombay, who was to be his colleague, fellow-ornithologist and explorer. Dillon Ripley and Salim Ali planned ornithological field-trips for the post-war years, the first to be achieved being a journey to the Mishmi Hills in the extreme north-east of Assam. It was on this trip that they conceived the idea of their *Handbook of the Birds of India and Pakistan*. The first step towards compiling a handbook was an up-to-date checklist, provided by Ripley's *A Synopsis of the Birds of India and Pakistan* published by the BNHS in 1961. The first volume of the Handbook was published in 1968, and the tenth and last in 1974, four days after Salim Ali's seventy-eighth birthday.

The Handbook, listing 2060 birds, remains the standard and most exhaustive work on Indian birds as such, which is why in this photoguide we have kept to Dillon Ripley's numbering system. What this guide aims to provide for the first time is a valuable aid to field identification through photographic illustrations of a large number of the region's birds.

# Oriental and Sub-regions

In the 19th century, PL Sclater studied the world's birds and divided the planet into six bio-geographic realms. This was later slightly modified to apply to all animals. The Oriental realm covers South and South East Asia, the Himalaya separating it from the Palearctic to the north. Leafbirds are found exclusively in this region and broadbills nearly so. In general the region's birds have closest affinities with those of tropical Africa.

The Indian sub-region has further been divided into seven different areas, in which different types of birds are found.

*Western Himalaya*

The northernmost of these areas is the **Himalaya**, which form an arc some 2500 kilometres long and 150 to 400 kilometres broad across the top of the sub-continent. The Himalayan mountains form roughly three parts, the foothills or Sivaliks to the south, the Himachal, or lower mountains, and the Himadri or high Himalaya to the north. The Ladakh plateau, with an average elevation of 5300 metres, occupies a large portion of the Indian state of Jammu and Kashmir and consists of steppe country with mountain lakes where birds like the Bar-headed Goose and Brown-headed Gull breed in summer. The state of Himachal Pradesh, and the Kumaon and Garhwal regions of the state of Uttar Pradesh lie to the west of Nepal, which falls almost entirely within the central Himalaya. Further east the rainfall increases giving the Eastern Himalaya of Bhutan and Sikkim a very different range of species from those in the west.

*Bank Myna community*

The **north west** covers the bulk of Pakistan, the flat plains of the Indian Punjab and the semi-arid and arid plains of Rajasthan in the west. The Punjab (divided now between India and Pakistan) is watered by the five rivers, after which it takes its name, and efficient farming on fertile soil means that it produces an immense surplus of wheat and rice. Further west, wherever irrigation has been possible the desert has bloomed. Mountains of red chillies, for example, can been seen drying next to the fields around Jodhpur, while there are verdant paddy fields in areas irrigated by the great River Indus in Pakistan's Sindh province. Areas without irrigation have to rely on the perennially deficient rainfall, but local grasses have adapted to this, and after a monsoon shower even the desert sprouts rich pasture. Much of the area is in fact thorn scrub rather than true desert. Among the numerous desert birds found in this area are many which are related to species further west. The shifting sands of the desert join ultimately with the Rann of Kutch, a large salt waste which runs into the sea, and are bordered to the south-east by the Aravallis, India's most ancient mountains.

**North India** comprises the Gangetic plain, enriched by thousands of years of alluvial deposits brought by the River Ganga and her tributaries from the Himalaya. The Gangetic plain is densely populated and highly fertile. This region extends up to an altitude of 1000 metres in the north, which also means it includes the low foothills of the Himalaya, and the terai of India and Nepal, once a marshy area covered with dense forest. Much of the terai area has been cleared for farming but some of the forests which still exist reveal the fantastic variety of birdlife which these forests must once have supported.

**Peninsular India**, bordered on the north-west by the Aravallis and the north by the Vindhya mountains, on the west by the Arabian Sea and the east by the Bay of Bengal, makes up the largest physiographic division of India. The

*Mixed heronry*

central plateaus of this area, which is also known as the Deccan, rise to over 1000 metres in the south, but hardly exceed 500 metres in the north. The peninsula has some wonderful landscapes, hills and huge boulders littering the countryside, and large areas of forest. Great rivers like the Narmada rise in the heart of the peninsula and flow into the sea. The steep escarpments of the Western Ghats, the mountains which stand between the plateau and the low-lying coastal strip, catch the full force of the monsoon.

The **south west** region lies within the peninsula, but due to the particularly humid climate and the height of the hills here, its birds, like spiderhunters and laughing thrushes bear strong affinities with those found in the north-east and Burma. The highest of the hills here are the Nilgiris or Blue Mountains, much of whose characteristic downland and shola forest is now under eucalyptus, tea and other plantation crops. Tea is also the main crop of the Annamalai or Elephant Mountains of Kerala, while cardamom and other spices are grown lower down. Perhaps the most ornithologically fascinating part of this area are the forests of the Wynad, where Kerala, Karnataka and Tamil Nadu meet.

The **north east** and **Bangladesh** region consists of the delta of the Ganga and Brahmaputra, with its tidal

*Central Indian grasslands*

estuaries, sandbanks, mud-flats, mangrove swamps and islands. Further upstream are lands drained, and occasionally flooded, by these great rivers and their tributaries. The north-east region also extends northwards to include all the forest regions of the states of Arunachal Pradesh, Mizoram, Meghalaya and Nagaland, as well as the Kingdom of Bhutan. As you progress eastwards, the birdlife has increasingly strong affinities with the Indo-Chinese sub-region.

**Shri Lanka** is a remarkable area for birdlife. Although far from large, the country has a wide range of climate and habitat which supports some 400 species and sub-species of birds, including 21 species like the Ceylon Blue Magpie found nowhere else. Many of the island's birds are identical to those found in India, although for some reason vultures have not been able to cross the Palk Straits. Shri Lanka can be divided into three zones, the dry plains of the north, the mountainous central region, and the humid wet zone around the capital Colombo. The most useful detailed work exclusively dealing with Shri Lankan ornithology is GM Henry's *A Guide to the Birds of Ceylon*.

*Godwits, west coast of India*

# Habitat

While many common species are spread over large areas of the Oriental realm, others are limited not just to a region but also to habitat. Some birds of the conifer forests of the hills will be found only there, while grassland birds may be restricted to that habitat.

*Parakeets, urban garden*

As the sub-continent has a very dense human population, birds which get on well with man flourish. These are not limited to house sparrows, crows and house martins. Indian culture has traditionally respected all forms of life and protected birds before sanctuaries and parks were ever thought of. India's only resident crane, the Sarus, is left unharmed no matter how much of a farmer's pea crop it consumes. The Peacock has in areas a semi-sacred status, which is why it is found in large numbers undisturbed. The Red Junglefowl has a long history of association with man and is the ancestor of the domestic chicken.

City gardens are homes for many species, including tailorbirds, sunbirds, white-eyes, babblers, and the ubiquitous myna. Other birds take advantage of cultivation techniques; especially pond herons, who often take up position in paddy fields practising what villagers call *bagla bhakti*— supreme hypocrisy, sitting like a holy man lost in meditation, but in fact just waiting to stab something in the back. Dabchicks or Little Grebes also take up residence in village ponds, while garbage is in great demand by vultures and the pariah kites which along with pariah dogs haunt the rubbish heaps of the sub-continent.

Shallow lagoons, inland jheels or shallow lakes, and rivers are rich habitats for water birds from pelicans, storks, cranes, egrets and cormorants to the jacanas and gallinules among the lotuses, and the waders picking their way along the water's edge probing for food. Huge numbers of migratory waterfowl also congregate at jheels during the winter months. Other birds, like bitterns, conceal themselves among reed beds. Numerous birds of prey can be found near water. The attractive Brahminy Kite is particularly adaptable. It can be seen from the lakes of north India to the sea coasts of the south.

Many birds of the coast are distinctive. Typical is the Indian Reef Heron, seldom found far inland, which feeds on molluscs and crustaceans.

In the more arid inland areas are found larks, chats, sandgrouse and the rare Great Indian Bustard, a stunning bird seen in small flocks which fly into land like great avian aircraft. Desert birds tend to be sandy in colouration. which helps to camouflage them.

Forest birds are more difficult to spot especially when they are concealed in the tree canopy. However they can often be seen in clearings flying from tree to tree or on the edge of forests where the sun can penetrate and there is a great deal of insect activity. Often assorted species form hunting parties and move together through the forest. So in one place you can see woodpeckers, warblers, tits and tree creepers. Often birds can be located and identified through their calls. Here it is also worth noting that Oriental forests are home to many more birds that those nearer either pole. A tropical forest can hold more than 200 bird species at more than 5000 pairs per kilometre, but a northern forest may hold less than 20 species at 200 individuals per kilometre.

*Narcondam Hornbills*

## Adaptation

The most outstanding way that birds have adapted is, of course, the conversion of their upper limbs into wings, the growth of feathers and the ability to fly. Plumage is further adapted depending on habitat and habits. The feathers of cormorants and snakebirds get drenched to allow them to swim under water, but other birds effectively coat their feathers with oil from oil glands to waterproof them. Plumage and body shape is adapted for specialised flight. Owl feathers are so formed as to give silent flight. Built especially for speed is the Peregrine Falcon, which swoops on its prey from a great height.

Colouring is also an important adaptation. Camouflage is seen for example in sandgrouse, snipe, bitterns, owls and nightjars.

*Shaheen Falcon*

Teeth would weigh down the head of any bird wanting to fly efficiently, and so over the past 100 million years birds have lost them and instead developed gizzards. The gizzard is situated near a bird's centre of gravity. Birds gulp food down into their crop from where it is ground down in the muscular gizzard with the aid of grit and small stones the birds swallow. The ability to disgorge indigestible bones, fur, insect shells or large seeds in the form of pellets is another form of adaptation.

Birds have developed specialised bills and feet for feeding. The most generalized bill perhaps belongs to the omnivorous crow. It is straight, pointed and roughly triangular in section. Birds like herons and kingfishers have more dagger-like bills, suitable for catching fish and frogs. Not all kingfishers need water for their fishing. One of the secrets of the White-breasted Kingfisher's ubiquity is that it can live on insects, lizards and other small terrestrial animals. Other accomplished fish-catchers like cormorants have 'tooth-edged' bills with which they can grip fish.

*Flowering silk-cotton*

Dabbling ducks have widened bills with laminations on the edges of the upper and lower mandibles. This adaptation is especially necessary for plankton-sieving shovellers, and the larger spoonbills and flamingoes. Shore birds have thin, elongated bills for probing the mud in search for small animals.

Birds of prey have developed deeper, shorter and down-curved bills for tearing and piercing flesh. But for them perhaps the most important piece of hunting equipment is their feet. They rely on the strength of their talons to kill.

Most species of birds are animal-eating, but most animals eaten are small invertebrates, in particular insects. Birds like swallows, martins and nightjars catch insects on the wing with wide gapes that scoop in their victims. Many other insects are caught on the plants on which they themselves feed. Small insectivorous birds like warblers have fine pointed beaks for collecting them. Woodpeckers, on the other hand, have strong, dagger-shaped bills, for chiselling wood and prising insects from crevices and beneath bark.

Flowering plants also support a great number of birds, and just as birds have adapted to feeding on flowers, trees and plants too have adapted themselves to being fed on. In 1932 Salim Ali wrote on *Flower-Birds and Bird-Flowers*. He listed as characteristics of the bird-flower that pollenisation is possible only through birds, that they have bright and conspicuous colours (red being a bird's favourite) and no scent (as birds have a very poorly developed sense of smell), but they do have an abundant supply of nectar. Typical bird-flowers of this sort can be seen on the spectacular silk-cotton tree *bombax malabaricum*, which is covered with waxy red or orange blooms around mid-February. Typical flower-birds are sunbirds, which have long, down-curved bills for drinking nectar.

A much larger number of bird species feeds on the fruit and seeds of plants and trees. Finches have stout beaks built for seed crushing, while barbets and fruit-eating thrushes both have large gapes for swallowing berries whole.

## Habits—Feeding and Breeding

Breeding is related very much to food supply. As large areas of the Oriental region provide more abundant food to more birds for a longer period than in more temperate zones, this means the breeding period can be longer.

Large birds of prey breed between October and March, while large water birds like storks, cormorants, egrets and ibis, nest in colonies during the monsoon. This is also the period when munias and weaver birds breed. The peak breeding season for other common birds is February to May, although hill birds nest even later.

During the breeding season males of many species produce long and complicated sounds called birdsong. Songs must be differentiated from the calls that birds of both sexes make throughout the year which are much simpler and used in a variety of circumstances, for example to express alarm, to threaten, to beg for food and so on. It should also be distinguished from the mechanical noises birds make, clattering of the bill or clapping of the wings, for similar reasons.

Once you are familiar with the song of a particular species, it is possible to identify it immediately by its voice. Not surprisingly, birds too use song to identify themselves to one another, and to attract mates. In species which aggressively defend a territory, it is still debatable how much song is used simply to attract females, and to what degree it serves to demarcate the male's domain. The matter is complicated further by the fact that females are probably most attracted by the male with the largest territory. The size of territory varies enormously. In species which breed in colonies, it extends just a few feet around the nest.

If song is important in finding a mate, so are courtship displays. The peacock is blessed with a powerful though

*Weaver-bird nest*

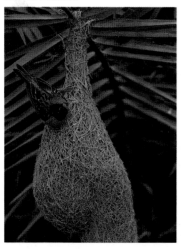

unmellifluous voice, but makes up for this by the male's unmatched courtship display. The peacock stamps and turns with his tail outspread before a number of females. Even birds which pair for life are known to display. In the breeding season Sarus Cranes frequently break into a striking dance, spreading their wings, lowering their heads and leaping into the air, trumpeting loudly all the while. Other birds indulge in less spectacular rituals, like making gifts of food to one another.

Courtship culminates in mating, with the male mounting the female. The male's testes are internal and make up only a tiny fraction of the bird's bodyweight, as little as 0.005 per cent, outside the breeding season. During the breeding season the testes increase up to a thousandfold in weight. In most birds there is a small erectile phallus, but this is well developed and protrusible in only a few species like ducks and geese. The female's ovaries are also contained in her body cavity, and fertilisation of an egg generally takes place once it leaves the ovary and passes down towards the shell gland where the outer layer of the egg becomes calcified to form the shell. Most females can store live sperm in their body and so fertilisation can take place some time after mating.

*Nesting Crested Serpent Eagle*

*Victorian painting of eggs*

Eggs are laid in the nest the pair has previously prepared. These vary from rough scrapes in the ground, as with plovers, to the holes in river banks tunnelled by kingfishers, the large untidy nests of vultures, and the elaborate nests of weaver birds often seen suspended in groups of ten or more from palms and other trees. The male weaver bird is a master of the nest-building art. Each male of a colony laboriously tears off strips of grass or leaves and proceeds to construct a retort-shaped nest, complete with entrance tunnel and egg chamber. When the nests are well under construction, the hen-birds arrive and set up house in whichever nest takes their fancy. When the nest is complete and the eggs laid, the male takes off to build another nest and attract another female.

Hornbills nest in holes in trees and are unique in imprisoning the female within the nest behind a mud wall, leaving open a gap just large enough for the male to pass her food. Not all birds form pairs. Some babblers breed communally with different females laying eggs in the same nest.

Eggs also vary in size, colour, shape and number. Those which require camouflage are well-mottled, although most are pigmented. Cuckoos parasitic on others' nests lay eggs which resemble those of the host species. In the case of Hawk-Cuckoos and Pied Crested Cuckoos, these are babblers.

Hatchlings require different amounts of care from their parents. Songbird chicks, for example, are born naked, while gamebirds are born with feathers and are soon running after their parents. Most young birds have characteristic begging behaviour, and in many species parents have been observed to give them a diet richer in protein than their own normal diet, to promote their offspring's growth.

As the young gain their full plumage, the adults generally begin to moult. Feathers are shed and re-grown in a distinct pattern, generally beginning with the first flight feathers and ending with the replacement of the last. Moulting is necessary as feathers do wear out. Species which have distinct breeding and non-breeding plumage moult twice a year, while in larger birds, such as eagles, a moult may take two to three years to complete. In short, individual birds shed feathers according to their needs. Migratory birds, for example, never moult at the time of migration.

# Migration

Many species migrate locally or over long distances to avoid adverse climatic conditions and in search of food. Hundreds of thousands of waterfowl migrate each winter to India from central and northern Asia, covering huge distances. Smaller winter migrants include wagtails, warblers and bluethroats. The huge number of wintering birds also accounts for the large numbers of wintering ornithologists and bird enthusiasts who visit the sub-continent over these months.

Summer visitors are much fewer. The multi-coloured Indian Pitta is one such bird well worth searching out. It winters in south India and Sri Lanka, and visits the deciduous forest and scrubland of the Himalayan foothills and the north-west around May, staying until it has bred.

Scientists have still to discover exactly how birds navigate during migration, although it is clear that they have a number of means to do so. Apart from sighting landmarks, it has been proved that birds make use of an internal magnetic compass and of the position of the sun and stars. It is also thought that sound and smell may play a role. The Siberian Crane is one bird which finds its way every year from Siberia to the same square kilometre of wetland in the Keoladeo Ghana National Park at Bharatpur in Rajasthan.

*Black-necked Cranes*

## Classification

As with other animals birds are classified into orders, families, genera and species. Each genus consists of a number of species which are obviously closely related. The first of a bird's two or three Latin names is that of its genus, and the second describes the species, while a third is used for sub-species. A species is a population of birds with a distinct identity which does not interbreed with other bird populations. Where there is a constant variation in a species, it is called a sub-species. Each bird of this region has been numbered by Dillon Ripley in his synopsis. In this guide we have followed his numbering system.

## Birdwatching

Birdwatching is a way not only of learning about birds, but a channel for study of the natural world as a whole. The immense variety of birdlife in the Oriental region, and the large size and colourful plumage of many species makes it an especially attractive occupation. As you observe bird behaviour you cannot fail to notice how the changing seasons affect plant and insect life too.

*Merganser chicks*

Birdwatching is also simple for the beginner to take up as it requires no special equipment, although binoculars are a great help in identification.

To see birds most easily you should be quiet, careful and inconspicuous. It is best to wear subdued colours, to walk slowly and make use of cover such as banks, trees and bushes. It is often a good idea to take up position on the edge of a forest clearing or near a fruiting tree and let the birds come to you. Lakes and jheels are also good locations for observation. Carry a notebook so that you can jot down details of any bird you can't immediately identify and then check your descriptions against those in a guide.

This guide in particular is designed as an aid to field identification and aims to help everyone from the newest of enthusiasts to the habitual birdwatcher. We have drawn on the vast reserve of scholarship on sub-continental birdlife carried out by Salim Ali, Dillon Ripley and so many others.

Each bird description begins with the species number, followed by the common English name, the scientific name and size. Sizes of birds stated are approximate and generally taken from the tip of the bill to the end of the tail. Then follows a description of the plumage of both male and female birds, along with any seasonal variations. We have also noted any behaviour which helps easy identification. The final entries list the bird's food, voice, range and habitat.

Common names of birds are often being revised. Readers will note that in certain cases birds have more than one name. We have given the names which are most commonly used in the sub-continent. However, to help readers who may be more familiar with other names a list of alternate names has been provided on pages 186–187.

*Jerdon's Courser*

# Vanishing Birds

One of the most significant and exciting achievements of Indian ornithology in recent years was the rediscovery of Jerdon's Courser in 1986. In *The Handbook of the Birds of India,* Salim Ali said that the last 'authentic record was in 1900, since when thorough search by competent ornithologists has failed to rediscover it'. **Jerdon's** or **Doublebanded Courser** *Rhinoptilus (Cursorius) bitorquatus* was first recorded by Dr TC Jerdon, an Indian Army Medical Officer, in 1848. Blandford recorded it in 1867 and 1871 and the last record was by Howard Campbell in 1900. Always a rare bird, these few sightings were restricted to the Penner and Godavari river valleys of Andhra Pradesh, to the north-west of Madras. Despite surveys by outstanding ornithologists such as Whistler and Kinnear in 1929 and 1931, by Salim Ali in 1932 and post-war surveys by the Bombay Natural History Society (BNHS) along the Godavari river, no birds were sighted. Salim Ali, however, was not convinced.

In 1985, under a joint Government of India and US Government sponsored Endangered Species Project carried out by the BNHS, Bharat Bhushan, a young BNHS scientist, surveyed the dry scrub covered hill country where Jerdon first recorded the bird. In January 1986, the species was rediscovered.

Jerdon's Courser is a nocturnal and crepuscular species found in open patches within scrub, bordering the dry deciduous forest of the region. Bharat Bhushan has identified six sites in the Lankamalai hills and suitable habitat in two valleys is restricted to about 2000 sq km. The timing of the rediscovery was providential as a month later it was realised that an irrigation scheme to take water from the large Nagarjunasagar lake to Madras would destroy the area. A large channel would have been built through the exact discovery site. Fortunately, BNHS lobbyed hard and with support from the Andhra Pradesh Forest Department the State Government was able to realign the proposed canal.

Since the rediscovery, the area has been gazetted as the Sri Lankamalleswara Wildlife Sanctuary covering 464 sq km. The sanctuary has an interesting policy of employing local tribes as protectors of the area. To the south the 353 square kilometre Sri Venkateswara National Park has been gazetted in the Palakonda forest area, while to the east there is a proposal to declare another 1300 sq km of the Velikonda forests as a Wildlife Sanctuary. All these areas are potential habitat for the courser but are also home to many other species including the golden gecko that was also rediscovered in the 1980s, the dwarf palm and the red sandalwood tree *Perocarpus marsupium*.

Three other bird species that have not been recorded for the last seventy years are the **Pink-headed Duck** *Rhodenessa caryophyllacea*, the

**Himalayan Mountain Quail** *Ophrysia superciliosa* and the **Forest Spotted Owlet** *Athene blewitti.* Despite rumours as late as the 1960s, it seems the last Pink-headed Duck has been extinct in the wild since about 1926. Originally thinly distributed through the wetlands, swamps and wilderness areas that formed around the confluence of the Ganga and Brahmaputra rivers in the vast plains of Bengal and what is now Bangladesh. The reed beds along the river banks have long since been cleared by the burgeoning human population and the isolated enclosed waters that were home to the ducks have mostly disappeared. Little is known about the Pink-headed Duck and only a few skins exist in museum collections around the world. Local sportsmen hunted and shot the bird, but it was never popular eating. In the early years of this century a few birds would be regularly found in the markets of Calcutta but as these became less frequent naturalists began to become concerned. In 1924 an expedition searched various areas of Bengal but failed to see a single specimen. A few reports in the last fifty years may have confused this species with the **Red-crested Pochard** *Netta rufina* with which it has a superficial resemblance. The Pink-headed Duck has, as its name suggests, a bright pink head and neck with a dull brown body except for a pink speculum. It is probable that the last living specimen died around 1935 in a private collection in England.

Even less is known about the Himalayan Mountain Quail which was first reported in 1846 and has not been seen since 1876. Always a difficult bird to flush, Salim Ali believed a small population may have escaped detection in what remains of the forested mountain areas of the western

*Pink-headed Duck*

Himalaya. The few specimens that were collected during the last century were found between 1500 and 1850 metres in the hills around Mussoorie in Uttar Pradesh. The last specimen was collected near Nainital, a little further east. Judging by their thick, soft plumage it has been suggested that they spent the summers at much higher altitudes and only spent the winters in the Himalayan foothills.

*Himalayan Mountain Quail*

The third bird from the Indian sub-continent that has almost certainly become extinct in the last hundred years is the Forest Spotted Owlet. The last specimen was collected by the eccentric ornithologist Richard Meinertzhagen in October 1914 while on an expedition along the Tapti river, north-east of Bombay, and near what is now the Melghat Tiger Reserve. The Owlet was apparently found in the heavy moist deciduous forests along the entire length of the Satpura mountains. Very little is known about its habits since the bird was first collected in 1873.

The rediscovery of Jerdon's Courser in 1986 vindicated Salim Ali's belief that the bird may have survived the enormous pressures placed on India's wilderness. He also hoped the Mountain Quail and Forest Owlet might be 'rediscovered' but despite efforts over the last ten years no reports have been received. It is however still possible that the thick mountain forests of Bhutan and Arunachal Pradesh in the eastern Himalaya may offer a new species or sub-species to the ornithologist at the beginning of the 21st century. It is also possible that the little known areas of the eastern ghats where the courser was found, may also yield a new bird to science.

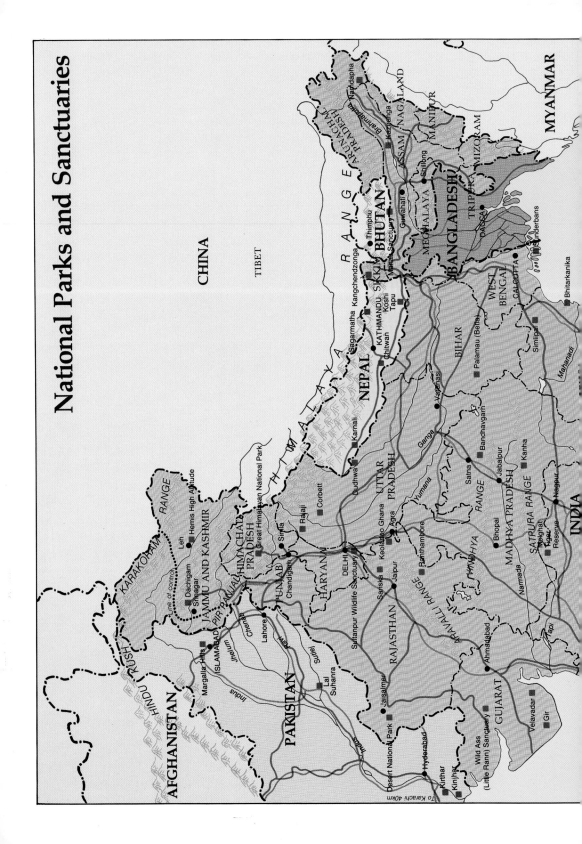

# National Parks and Sanctuaries

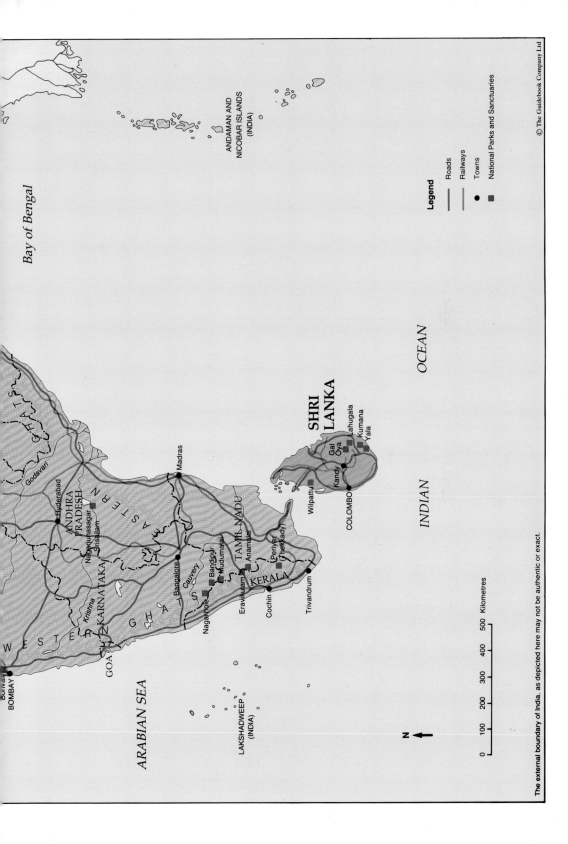

Bay of Bengal

ANDAMAN AND
NICOBAR ISLANDS
(INDIA)

ANDHRA
PRADESH

Godavari

Hyderabad

Nagarjunasagar

Srisailam

Krishna

KARNATAKA

Madras

TAMIL NADU

Bangalore

Cauvery

Bandipur

Mudumalai

Anamalai

Periyar
(Thekkady)

KERALA

Nagarhole

Eravikulam

Cochin

Trivandrum

SHRI
LANKA

Wilpattu

Kandy

Gal
Oya

Lahugala

Kumana

Yala

COLOMBO

INDIAN

OCEAN

WESTERN

GOA

GHATS

EASTERN GHATS

ARABIAN SEA

LAKSHADWEEP
(INDIA)

BOMBAY

Borivali

N

| 0 | 100 | 200 | 300 | 400 | 500 | Kilometres |

**Legend**

Roads

Railways

● Towns

■ National Parks and Sanctuaries

*Rare Albino Kingfisher* Alcedoathis *Bharatpur, 1992*

**(5) LITTLE GREBE** *Podiceps ruficollis* 22cm. Sexes alike. India's smallest water-bird, squat and tailless. Plumage silky and compact; dark brown above; white in flight feathers; white abdomen. **Breeding:** chestnut sides of head, neck and throat; black chin; blackish-brown crown, hindneck. **Winter:** white chin; brown crown, hind-neck; rufous neck. Purely aquatic; seen singly or in small, scattered groups, often diving and swimming beneath the surface. **Food:** aquatic insects, frogs, crustacea. **Voice:** shrill trilling notes and an occasional click. **Range:** all India, to 2000m in Kashmir. Resident in most areas. **Habitat:** village tanks, deep jheels, lakes, reservoirs.

*Little Grebe*

**(20) ROSY or WHITE PELICAN** *Pelecanus onocrotalus* 75cm. Sexes alike but female slightly smaller. Rose-tinged white plumage; pink feet and yellowish tuft on breast; black primaries and underside of secondaries; forehead feathers continue in pointed wedge above bill. The very similar **(22) Dalmatian Pelican** *Pelecanus philippensis crispus* can be distinguished by its dark grey feet and dusky white wing underside. Purely aquatic, huge numbers gathering to feed together; rarely settles on land; strong flier, flocks often flying to great heights. **Food:** almost exclusively fish. **Voice:** grunts and croaks rarely heard. **Range:** resident in Rann of Kutch; winters in parts of N, S and SE India. **Habitat:** large jheels, lakes, coastal lagoons.

*Rosy or White Pelican*

**(21) SPOTTEDBILLED PELICAN** *Pelecanus philippensis* (*roseus*) 150cm. Sexes alike. Whitish plumage sullied with grey-brown; pink on lower back, rump and flanks; white-tipped brown crest on back of head; black primaries and dark brown secondaries distinctive in flight; flesh coloured gular pouch has a bluish-purple wash; at close range the blue spots on upper mandible and on gular pouch confirm identity of species. Purely aquatic; seen singly as well as in large gatherings, driving the fish into shallow waters before scooping up the prey in the gular pouches. **Range:** breeds in the well-watered parts of S, SE and E India but population spreads in non-breeding season. **Habitat:** large jheels, lakes.

*Spottedbilled Pelican*

*Large Cormorant*

**(26) LARGE CORMORANT** *Phalacrocorax carbo* 80cm. Sexes alike. **Breeding adult:** black plumage with metallic blue-green sheen; white facial skin, throat; bright yellow gular pouch and white thigh patches; silky white plumes on head and neck. **Non-breeding adult:** no white thigh patches; gular pouch less bright. **First year young:** dull brown above, white below. Aquatic. Not a gregarious species outside breeding season; usually one or two birds feeding close by, rarely half a dozen; dives underwater in search of fish. **Range:** resident in most areas; all India, to 3000m in the Himalaya (observed in Kashmir, Ladakh, Nepal). **Habitat:** jheels, lakes, mountain torrents, occasionally coastal lagoons.

*Indian Shag*

**(27) INDIAN SHAG** *Phalacrocorax fuscicollis* 65cm. Sexes alike. **Breeding adult:** iridescent bronze-black above; glossy black below; white speckles on head and tuft behind eyes. **Non-breeding adult:** no gloss in plumage; white specks on throat; yellowish gular patch. Distinguished from Large Cormorant chiefly by size. Gregarious; often seen along with Little Cormorants; frenetic communal hunting appears like stampede; basks with wings and tail open. **Food:** mostly fish. **Range:** resident; local migrant; all India south of the Himalayan foothills. **Habitat:** rivers, jheels, also tidal creeks.

**(28) LITTLE CORMORANT** *Phalacrocorax niger* 50cm. Sexes alike. Our smallest and commonest cormorant; short, thick neck and head distinctive; lacks gular patch. **Breeding adult:** black plumage has blue-green sheen; silky white feathers on fore crown and sides of head; silvery-grey wash on upper back and wing coverts, speckled with black. **Non-breeding adult:** white chin and upper throat. Gregarious; flocks in large jheels; swims with only head and short neck exposed; dives often, the hunt can become a noisy, jostling scene; frequently perches on poles, trees and rocks, basks with wings spread open. **Food:** mostly fish, also tadpoles, crustaceans. **Range:** all India south of the Himalaya. **Habitat:** Village tanks, jheels, lakes, occasionally rivers and coastal areas.

**(29) DARTER** or **SNAKE BIRD** *Anhinga rufa* 90cm. Sexes alike. Long, snake-like neck, pointed bill and stiff, fan-shaped tail confirm identity. **Adult:** Black above, streaked and mottled with silvery-grey on back and wings; choco-brown head, neck; white stripe down sides of upper neck; white chin, upper throat; entirely black below. **Young:** brown with rufous and silvery streaks on mantle. A bird of deep, fresh water; small numbers scattered along with Little Cormorants; highly specialised feeder, the entire structure of the bird modified for following and capturing fish underwater, swims low in water, with only head and neck uncovered; chases prey below water with wings half open, spearing a fish with sudden rapier-like thrusts made possible by bend in neck at 8th and 9th vertebrae which acts as a spring as it straightens. Tosses fish into air and swallows head-first. Basks on tree stumps and rocks, cormorant style. **Voice:** loud croaks and squeaks. **Range:** all India, south of the Himalayan foothills. **Habitat:** fresh-water lakes, jheels.

*Darter or Snake Bird*

*Little Cormorant*

*Grey Heron*

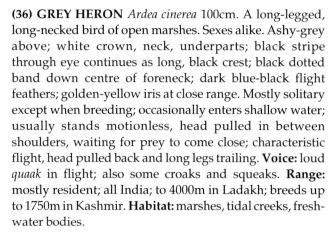

**(36) GREY HERON** *Ardea cinerea* 100cm. A long-legged, long-necked bird of open marshes. Sexes alike. Ashy-grey above; white crown, neck, underparts; black stripe through eye continues as long, black crest; black dotted band down centre of foreneck; dark blue-black flight feathers; golden-yellow iris at close range. Mostly solitary except when breeding; occasionally enters shallow water; usually stands motionless, head pulled in between shoulders, waiting for prey to come close; characteristic flight, head pulled back and long legs trailing. **Voice:** loud *quaak* in flight; also some croaks and squeaks. **Range:** mostly resident; all India; to 4000m in Ladakh; breeds up to 1750m in Kashmir. **Habitat:** marshes, tidal creeks, fresh-water bodies.

*Purple Heron*

**(37) PURPLE HERON** *Ardea purpurea* 100cm. Sexes alike. A slender-necked, lanky bird. Slaty-purple above; black crown, long, drooping crest; rufous neck with prominent black stripe along its length; white chin, throat; deep slaty and chestnut below breast; almost black on wings and tail; crest and breast plumes less developed in female. Solitary; crepuscular; extremely shy but master of patience; freezes and hides amidst marsh reeds; when flushed, flies with neck outstretched. **Voice:** a harsh croak. **Range:** mostly resident, though numbers in some areas increase during winter because of migrants; all India south of Himalaya foothills. **Habitat:** open marshes, reed-covered lakes, riversides.

**(38) LITTLE GREEN HERON** *Ardeola striatus* 45cm. Sexes alike. A grey, black and dark metallic green heron. Slaty-grey above, with a glossy green wash; white cheeks; very dark green forehead, crown, longish crest; grey head, neck; glossy green, grey and white in wings; white chin, centre of throat; ashy-grey below. Solitary, shy and sluggish; feeds during day too but mostly crepuscular and nocturnal; sits patiently near water. **Food:** frogs, small fish, crabs, insects. **Voice:** redshank-like *tewn..tewn.* **Range:** resident; uncommon; India south of the Himalaya; recorded upto 1500m in Peninsular hills. **Habitat:** secluded pools, ponds, mostly where there is dense growth; also mangrove creeks.

**(42) POND HERON** or **PADDY BIRD** *Ardeola grayii* 46cm.
Sexes alike. A small heron, commonest of family in India,
thick-set and earthy-brown in colour, with dull green legs,
bill bluish at base, yellowish at centre with black tip, neck
and legs shorter than in true egrets. Difficult to sight when
settled; suddenly springs to notice with a flash of white
wings, tail and rump. **Breeding:** buffy-brown head, neck;
white chin, upper throat, longish crest; rich maroon back;
buff-brown breast. **Non-breeding:** streaked dark brown
head, neck; grey-brown back, shoulders; more white in
plumage. Found around water, even dirty roadside puddles, ubiquitous in the plains, found in hills up to 1200m;
remains motionless in mud or up to ankles in water, or
slowly stalks prey. Hunts alone, roosts in groups with
other pond herons and occasionally crows. **Food:** fish,
frogs, crustaceans, insects. **Voice:** a harsh croak, usually
when flushed; also squeaks and chatter at nesting colony.
**Range:** resident; all India. **Habitat:** marshes, jheels, riversides, roadside ditches, tidal creeks.

*Pond Heron*

*Little Green Heron*

*Cattle Egret*

**(44) CATTLE EGRET** *Bubulcus ibis* 50cm. Sexes alike. A snow-white egret seen on and around cattle, garbage heaps. **Breeding**: buffy-orange plumes on head, neck and back. **Non-breeding**: distinguished from Little Egret by yellow beak; from other egrets by size. Widespread; equally abundant around water and away from it; routinely attends to grazing cattle, feeding on insects disturbed by the animals; follows tractors; scavenges at garbage dumps and slaughter houses. **Food:** insects, frogs, lizards, refuse. **Voice:** mostly silent except for some croaking sounds when breeding. **Range:** resident; all India, to 1800m in outer Himalaya. **Habitat:** marshes, lakes, forest clearings.

*Large Egret*

**(46) LARGE EGRET** *Ardea alba* 90cm. Lanky, snow-white marsh bird; black and yellow **(breeding)** or yellow **(non-breeding)** beak and black legs; when breeding, long, fine plumes on back. The very similar **(47) Median Egret** *Egretta intermedia*, besides being smaller (80cm) develops plumes both on back and breast during the breeding season. Usually solitary; rarely more than three or four birds scattered over a marsh, towering over other egrets; wades in shallow water but mostly waits silently for prey to come close. **Food:** fish, frogs, crustaceans, aquatic insects. **Voice:** an occasional croak. **Range:** resident and local migrant; not common but widespread over the country. **Habitat:** marshes, jheels, rivers, tidal estuaries.

*Little Egret*

**(49) LITTLE EGRET** *Egretta garzetta* 65cm. Sexes alike. A slender, snow-white waterbird. White plumage; black legs, yellow feet and black bill diagnostic. **Breeding**: nuchal crest of two long plumes; feathers on back and breast lengthen into ornamental filamentous feathers. Small flocks feed at edge of water, sometimes wading into the shallower areas; stalks prey like typical heron, waiting patiently at edge of water. **Food:** small fish, frogs, tadpoles, aquatic insects, crustaceans. **Voice:** an occasional croak. **Range:** resident; all India, from 1600m in outer Himalaya. **Habitat:** inland marshes, jheels, riversides, damp irrigated areas; sometimes tidal creeks.

**(50) INDIAN REEF HERON** *Egretta gularis* 65cm. Sexes alike. A slender heron of rocky sea coast. Has two colour phases. **Dark Phase**: slaty-black plumage; white throat, upper foreneck. **Light Phase**: all white plumage, like Little Egret, but habitat and more solitary nature distinctive; bill brown and yellow or bright yellow; plumes in breeding plumage much like Little Egret. Shy and solitary; more active in twilight; sometimes both phases feed side by side; moves cautiously on tidal ooze; jabs at prey; settles hunched-up on a rock. **Food**: small crabs, insects, fish, mudskippers. **Voice**: an occasional croak. **Range**: resident and local migrant; breeds off Gulf of Kutch; commoner on west coast; rare on the eastern seaboard. **Habitat**: rocky and sandy coast; mudflats.

*Indian Reef Heron*

**(52) NIGHT HERON** *Nycticorax nycticorax* 60cm. Sexes alike. A small but heavy heron. Plumage mostly grey, black and white; black head, back and drooping crest; white forehead, streak over eye, underbody; very long white feathers extend back from crest; greyish sides of neck, wings, rump and tail; blood-red iris visible at close range. Nocturnal; shy and secretive; roosts in trees during day; at dusk the birds leave the colony in small parties to frequent feeding marshes; feeds through the night until early morning. **Food**: frogs, fish, aquatic insects. **Voice**: harsh raucous *kwock*...in flight. **Range**: resident; all India, to about 2200m in W and C Himalaya. **Habitat**: marshes, forest streams, lakes, tidal creeks. Roosts in trees.

*Night Heron*

**(56) CHESTNUT BITTERN** *Ixobrychus cinnamomeus* 38cm. **Male**: dark cinnamon-rufous above; chestnut in wings, paler on underside; whitish chin, throat, fading into dull chestnut below. **Female**: more chestnut-brownish above, appearing darker than male; dull rufous below, streaked dark brown; prominent dark streak down centre of foreneck and breast. Young birds have mottled upper body and more heavily streaked below. Usually solitary; rather secretive, mostly seen when flushed from dense reed-growth; overall appearance and behaviour much like familiar Pond Heron; active during the rains. The slightly smaller **(55) Little Bittern** *I minutus* is common in the Kashmir Valley. **Food**: insects, frogs; also fish. **Voice**: courting male calls during the rains, when breeding. **Range**: almost all India south of the Himalayan terai; moves considerably, especially with the onset of the rains. **Habitat**: marshy areas, dense reed growth, wet cultivation.

*Little Bittern*

*Painted Stork*

**(60) PAINTED STORK** *Mycteria leucocephala* 95cm. Sexes alike. White plumage; blackish-green and white wings; blackish-green breast band and black tail; rich rosy-pink wash on greater wing coverts; large, slightly curved bill orangish-yellow. **Young:** pale dirty brown, the neck feathers edged darker; lacks breast band. Common and gregarious; feeds with beak partly submerged, ready to grab prey; when not feeding, settles hunched-up outside water; regularly soars high on thermals. **Food:** fish, frogs, crustaceans. **Voice:** characteristic mandible-clattering of storks; young in nest have grating begging calls. **Range:** resident and local migrant, from terai south through the country's well-watered regions. **Habitat:** inland marshes, jheels; occasionally riversides.

*Openbilled Stork*

**(61) OPENBILLED STORK** *Anastomus oscitans* 80cm. Sexes alike. India's smallest stork. White plumage, lightly washed with smoky grey in non-breeding birds; glistening purplish-greenish black on wings and tail; long, thick beak with curved mandibles and a wide gap along the centre. **Young:** dark smoky-brown; darker brown mantle. Widespread over well-watered regions; associates with other storks and herons when feeding; soars along with other birds; exact function of gap in mandibles uncertain. **Food:** mostly molluscs; also frogs and crabs. **Voice:** only mandible-clattering and some moaning sounds at nest. **Range:** resident and local migrant; all India south of terai. **Habitat:** marshes, jheels.

*White-necked Stork*

**(62) WHITE-NECKED STORK** *Ciconia episcopus* 105cm. Sexes alike. A large black and white stork with red legs. Glossy black crown, back, breast and huge wings, the black parts having a distinct purplish-green sheen; white neck, lower abdomen and undertail coverts; long, stout bill black, occasionally tinged crimson. In young birds, the glossy black is replaced by dark brown. Solitary or in small scattered parties, silently feeding along with other storks, ibises and egrets; stalks on dryland too; settles on trees; soars high on thermals. **Food:** lizards, frogs, crabs, large insects. **Voice:** only clattering of mandibles. **Range:** resident; all India, up to about 1400m in the Himalaya. **Habitat:** marshes, cultivation, wet grasslands.

**(63) WHITE STORK** *Ciconia ciconia* 105cm. Sexes alike. All white plumage; black flight feathers; red bill and legs confirm identity and help distinguish from the Openbill. Young birds have black parts replaced by brown. Small scattered parties stalk around sedately for food in open marsh or fallow land; usually protected in India due to religious sentiment, yet a shy and wary bird; in winter, enters cultivation; soars high on thermals. **Food:** lizards, frogs, fish, insects including locusts. **Voice:** only clattering of mandibles. **Range:** winter visitor, arriving by mid-September and leaving around end-March; commoner in NW and C India, and in the Indo-Gangetic Plains; less common south of the Deccan. **Habitat:** marshes, fallow land, cultivation.

*White Stork*

**(66) BLACK-NECKED STORK** *Ephippiorhynchus asiaticus* 135cm. Sexes alike. India's largest stork. Unmistakable. Massive black beak; glossy blue-green-black head, neck and tail; rest of body white; in flight, white wings have broad black band along their length; red legs. Solitary or in pairs, feeding in a marsh or perched atop a tree; shy and wary; occasionally a family may be seen feeding close by, parents with young; wades into deeper water than other storks; soars high on thermals. **Food:** fish, frogs, lizards, small turtles, insects. **Voice:** only clattering of mandibles. **Range:** resident; though widespread in the Indian region, this species is becoming uncommon. **Habitat:** marshes, jheels, large rivers.

*Black-necked Stork*

**(67) ADJUTANT STORK** *Leptoptilos dubius* 140cm. Sexes alike. Plumage whitish-grey and black; naked red **(breeding)** or yellow-brown **(non-breeding)** head, neck; massive beak; long, naked gular pouch. Silvery-grey wing-band and white ruff around base of neck when breeding. The **(68) Lesser Adjutant** *L javanicus* lacks the gular pouch. Usually small parties but many gather at garbage dumps; upright, soldier-like walk; often feeds along with other storks, kites, vultures. **Food:** snakes, lizards, frogs, fish, offal; also crustaceans, small birds. **Voice:** an occasional loud croak; bill-clattering. **Range:** local migrant; breeds over NE areas, Burma; spreads during monsoon over parts of N India, Indo-Gangetic plains. **Habitat:** marshlands, cultivation, mangrove, vicinity of habitation.

*Adjutant Stork*

*White Ibis*

**(69) WHITE IBIS** *Threskiornis aethiopica* 75cm. Sexes alike. White plumage; naked black head; long, curved black bill; blood-red patches seen on underwing and flanks in flight. **Breeding**: long plumes over neck; some slaty-grey in wings. **Young:** head and neck feathered; only face and patch around eye naked. Gregarious; feeds with storks, spoonbills, egrets and other ibises; moves actively in water, the long, curved bill held partly open and head partly submerged as the bird probes the nutrient-rich ooze. **Food:** frogs, insects, fish, molluscs, algal matter. **Voice**: loud booming call; nasal grunts reported during breeding season. **Range**: resident; local migrant; all India, fromterai south. **Habitat:** marshes; riversides.

*Black Ibis*

**(70) BLACK IBIS** *Pseudibis papillosa* 70cm. Sexes alike. Glossy black plumage; slender, blackish-green, downcurved beak; red warts on naked black head; white shoulder patch; brick-red legs. The **(71) Glossy Ibis** *Plegadis falcinellus* is deep maroon-brown above, with purple-green gloss from head to lower-back; feathered head and lack of white shoulder-patch distinctive. Small parties, spends more time on the drier edges of marshes and jheels; when feeding in shallow water, often feeds along with other ibises, storks, spoonbills. **Food:** small fish, frogs, earthworms, insects, lizards, crustaceans. **Voice:** two to three note loud nasal screams, uttered in flight; also on nest. **Range**: resident; NW India, east through Gangetic plains; south to Mysore. **Habitat:** cultivated areas; edges of marshes.

*Spoonbill*

**(72) SPOONBILL** *Platalea leucorodia* 65cm. Sexes alike, female slightly smaller. Snow-white plumage; large, flat, spatula-shaped, black bill with yellow tip; longish, black legs; cinnamon-buff patch on lower foreneck; small red-yellow throat patch. **Breeding**: a long, white crest of pointed plumes. Highly gregarious and social; peculiar feeding manner, bird wading quickly, its partly-open half-immersed beak sweeping from side to side; sometimes indulges in frenetic feeding bouts; rests on bare ground during hot hours of day; feeds till past sunset. **Food:** frogs, small fish, crustaceans, vegetable matter. **Voice**: mandible-clattering and short grunts when breeding. **Range**: resident; winter visitor in some areas; all India south of terai. **Habitat**: marshes, riversides, jheels; creeks.

**(73) FLAMINGO** *Phoenicopterus roseus* 140cm. Rose-white plumage; black and scarlet wings; big, downcurved pink beak and legs; characteristic flight, the long legs and neck stretched to full length, with scarlet and black underwing pattern. **Young:** greyish-brown with brown bill. Highly gregarious; prefers brackish water, lagoons, salt pans; feeds with head immersed; often rests on one leg, neck coiled and head tucked in feathers. **Food:** minute organisms, molluscs, crustaceans, possibly small fish. **Voice:** assortment of cackles when feeding together, otherwise a loud honk. **Range:** resident; local migrant; breeds in Great Rann of Kutch; sporadically seen all India. **Habitat:** brackish water lagoons, estuaries, also freshwater jheels.

*Flamingo*

**(74) LESSER FLAMINGO** *Phoeniconaias minor* 100cm. Smaller size, much deeper rose-pink plumage and dark bill distinguish it from its larger cousin; shorter red legs. **Female:** slightly smaller; no crimson on breast, back. **Young:** grey-brown. Highly social, often seen with Large; prefers heavily saturated brine, lagoons, salt and brackish lakes; peculiar feeding style, the submerged head swinging from side to side as it walks in foot-deep water; bill specially adapted for filter-feeding. **Food:** almost restricted to feeding on algae and diatoms; perhaps also insect larvae. **Range:** first found breeding in Great Rann only in 1974; erratically found in many parts of west and central India. **Habitat:** restricted to high brine concentration, brackish lakes, salt pans, lagoons.

**(81) GREYLAG GOOSE** *Anser anser* 80cm. Sexes alike. Grey-brown plumage; pink bill, legs and feet; white upper tail-coverts, lower belly and tip to dark tail; in flight, pale leading edge of wings and white upper tail-coverts distinctive. Gregarious and wary; flocks on jheels and winter cultivation; rests for most of day and feeds during night, in water and in agricultural land, especially freshly sown fields. **Food:** grass, shoots of winter crops like gram and wheat; aquatic tubers; recorded eating *Singhara* (water-chestnut) in Kashmir. **Voice:** domestic goose-like single note honk, often uttered several times, loud and ringing; typical geese gaggles when feeding. **Range:** winter visitor; early-October to mid-March; commoner in N India, across the Gangetic plain to Assam, Orissa; south to N Gujarat; Madhya Pradesh; rarer south. **Habitat:** jheels, winter cultivation.

*Barheaded Goose*

**(82) BARHEADED GOOSE** *Anser indicus* 75cm. Sexes alike. Two blackish strips on back of white head; white stripes down necksides; dark-brown neck; very pale-grey plumage; yellow bill, legs; black bill-tip; in flight, the pale coloured body, white head and dark wing tips distinctive. Gregarious, sometimes seen along with Greylags; rests during day on jheel banks and sandbars in rivers; crepuscular and nocturnal; causes damage to winter crops. **Food:** tender shoots of gram, tubers, paddy. **Voice:** nasal, quite musical honking. **Range:** breeds only in Ladakh within Indian limits; winter visitor, commoner from Kashmir, south to C India and east across Gangetic plains to Assam; less common south of Deccan. **Habitat:** rivers, large jheels.

*Lesser Whistling Teal*

**(88) LESSER WHISTLING TEAL** or **TREE DUCK** *Dendrocygna javanica* 42cm. Sexes alike. Rufescent-brown plumage; browner head; chestnut upper tail-coverts; in flight, chestnut upper tail-coverts, upper wing-coverts and blackish flight feathers distinctive. Young birds are dull coloured. The **(89) Large Whistling Teal** *D bicolor* (50cm) is larger, and has white upper tail-coverts. Small flocks on edges of jheels and village ponds, especially where there is ample vegetation, reeds; mostly nocturnal feeder; flight slow, often accompanied by whistling calls. **Food:** tender shoots, grain, aquatic weeds, small fish, worms, frogs. **Voice:** shrill, musical whistle frequently in flight. **Range:** resident, but moves locally; all India south of Himalaya. **Habitat:** vegetation and reed covered jheels, village ponds.

*Ruddy Shelduck*

**(90) RUDDY SHELDUCK** or **BRAHMINY DUCK** *Tadorna ferruginea* 65cm. Whitish-buff head; orange-brown plumage; in flight, orangish body, white wing-coverts, green speculum and blackish flight feathers distinctive; black tail and ring around neck **(breeding)**. Female has a whiter head and lacks neck ring. Young birds look like female and have some grey in wings. Pairs or small parties, rather wary; rests during day on river banks, sandbars, edges of jheels; prefers clear, open water. **Food:** grain, shoots, insects, molluscs; reportedly also carrion. **Voice:** loud goose-like honking, on ground and in flight. **Range:** breeds in Ladakh; winter visitor; all India, less common in south. **Habitat:** rivers with sandbars, large, open jheels.

**(93) PINTAIL** *Anas acuta* 60cm. A slender duck with pointed tail. **Male:** greyish above; choco-brown head, upper neck; thin white stripe up neckside; bronze-green speculum. **Female:** mottled buff-brown; pointed tail lacks longer tail-pins; whitish belly. Non-breeding male like female, but mantle greyish. In flight, pointed tail between feet distinctive. Highly gregarious; extremely common on vegetation-covered jheels; males often in separate flocks, especially on arrival in winter grounds; crepuscular and nocturnal; characteristic hissing swish of wings as flock flies over. **Food:** shoots, seeds of aquatic plants, rice (wild and cultivated); also water insects and molluscs. **Range:** winter visitor; all India. **Habitat:** vegetation-covered jheels, lagoons.

*Pintail*

**(94) COMMON TEAL** *Anas creca* 32cm. **Male:** greyish with chestnut head with broad metal green band from eye to nape with yellow white border. Black, green and buff wing speculam. **Female:** mottled in dark and light brown, pale belly and black and green wing speculam. Commonest migratory duck, much sought by sportsmen. Swift flier and difficult to circumvent. **Food:** tender shoots and grains, mostly vegetarian. **Voice:** *krit..krit..*also wheezy quack. **Range:** all India in winter. **Habitat:** jheels, marshes, village ponds.

*Common Teal*

**(97) SPOTBILL** *Anas poecilorhyncha* 60cm. Sexes alike. Blackish-brown plumage, feathers edged paler; almost white head, neck; black cap, dark, broad eye-stripe; green speculum bordered above with white; black bill tipped yellow; coral-red legs, feet. Pairs or small parties walking on marshy land, wet cultivation, or up-ending in shallow water; usually does not associate with other ducks; much prized table-bird; when injured, can dive and remain underwater, holding on to submerged vegetation with only bill exposed. **Food:** wild grain, seeds, shoots of aquatic plants; occasionally water insects, worms, water-snails; causes damage to paddy. **Voice:** loud duck-like quack. **Range:** resident; all India, to about 1800m in Kashmir; local migrant in some areas. **Habitat:** reed and vegetation-covered jheels, shallow ponds.

*Spotbill*

*Mallard*

(100) **MALLARD** *Anas platyrhynchos* 60cm. Broad purple speculum, bordered on each side by white bars, orangeish legs, distinctive in flight. **Male:** Glossy green head; narrow white collar. **Female (and eclipse male):** mottled brown; brownish bill; indistinct dark stripe through eye. Sociable and gregarious; crepuscular and nocturnal; feeds on marshy ground and in shallow water, up-ending when raking the bottom ooze; can rise vertically from water. **Food:** seeds, shoots of grasses and aquatic plants; also tadpoles, fish spawn, worms. **Voice:** loud, wheezy *yheeep* of drake; female quacks loud, loudest when alarmed. **Range:** very small numbers breed in some of Kashmir's lakes; winter visitor to N and C India; rare in Deccan and further south. **Habitat:** reed-covered jheels.

(101) **GADWALL** *Anas strepera* 50cm. White wing-speculum and chestnut wing-patch diagnostic. **Male:** dark grey, with brown head; white belly; heavily speckled breast. **Female:** plumage mottled brown; the Mallard female is larger, lacks white belly and has metallic white-bordered purple speculum; Pintail female also has white belly but pointed tail and more slender neck distinctive. **Winter Male:** like female but not so heavily mottled,

especially above. Small flocks, sometimes with other ducks; surface-feeder; much sought-after table-bird. **Food:** chiefly vegetarian-tubers, shoots of aquatic plants, grain, seeds. **Voice:** single-noted, low call of male; loud quacking of female. **Range:** winter visitor, quite abundant; all India, but decreasing in numbers towards S India. **Habitat:** jheels, marshes.

**(105) SHOVELLER** *Anas clypeata* 50cm. Broad, long beak diagnostic. **Br Male***:* metallic-green head, neck; in flight, dark head, back-centre, rump and upper-tail coverts contrast with white of back and tail; also, dull-blue upper-wing coverts against dark flight-feathers; metallic-green speculum and white wing-bar; in overhead flight, dark head, thick white neck, dark chestnut belly, flanks. **Female**: mottled brown, but blue-grey shoulders (wing-coverts) and dull green speculum distinctive. Pairs or small flocks, often amidst other ducks; swims slowly, the beak held very close to water; sometimes up-ends. **Food:** aquatic insects, crustaceans, molluscs; also vegetable matter. **Voice:** loud two-noted quacking notes of male; **Range:** winter visitor, quite common over most well-watered parts of the country. **Habitat:** marshes, lakes; also vegetation-covered village ponds.

*Shoveller*

**(114) COTTON TEAL** *Nettapus coromandelianus* 32cm. **Br Male:** white head, neck; blackish, green-glossed crown, back, neck-collar; white below; white wing-bar. **Female:** dull-brown above; indistinct white wing-bar; dark stripe through eyes; white below, mottled brown. **Non-br Male:** like female, but darker above; distinct wing-bar. Flocks, feeds either by themselves or along with other ducks; mostly feeds on surface, but can also dive; a familiar waterfowl on village tanks and ponds, rather confiding where not persecuted; strong flier, usually flying low. **Food:** shoots of aquatic plants, grain, insects, crustacea. **Voice:** cackling call in flight. **Range:** almost all India; not common, possibly absent over the arid NW regions. **Habitat:** ponds and tanks, preferably those covered with reeds and vegetation.

*Comb Duck*

**(115) NAKTA** or **COMB DUCK** *Sarkidiornis melanotos* 75cm. **Male:** white head, neck, speckled black; fleshy knob (comb) on top of beak; black back has purple-green gloss; greyish lower-back; white lower-neck collar and underbody; short black bars extend on sides of upper breast and flanks. **Female:** duller, smaller; lacks comb. Small parties, either on water or in trees over water; nests in tree-cavities; feeds on surface and in cultivation; can also dive. **Food:** shoots and seeds of water plants, grain, aquatic insects, worms, frogs. **Voice:** loud goose-like *honk* when breeding. **Range:** almost all India; mostly resident but moves considerably with onset of monsoons; uncommon in extreme S and NW India. **Habitat:** jheels and marshes with surrounding tree-cover.

**(124) BLACKWINGED KITE** *Elanus caeruleus* 32cm. Sexes alike. Pale grey-white plumage, whiter on head, neck and underbody; short black stripe through eyes; black shoulder patches and wing-tips distinctive at rest and in flight; blood-red eyes. **Young:** upperbody tinged brown, with pale edges to feathers. Usually solitary or in pairs; resting on exposed perch or flying over open scrub and grass country; mostly hunts on wing, regularly hovering like a Kestrel to scan ground; drops height to check when hovering, with legs held ready. **Food:** insects, lizards, rodents, snakes. **Voice:** high-pitched squeal. **Range:** all India, to about 1500m in outer Himalaya. **Habitat:** open scrub and grass country; light forest.

*Blackwinged Kite*

**(127) BLACK-CRESTED BAZA** *Aviceda leuphotes* 32cm. Sexes alike. Black upperparts, including long crest, foreneck, upper-breast; broad white breast-band followed by a black and chestnut band below; buff-white lower breast, flanks, barred chestnut; black abdomen; pale underside of tail. Solitary or small flocks in tall forests; more active in cloudy weather and at dusk; makes sorties after winged insects from perch high up in forest tree; occasionally hovers. **Food:** insects, small lizards, frogs, small birds. **Voice:** plaintive squeal, very much like Pariah Kite's. **Range:** uncommon resident; Kerala and some parts in adjoining Mysore; NE India, east of E Nepal to about 1200m. **Habitat:** evergreen forest, clearings, streams, foothills.

**(130) HONEY BUZZARD** *Pernis ptilorhyncus* 67cm. Sexes alike. Slender head and longish neck distinctive; tail rarely fanned. Highly variable phases. Mostly darkish brown above; crest rarely visible; pale brown underbody, with narrow whitish bars; pale underside of wings barred; broad dark subterminal tail band; two or three more bands on tail; tarsus unfeathered. Solitary or in pairs, perched on forest trees or flying; often enters villages and outskirts of small towns. **Food:** bee larvae, honey, small birds, lizards; occasionally robs poultry. **Voice:** high-pitched, long-drawn *weeeeeu*... may call during the night. **Range:** resident and local migrant; all India to about 2000m in the Himalaya. **Habitat:** Forest, open country, cultivation, vicinity of villages.

*Honey Buzzard*

**(133) PARIAH KITE** *Milvus migrans govinda* 60cm. Sexes alike. Dark brown plumage; forked tail, easily seen in flight; underparts faintly streaked. The **(134) Blackeared Kite** *M m lineatus* breeds in Himalaya and winters in N and C India is slightly larger and has conspicuous white patch on underwing, visible in overhead flight. Common and gregarious; commoner near man, thriving on the refuse generated, often amidst most crowded localities; roosts communally. **Food:** omnivorous; garbage, dead rats, earthworms, insects, nestlings of smaller birds, poultry. **Voice:** loud, musical whistle, often uttered on wing during breeding season. **Range:** resident; all India to about 2200m in Himalaya, co-existing with Blackeared in some localities. **Habitat:** mostly neighbourhood of humans.

*Pariah Kite*

*Brahminy Kite*

**(135) BRAHMINY KITE** *Haliastur indus* 50cm. Sexes alike. White head, neck, upper back and breast; rest of plumage a rich, rusty-chestnut; brownish abdomen and darker tips to flight feathers visible mostly in flight. **Young:** brown, like Pariah Kite, but with rounded tail. Solitary or small scattered parties; loves water; frequently scavenges around lakes and marshes; also around villages and towns. **Food:** mostly stranded fish; also frogs, insects, lizards, mudskippers, small snakes, rodents. **Voice:** loud scream. **Range:** resident and local migrant; all India, from about 1800m in the Himalaya. **Habitat:** margins of lakes, marshes, rivers, sea coast.

*Shikra*

**(139) SHIKRA** *Accipiter badius* 32cm. Ashy-grey above; whitish below, close-barred with rust-brown; grey throat-stripe; in flight, the multi-banded tail and roundish wings help identification; golden yellow eyes and yellow legs and feet seen at close range. The migrant **(147) Sparrowhawk** *A nisus* is very similar but closer look reveals the longer legs, rufous cheek patch and absence of mesial stripe in *nisus*. Usually solitary; hides in leafy branch; pounces on unsuspecting prey; occasionally chases small birds; soars over forest. **Food:** rodents, small birds, lizards, large insects; also robs poultry. **Voice:** loud, drongo-like *titew..titew*. **Range:** resident; all India, to 1600m in the Himalaya. **Habitat:** light forest, open country, neighbourhood of villages.

**(144) CRESTED GOSHAWK** *Accipiter trivirgatus* 42cm. Sexes alike, female larger. Dark brown above; slaty-grey crown, crest; white below, streaked on breast; barred with rufescent below breast; white throat, under tail-coverts; black mesial stripe. Like Shikra, remains hidden in leafy branch, preferably around a forest clearing; pounces on prey; has favoured hunting grounds; often soars over forest. **Food:** middle-size birds such as pigeons, partridges; also rodents, squirrels. **Range:** resident; two races in India; one found from the Himalaya south to Godavari river, the other resident in the W Ghats south of Goa. **Habitat:** deciduous and semi-evergreen forest.

**(157) WHITE-EYED BUZZARD** *Butastur teesa* 45cm. Sexes alike. Ashy-brown above; distinct throat, white with two dark cheek stripes and a third stripe from chin; white nape patch, white eyes and orange-yellow cere visible from close quarters; in flight, a pale shoulder patch from above; from below, the pale underside of roundish wings against a darkish body distinctive. Solitary or scattered pairs; seen on exposed perches, trees, poles or telegraph wires; seems to prefer certain sites; soars high and does aerial displays when breeding. **Food:** rodents, lizards, squirrels, small birds, frogs and insects. **Voice:** musical, plaintive *te..twee.* frequently when breeding. **Range:** resident; all India, to about 1200m in Himalaya. **Habitat:** open, dry forest; cultivated country.

*White-eyed Buzzard*

**(161) CRESTED HAWK EAGLE** *Spizaetus cirrhatus cirrhatus* 70cm. Sexes alike, but female larger. Large, slender, crested forest eagle. Brown above; white underbody longitudinally streaked all over with brown; prominent occipital crest; the streaked whitish body, broad wings and long, rounded tail distinctive in flight. Solitary, occasionally a pair circles high over forests, especially when breeding; surveys for prey from high, leafy branches near forest clearings. The **(160) Changeable Hawk Eagle** *S c limnaeetus* is very similar to the Crested Hawk Eagle except for smaller, often indistinct crest. **Food:** partridges, other ground-birds, squirrels, hares, lizards. **Voice:** loud, screaming cry, usually long-drawn. **Range:** resident; all India, south of the Himalaya, where another race, (*limnaeetus*, with very small or no crest and paler below with barred abdomen) may be seen up to 2000m. **Habitat:** semi-evergreen and deciduous forest, clearings.

*Crested Hawk Eagle*

**(163) BONELLI'S EAGLE** *Hieraaetus fasciatus* 70cm. Sexes alike, but female larger. Uncrested, long-tailed forest eagle. Dark brown above; buffy-white below, heavily streaked with black; broad subterminal tail-band black; several narrower bands; the pale, streaked body, barred flight feathers and broad band on longish tail distinctive in flight. Solitary or in pairs, flying over forests; pairs often hunts in unison; pounces on prey from lofty perches or strikes in aerial pursuit. **Food:** hares, large ground birds, monitor lizards; also smaller forest birds, squirrels. **Voice:** shrill scream of three to six notes. **Range:** resident; all India, sporadically from about 2400m in the Himalaya. **Habitat:** forest.

*Bonelli's Eagle*

**(164) BOOTED HAWK EAGLE** *Hieraaetus pennatus* 52cm. Sexes alike; female larger. Our smallest eagle. Has two distinct colour phases. **Light phase:** paler head, uppertail and upper wing-coverts; buffy-white wing lining, underbody and tail with blackish flight feathers distinctive, easily identifiable in flight. **Dark phase:** choco-brown below; pale, banded tail, visible in flight. Upperbody as in light phase. Solitary or in pairs hunting in concert; several may roost together at night; picks prey off ground or chases in flight. **Food:** small birds, rodents, lizards; robs poultry. **Voice:** loud scream of several notes. **Range:** breeds in the Himalaya (1800–3000m) and sporadically in the peninsula; commoner in winter over the country. **Habitat:** open forest; scrub; orchards; around human habitation.

*Tawny Eagle*

**(168) TAWNY EAGLE** *Aquila rapax* 70cm. Sexes alike, female slightly larger. Variable plumage; adults usually dark brown, with faint pale barrings on short rounded tail; holds tail straight and level with body when in flight; lacks dull white rump of most Spotted Eagles. Adult **(169) Steppe Eagle** *A r nipalensis* is very similar but may have pale white wing bars and rump. Difficult to distinguish; solitary or several scattered; sits on ground for long periods eating carrion or offal; lazy, low flight. **Food:** carrion, small animals, birds. **Voice:** loud crackling notes; high pitched call. **Range:** sporadically over parts of the country; *nipalensis* is a winter visitor. **Habitat:** open country, vicinities of villages, towns and cultivation

**(170) GREATER SPOTTED EAGLE** *Aquila clanga* 65cm. Sexes alike, but female slightly larger. Deep brown above, with purplish wash on back; somewhat paler below; often has whitish rump; soars on straight wings, with drooping tips; immature birds may have white markings above. The **(271) Lesser Spotted Eagle** *A pomarina* is slightly smaller, with narrower wings and is paler above. Mostly solitary; prefers vicinity of water; perches for long spells on bare trees or on ground; sluggish behavior. **Food:** small animals, waterfowl, small birds. **Voice:** loud shrill *kaek...kaek..*, often from perch. **Range:** breeds sporadically in parts of N, E and NC India; spreads south in winter. **Habitat:** tree covered areas in the vicinity of water.

**(173) WHITEBELLIED SEA EAGLE** *Haliaeetus leucogaster*
70cm. Sexes alike; female larger. Ashy-brown above; white
head, neck, underparts, tail-end; in overhead flight,
wedge-shaped tail, white body, underwing and terminal
tail bar contrasting with black flight feathers and tail.
Solitary or in pairs; perches on tall tree or poles, overlooking sea or lake; with a great stoop, picks prey from near
water surface; indulges in spectacular courtship display;
often feeds in nest. **Food:** mostly sea-snakes; fish, including dead ones; also robs poultry. **Voice:** loud metallic
screams, mostly when breeding. **Range:** resident; the coast
south of Bombay and all along the east coast; flies many
miles inland, to freshwater lakes, rivers. **Habitat:** sea coast,
inland water.

*Whitebellied Sea Eagle*

**(174) PALLAS'S FISHING EAGLE** *Haliaeetus leucoryphus*
80cm. Sexes alike; female larger. Dark brown plumage;
buffy-golden head, neck and breast; darkish tail and contrasting broad, white band confirms identity. Young birds
are much darker above, paler below. Solitary or in pairs;
perches atop tall trees or poles, mostly near or in the
middle of a lake or river; picks fish from surface in its
talons; often pirates the catch of other birds; robs nestlings
at heronries. **Food:** fish, frogs, turtles, wildfowl, nestlings
of herons and other water birds. **Voice:** loud screams; very
noisy when breeding. **Range:** resident; local migrant; N
India, to about 1800m in Himalaya; along Gangetic plains
to E India; Chilika Lake. **Habitat:** jheels, large rivers.

*Pallas's Fishing Eagle*

**(175) GREYHEADED FISHING EAGLE** *Ichthyophaga
icthyaetus* 75cm. Sexes alike. Dark brown plumage; grey
head, neck and throat; pale brown crown, nape; pale
brown breast; white flanks, abdomen and tail with broad,
black terminal band distinctive in overhead flight. The
**(177) Himalayan Greyheaded Fishing Eagle** *I i nana* is
smaller and has pure grey head; lacks pure-white in tail
when seen from below. Mostly solitary; sits straight on
lookout perches, usually on trees over and around forest
streams or pools; captures fish off surface; does not plunge.
**Food:** predominantly fish; sometimes birds, squirrels.
**Voice:** loud, ringing cry; noisy when breeding. **Range:**
resident; from Delhi east through Gangetic plains to
Assam and further east; south through the peninsula.
**Habitat:** lakes, rivers in forested country.

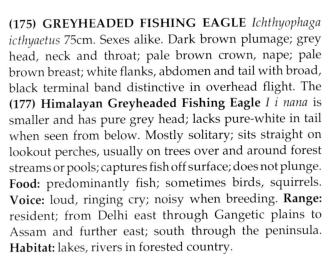

*King Vulture*

**(178) BLACK** or **KING VULTURE** *Sarcogyps calvus* 85cm. Sexes alike. Black plumage with white on thighs and breast; naked red head, neck and feet; in overhead flight, the white breast, thigh patches and grey-white band along wings distinctive; widely-spread primaries. Young birds are darkish brown with white abdomen and undertail. Mostly solitary but two to four may be seen at a carcass along with other vultures; usually does not mix with the rest; occasionally grabs a morsel. **Food:** chiefly scavenges on carcasses. **Voice:** reportedly a hoarse croak. **Range:** resident; all India, to about 2800m in the Himalaya; nowhere common. **Habitat:** Open country, village outskirts.

**(181) HIMALAYAN GRIFFON** *Gyps himalayensis* 125cm. Sexes alike. Pale sandy brown above; very pale buff-white below with broad, white shaft streaks; in overhead flight, the massive size almost whitish underbody and contrasting black flight feathers and tail. Young birds are darker brown above. One to six birds sail motionless over high country; soars to immense heights on thermals; follows cattle graziers in high altitudes; several converging on a carcass; fixed rest-sites on rock faces. **Food:** chiefly scavenges on carcasses. **Voice:** cackling screeches at carcass site. **Range:** resident; Himalaya, between about 600–3000m; forages much higher; recorded over 5000m. **Habitat:** barren, high altitude country; around mountain settlements.

*Long-billed Vulture*

**(182) INDIAN LONG-BILLED VULTURE** *Gyps indicus* 90cm. Sexes alike. Pale-brown plumage; hair-like feathers on naked head and neck seen at close range; ruff of white feathers round base of neck; very dull sandy-brown below; in overhead flight, pale underbody and underwing diagnostic. The Himalayan race *Gi tenuirostris* has bald head, neck. Gregarious, frequently seen with other vultures and crows at carcasses and garbage dumps; less common than the White-backed but similar in habits. **Food:** scavenges on carcasses, offal. **Voice:** appears rather silent, even when feeding. **Range:** common in the drier parts of India (Rajasthan, Gujarat, most of C India, south of Gangetic Plains); *G i tenuirostris* occurs along foothills, from Kashmir to Assam. **Habitat:** open country, habitation, forest; breeds on cliffs.

**(185) INDIAN WHITE-BACKED VULTURE** *Gyps bengalensis* 90cm. Sexes alike. Blackish brown plumage; almost naked head has whitish ruff around base; white rump (lower back) distinctive, when perched and often in flight; in overhead flight, white underwing coverts contrast with dark underbody and flight feathers. Young birds are brown and show no white on underwing in flight. Common and gregarious; seen with other vultures and crows at carcass, slaughter houses, garbage dumps. When resting, the head and neck are dug into shoulders; soars high on thermals; several converge onto a carcass; basks in sun; wades :and bathes in shallow water. **Food:** mostly scavenges on carcasses. **Voice:** loud screeches when feeding. **Range:** resident; all India, to about 2800m in the Himalaya. **Habitat:** open country.

**(186) EGYPTIAN** or **SCAVENGER VULTURE** *Neophron percnopterus* 65cm. Sexes alike. White plumage; blackish in wings; naked yellow head, neck and throat; yellow bill; thick ruff of feathers around neck; wedge-shaped tail and blackish flight feathers distinctive in overhead flight. The nominate race of NW India is slightly larger and has dark horny bill. Several usually together, perched atop ruins, earthen mounds or just walking on ground; glides a lot but rarely soars high; sometimes with other vultures. **Food:** garbage, carrion, insects, stranded turtles, the bird being specially adept at opening live turtles. **Range:** all India; plains to about 2000m in the Himalaya. **Habitat:** open country; vicinity of human habitation.

*Scavenger Vulture*

**(188) BEARDED VULTURE** or **LAMMERGEIER** *Gypaetus barbatus* 125cm. Wingspan of about 2.5m. Sexes alike. Silvery-black above with white shaft stripes; rust-white head, neck; black bristly "beard" under chin; white below with a rusty wash; in overhead flight, long, narrow wings and long, black wedge-shaped tail. Young birds dark brown with blackish head. Usually solitary; soars high over ravines or glides effortlessly over the slopes; may swoop down on hill-station garbage dumps to snatch away some offal; carries bones and drops on rock to break and eat fragments; feeds sometimes with other vultures. **Food:** refuse; bones. **Range:** resident; the Himalaya, west to east, 1000–5000m; soars higher. **Habitat:** high mountain slopes.

*Lammergeier*

**(192) PIED HARRIER** *Circus melanoleucos* 48cm. **Male:** pied black, white and grey. Black head, back, throat, breast; grey tail, wings; black primaries; black band on wings above (across median coverts). **Female:** dark brown above; pale white nape patch, rump; pale buffy-rufous below; marked underside of flight feathers; overall appearance like other female harriers, and species identification not always easy. Solitary or in pairs; methodically surveys open grassy country; flies low, almost floats over; occasionally hovers for a few seconds. **Food:** rodents, lizards, frogs, insects. **Range:** resident in Manas and adjoining areas in Assam; winter visitor over parts of E India and erratically in parts of C and S India. **Habitat:** grassy areas, cultivation, reedy edges of jheels.

*Marsh Harrier*

**(193) MARSH HARRIER** *Circus aeruginosus* 55cm. **Male:** dark brown plumage; dull rufous head, breast; silvery-grey wings, tail; black wing-tips (best seen in flight). **Female (and young):** choco-brown; buff on head and shoulders; like Pariah Kite, but tail rounded (not forked). Solitary or in pairs; sails low over a marsh, grassland or cultivation; often drops onto ground, frequently vanishing in dense grass and reed growth; perches on mounds or edge of marshes. **Food:** fish, rodents, frogs, small water-birds, insects. **Range:** winter visitor; common; all India, south of foothills country; commoner in N India. **Habitat:** marshes, jheels, wet cultivation.

**(195) SHORT-TOED EAGLE** *Circaetus gallicus* 65cm. Sexes alike, but female larger. Brown above; whitish below; pale brown across throat, breast; banded tail; terminal band broad; in overhead flight, the pale silvery-white under-wings and darker head and breast distinctive; overall, a thick-set eagle. Usually solitary; surveys low, like harriers; hovers to check for prey; frequently soars high; tremendous dive for prey; perches on tree-tops or poles. **Food:** snakes, lizards, frogs, rodents, large insects. **Voice:** a plaintive, loud scream. **Range:** resident; all India, to about 1200m in outer Himalaya; absent in NE. **Habitat:** open country, cultivation.

(196) **CRESTED SERPENT EAGLE** *Spilornis cheela* 75cm. Sexes alike; female larger. Dark brown plumage; roundish, pied crest, visible when erected; pale brown below, finely spotted white; in overhead flight, the dark body, white bars along the wings and white tail band confirm identity; characteristic call. Solitary or in pairs, flying over forest, often very high, calling frequently; perches in a leafy branch; swoops down on prey, snatching in talons; raises crest when alarmed. **Food:** snakes, lizards, birds, rodents, squirrels. **Voice:** loud whistling scream, *keee..kee..ke..*, the first note long-drawn. **Range:** resident; all India, to about 3000m in the Himalaya; Andamans. **Habitat:** forested country.

*Crested Serpent Eagle*

(203) **OSPREY** *Pandion haliaetus* 55cm. Sexes alike; female larger. Dark brown above; some white on head; white below; brown breast 'necklace', seen at rest and in flight; in overhead flight, white body with breast band, long, narrow black-tipped, barred wings with black carpal (wrist) patches. Young birds have upper body marked white. Solitary or in scattered pairs; mostly around water; perches on a stake or tree top; circles over water; hovers characteristically; dives with feet dangling; often splashes into water; carries fish on to perch. **Food:** fish, often heavier than the bird itself. **Voice:** short, nasal scream; calls rarely. **Range:** resident in parts of the Himalaya, between about 2000 and 3500m; winter visitor over India. **Habitat:** lakes, rivers, coastal lagoons.

**(208) LAGGAR FALCON** *Falco biarmicus jugger* 45cm. Sexes alike; female larger. Dark brown above; white on head; narrow moustache; whitish below, streaked thickly on flanks; in flight, pale breast contrasts with darker flanks and thighs. In young birds, underbody below throat dark brown. Usually a pair, scattered or together, perches on tree-tops or poles in open country; often seen in towns and cities; the pair often hunts in concert, chasing prey; spectacular displays at onset of breeding season. **Food:** small to medium-sized birds, rodents, lizards. **Voice:** two or three note scream, mostly when breeding. **Range:** resident; local migrant; all India, to about 1000m in the Himalaya. **Habitat:** open country; scrub.

**(211) SHAHEEN FALCON** *Falco peregrinus peregrinator* 42cm. A powerful, broad-shouldered falcon. Sexes alike; female larger. Slaty-grey above; whitish about cheeks; dark moustachial stripe; rusty-white below, finely cross-barred with dark below breast. The migrant **(209) Peregrine Falcon** *F p japonensis* is whitish below, and frequents the vicinity of jheels and marshes. Solitary or in pairs; wheeling and gliding around steep cliffsides; has favoured feeding sites, usually some rockface; flight very fast and powerful; dives at prey; indulges in spectacular displays. **Food:** birds such as partridges, quails, pigeons, parakeets. **Voice:** fairly loud, ringing scream. **Range:** resident; all India, to about 3000m in the Himalaya; not found in the semi-arid regions. **Habitat:** mostly rugged, mountainous areas; cliffs.

*Hobby*

**(214) ORIENTAL** or **INDIAN HOBBY** *Falco severus* 28cm. A small, robust falcon; miniature Shaheen; slaty-grey above; deep, black head, including cheeks; chestnut underparts, paler on throat. The **(212) Hobby** *Falco subbuteo* has rusty-white underparts, thickly streaked. Solitary or several together; feeds mostly around dusk and dawn, in twilight; flies about erratically, circling, dancing, rising and dropping; charges after prey at tremendous speed; eats on wing or on perch. **Food:** large flying insects; small bats, birds and lizards. **Voice:** shrill trill of three to four notes. **Range:** resident; lower Himalaya; possibly winter visitor over rest of the country. **Habitat:** forested, hilly country.

*Redheaded Merlin*

**(219) REDHEADED MERLIN** *Falco chicquera* 35cm. Sexes alike; female larger. Blue-grey above; chestnut sides of head, crown, nape, cheek-stripe diagnostic; wings pointed, outer flight feathers blackisk, closely barred with white on inner webs; black-barred grey tail with narrow black bars has a broad, black terminal band edged with white; white below; lightly streaked breast, barred below. Pairs, usually hunt in concert; straight and strong flight; also hunts by driving prey out from leafy branches; occasionally soars high; drinks water on ground. **Food:** small birds, rodents, lizards. **Voice:** shrill trilling screams. **Range:** resident; all India south of Himalayan foothills; commoner in Deccan; sometimes breeds in and around habitation. **Habitat:** avoids dense forest, prefers open country, wide cultivated plains with small groups of trees, groves; villages.

Kestrel

**(222) KESTREL** *Falco tinnunculus* 35cm. **Male:** black-streaked ash-grey crown, sides of neck, nape; rufous mantle, black-spotted; cheek-stripe; grey tail has white tip and black subterminal band; streaked and spotted buffy underbody. **Female:** pale rufous above; streaked head and narrowly barred back; paler buff below, densely streaked. **Young:** Like female; thickly streaked below. Solitary or in pairs; on exposed perches overlooking open country; circles in air and pounces into grass and scrub; often hovers when hunting. **Food:** insects, lizards, small rodents. **Voice:** an infrequent clicking sound. **Range:** resident; local migrant; several races; breeds in the Himalaya (commoner in the west); also in W Ghats south of Bombay; associated hill ranges in S India; winter numbers augmented. **Habitat:** open country; cliffsides.

Snow Partridge

**(227) SNOW PARTRIDGE** *Lerwa lerwa* 38cm. Sexes alike. Barred black and white above; deep chestnut below; broad white streaks on abdomen, flanks; chestnut undertail; streaked black and tipped white. Social; coveys of 5 to 20 on alpine pastures and amidst bushes; very tame where not harassed; easy to shoot; numbers decreasing. **Food:** seeds, vegetable shoots, lichens, moss. **Voice:** loud call, like that of Grey Partridge. **Range:** resident; the Himalaya, 2500–5000m. **Habitat:** alpine meadows, scrubby hillsides, rhododendron and fern undergrowth.

Himalayan Snowcock

**(232) HIMALAYAN SNOWCOCK** *Tetraogallus himalayensis* 72cm. Sexes alike. Overall plumage grey, white, black and chestnut; streaked and blotched; white throat bordered by broken chestnut collar; dark grey below breast; white under tail-coverts; trailing edge of wings transparent white in overhead flight, against bright sky. Small parties of 3 to 10 birds, rummage the hillsides, scratching and digging furiously; mostly fly downhill; run up when alarmed; colouration hides the birds well in preferred haunts. **Food:** grass shoots, tubers, bulbous roots; swallows grit. **Voice:** noisy; cock utters loud whistle of several notes. **Range:** resident; the Himalaya; Kashmir to Kumaon and W Nepal; 3800–5500m in summer; low to about 2200m in winter. **Habitat:** alpine meadows, rocky country above tree-line.

**(236) CHUKAR PARTRIDGE** *Alectoris chukar* 38cm. Sexes alike. Ashy-pink-brown partridge; chestnut in outer tail; prominent, broad black and buff bars on flanks; black stripe across forehead continues through and behind the eyes to form a necklace on upper breast; white cheeks, chin, throat. Female lacks spur on tarsus; also slightly smaller. Gregarious; coveys amidst cultivated areas, scrub and rocky country; collects at water; strong but short flight, flying much faster downhill. **Food:** grain, bulbous roots, grass shoots, wheat, barley; also insects. **Voice:** cock utters a loud chuckle, of up to a dozen notes. **Range:** resident; W Himalaya to C Nepal; about 1200–5000m. **Habitat:** scrub and rock-covered hills; cultivation.

*Chukar Partridge*

**(238) BLACK PARTRIDGE** *Francolinus francolinus* 35cm. **Male:** jet black, spotted and marked white and fulvous; white cheeks; chestnut collar, belly, under tail-coverts. **Female:** browner where male is black; rufous nuchal patch; no white cheeks or chestnut collar. Solitary or small parties in high grass and edge of canals; emerges in the open early mornings; sometimes cocks tail. **Food:** grain, seeds, tubers, fallen berries, insects. **Voice:** loud three to six note crow of the cock, frequently uttered, unmistakable once heard. **Range:** resident; N India, along foothills; south to N Gujarat and C Madhya Pradesh; an eastern race occurs east of Nepal in Duars; to about 2000m. **Habitat:** high grass, cultivation; prefers wetter areas along canals and rivers.

*Black Partridge*

**(241) PAINTED PARTRIDGE** *Francolinus pictus* 30cm. **Male:** blackish-brown above, profusely marked with white; dull-chestnut face, supercilium; chestnut throat; black below, thickly spotted white; rufous on abdomen-centre, vent. **Female:** similar to male but throat usually dirty white. Calls diagnostic. Pairs or adults with young; great skulkers; extremely secretive and not easily flushed; may roost in trees. **Food:** grain, grass and other seeds, fallen fruit, insects. **Voice:** noisy when breeding (SW monsoon); high-pitched, harsh grating four or five-noted *khik...kheek.kheek.khheeki* call, quite similar to that of Black Partridge; may call every 20–30 seconds, for up to 40 minutes; often in duet. **Range:** most of India, south of range of Black Partridge, south of line from central Gujarat, northern Madhya Pradesh, southern Uttar Pradesh. **Habitat:** grassland, scrub, cultivation.

*Painted Partridge*

*Grey Partridge*

**(246) GREY PARTRIDGE** *Francolinus pondicerianus* 35cm. Sexes alike. Grey-brown and rufous above, barred and blotched; buffy-rufous below; narrow cross-bars on throat, upper breast; fine black markings on abdomen, flanks; black loop around throat encloses bright rufous-yellow throat; female smaller, with indistinct spur. Small parties, digging and moving amidst scrub and grass; seen on country roads, dust bathing or feeding; quick to take to cover on being alarmed, scattering over the area. **Food:** cereal grains, seeds, fallen berries, insects. **Voice:** loud, high-pitched two to three note *pat..ee..la*; noisy. **Range:** resident: all India, south of Himalayan foothills. **Habitat:** open scrub, grass, cultivation.

**(250) GREY** or **COMMON QUAIL** *Coturnix coturnix* 20cm. **Male:** pale brown above, boldly streaked and marked; blackish chin, stripe down throat centre and narrow stripe curving to ear-coverts; rufous-buff breast with white shaft streaks; whitish abdomen. **Female**: buffy throat; breast heavily streaked with black. Pairs and small parties on ground; often huge numbers at favoured feeding sites; commoner in winter when numbers augmented; well known Indian bird, both for table as also for fighting and betting. **Food:** seeds, grain, insects. **Voice:** fluid whistling *wet..me..lips* of male is common and familiar call. **Range:** resident; local migrant; breeds in Kashmir to about 2500m and parts of N and NE India; common in winter over the country. **Habitat:** cultivation, standing crop, grasslands.

*Blackbreasted Quail*

**(253) BLUEBREASTED QUAIL** *Coturnix chinensis* 15cm. **Male:** slaty-blue forehead, supercilium, sides of neck, lower breast and flanks; grey-brown above, streaked and mottled; striking black and white on throat and upper breast; chestnut abdomen. **Female:** brownish, streaked and mottled; black-barred breast, flanks. Small parties in wet grasslands and scrub; drops into undergrowth soon after being flushed. The **(252) Blackbreasted** or **Rain Quail** *C coromandelica* has bold black streaks on flanks. **Food:** grass seeds, millets, small insects. **Voice:** soft double-note whistle *tiu..tiu...***Range:** resident; some local movements; roughly east and south of a line Bombay to Shimla; commoner in the eastern parts. **Habitat:** wet grassland, scrub, agriculture, tea gardens.

**(255) JUNGLE BUSH QUAIL** *Perdicula asiatica* 18cm. **Male:** brownish, streaked and mottled; dark buff and chestnut about face; bright chestnut chin, throat; whitish below with close black barrings. **Female:** like male above; pale pinkish-rufous wash on underbody; chestnut throat. Small parties in dense grass and undergrowth; have well laid favoured paths; explodes with a tremendous *whirr* when almost trodden upon. **Food:** grass seeds, grain, small insects. **Voice:** trilling, musical call, *tirri..tirri..*, often long-drawn and loud; other calls when breeding. **Range:** resident; all India, to about 1200m in the outer Himalaya. **Habitat:** dense grass, scrub, edge of forest.

*Jungle Bush Quail*

**(267) COMMON HILL PARTRIDGE** *Arborophila torqueola* 28cm. **Male:** chestnut cap, nape; black eyebrows, lores; rufous-buff ear-coverts; olive-brown above, streaked and mottled with black and chestnut; black throat and neck streaked white; prominent white band between breast and foreneck. **Female:** buff-rufous throat, sides of neck; black streaks on sides of head, neck. Small parties on forest floors; roosts up in trees at night, several huddled together. **Food:** seeds, insects, berries. **Voice:** mournful whistle *po..eer...po..eer...*, the second syllable slightly longer. **Range:** the Himalaya, east of Garhwal; 1000–4000m. **Habitat:** dense jungle undergrowth in hill country.

**(275) RED SPURFOWL** *Galloperdix spadicea* 35cm. A long-tailed game bird. **Male:** dark brown crown; brick-red naked patch around eye; reddish brown plumage, underparts scalloped with grey-brown. **Female:** sandy-rufous above, narrowly barred. Reddish legs with 2 to 4 sharp spurs in male, 1 or 2 spurs in female. Solitary or in pairs amongst dense cover in broken, hilly country; feeds in forest clearings and forest roads; runs fast on ground; roosts in trees at night. **Food:** grain, seeds, berries, insects. **Voice:** loud cackling notes; calls when flushed. **Range:** from Uttar Pradesh terai south across Gangetic Plains through the peninsula. **Habitat:** scrub in forested, broken hilly country.

**(278) PAINTED SPURFOWL** *Galloperdix lunulata* 32cm. **Male:** metallic green-black crown has faint white streakings; black sides of head, neck, with white spots; chestnut above, with white eye-spots; metallic bronze-green in wings and tail. **Female:** plain rufous-brown; no white spots in plumage; chestnut about face, cheeks; dark crown. Pairs or small parties in undergrowth; very shy and usually difficult to spot. **Food:** seeds, berries, insects. **Voice:** loud calls reported by males. **Range:** south of a line from Gwalior to Bengal; absent in Gujarat and Konkan; commoner in central and eastern peninsula. **Habitat:** dense thorn and bamboo jungle in broken hilly, rocky country.

**(282) BLOOD PHEASANT** *Ithaginis cruentus* 45cm. **Male:** bright red and black about face; greyish above, streaked; yellow mop-like crest; apple-green below, thickly streaked yellow; crimson on upper breast, wings and tail. **Female:** rich rufous-brown overall, finely marked; scarlet around eyes. Gregarious; strong runner; flies rarely; feeds in open clearings; extremely tame in certain areas and hence easily shot. **Food:** shoots of ferns and pines, moss, lichens. **Voice:** long-drawn squeal. **Range:** bird of high elevation in the Himalaya, east of central Nepal; 3200–4300m. **Habitat:** steep hill forest, ringal bamboo, rhododendron and juniper scrub; prefers snow-covered areas.

*Blood Pheasant*

**(285) WESTERN TRAGOPAN** *Tragopan melanocephalus* 70cm. **Male:** crimson and black plumage, profusely spotted white; red-tipped crest, red face patch; deep blue throat featherless; reddish on upper breast. **Female:** grey-brown plumage; rufous on head, neck; black and white streaks and spots on upperbody. Solitary or in pairs; very shy and elusive; occasionally emerges to feed in the open, around melting snow patches, along with other pheasants. **Food:** fresh leaves, ringal bamboo shoots, seeds, berries; also insects. **Voice:** rather goat-like *waa...waa...waa...* call notes; unmistakable once heard. **Range:** west Himalaya, from W Pakistan, through Kashmir to Garhwal; rather uncommon and little known over its entire range. **Habitat:** dense forest undergrowth; ringal bamboo.

*Western Tragopan*

**(290) IMPEYAN** or **MONAL PHEASANT** *Lophophorus impejanus* 70cm. **Male:** mix of glossy, metallic purple, blue and bronze-green above; prominent crest of iridescent green feathers; white lower back and rump; chestnut wings, distinctive in flight; short rufous tail; velvety black

*Monal Pheasant*

underparts. **Female:** mottled and streaked brown; white throat; short crest. Solitary or small parties; actively digs for food, often in deep snow; feeds in cultivation; wild, ringing cries distinctive in flight. **Food:** tubers, shoots, berries, insects, flower seeds. **Voice:** wild whistling call, *coooor..lew,* much like a Curlew's. **Range:** the Himalaya, west to east; 2300–5000m. **Habitat:** high forest, glades, snow patches.

**(293) KALIJ PHEASANT** *Lophura leucomelana* 65cm. **Male:** black above, with steel-blue gloss; glossy tail, ending in sickle-like feathers; whitish edges to rump feathers; bare, scarlet around eyes; long, hairy white crest; brownish-grey underbody; lanceolate breast feathers. **Female:** reddish-brown, scalloped paler; brown crest and bare scarlet patch around eye; brown tail, smaller than male's. Several races over the Himalaya and NE India, the males varying in colour from glossy black to black and grey/white; crest black in other races. Pairs or small gatherings; spends day on ground, gleaning on forest roads and clearings during early mornings and late afternoons; good flier; roosts in trees at night. **Food:** seeds, insects, small lizards, fruit; human excreta around habitation. **Voice:** loud crowing by male; chuckling calls on disturbance. **Range:** the Himalaya, NE hill regions; foothills country to about 3500m. **Habitat:** forest undergrowth, clearings, terraced cultivation, vicinity of hillside habitation.

*Kalij Pheasant*

*Red Junglefowl*

**(299) RED JUNGLEFOWL** *Gallus gallus* 65cm. Both sexes resemble domestic bantam breeds. **Male:** glistening red-orange above, with yellow about neck; metallic black tail with long, drooping central feathers distinctive. **Female:** 42cm; bright chestnut forehead, supercilia continuing to foreneck; reddish brown plumage, vermiculated with fine black and buff. Small parties, often several hens accompanying a cock; shy and skulking; emerges in clearings and on forest roads; flies up noisily when flushed. **Food:** grain, crops, tubers, insects. **Voice:** characteristic crow of male, a shriller version of domestic; other cackling sounds. **Range:** outer Himalaya, east of Kashmir; eastern and central India, south to Narmada river. **Habitat:** forest mixed with bamboo and cultivation patches.

*Grey Junglefowl*

**(301) GREY** or **SONNERAT'S JUNGLEFOWL** *Gallus sonneratii* **Male:** 80cm. **Br Male:** darkish-grey plumage, with white feather-shafts; blackish crown, neck, with white and yellow shaft-streaks and spots; rather waxy sickle-shaped arching tail distinctive. **Female:** 46cm; brownish overall, lightly streaked white above; white chin, throat; white underbody with bold markings on breast. Solitary, pairs or small coveys; rather shy and skulking; emerges in clearings and on forest roads to glean in early mornings and late evenings; roosts in trees and bamboo clumps. **Food:** seeds, tubers, crop shoots, insects, bamboo and *karvi* seeds. **Voice:** loud crow of male distinctive, *kuk..kuk..kura.kuk...*; noisy in early mornings, but intermittently calls during day; rather vocal when breeding. **Range:** peninsula and S India, south of a line from Mt Abu to C Madhya Pradesh, E Maharashtra and NW Andhra Pradesh, its range coinciding with the teak country. **Habitat:** mixed deciduous forest; also forest clearings, abandoned tea and coffee estates and other overgrown sites.

**(304) KOKLAS PHEASANT** *Pucrasia macrolopha* **Male:** 60cm; silvery grey above, streaked black; metallic green head, horns; long, brown occipital crest; pointed chestnut-brown tail; deep chestnut below. **Female:** 55cm; black and brown plumage, mottled and streaked; buffy-chestnut crown, with short crest. Pairs or small parties; keeps to steep slopes, where difficult to flush; emerges in clearings in early mornings; flies up at great speed when flushed, before plunging down. **Food:** tubers, shoots, leaves, seeds, insects. **Voice:** call is the best identification; loud *khok..kok..kok..kokha..*, with various tones; vocal around dawn and dusk, but intermittently through the day when breeding (April–June); interesting display of courting male. **Range:** the Himalaya; S Kashmir to CE Nepal; 1500–4000m, descending lower in winter. **Habitat:** steep forested hills, nullahs.

**(307) CHIR PHEASANT** *Catreus wallichii* **Male:** 100cm; pale buff above, close-barred black; dark brown head, long backward crest; bright red, naked orbital patch; buffy-white below; black on abdomen. **Female:** 70cm; paler orbital patch; more chestnut below. Small coveys in undergrowth and grass; very shy and skulking; hurtles downhill when flushed. **Food:** seeds, roots, tubers, insects. **Voice:** noisy before dawn and at dusk; loud, distinct call, sounding *chir..pir...chir..pir*; also some cackling calls. **Range:** the Himalaya between NW Pakistan and C Nepal; 1200–3500m. **Habitat:** grass covered steep, rocky hillsides with scattered tree cover.

**(311) COMMON PEAFOWL** *Pavo cristatus* **Male:** 110cm (including full tail or train 2.25m). Glistening blue neck and breast; wire-like crest and very long tail distinctive. **Female:** 85cm; lacks blue neck, breast; browner plumage; lacks the long train. Familiar bird of India; solitary or in small parties, several females with one or more males; wary in the forested parts, rather tame and confiding in many parts of W and C India around human habitation; ever-alert, gifted with keen eyesight and hearing. **Food:** seeds, berries, shoots and tubers, insects, lizards, small snakes, worms. **Voice:** loud *may-yow* calls at dawn and dusk; also loud nasal calls and cackles; very noisy during the rains, when breeding. **Range:** all India, from about 2000m in Himalaya. **Habitat:** forest, neighbourhood of villages and cultivated country.

*Common Peafowl*

*Yellowlegged Button Quail*

**(314) YELLOWLEGGED BUTTON QUAIL** *Turnix tanki* 15cm. A three-toed ground bird, resembling a true quail. Female slightly bigger. Yellow legs and beak in both sexes. **Male:** blackish crown has rufous and buff; pale stripe through centre of crown; white chin, throat; buffy underparts, with dark spots on sides of breast. **Female:** like male; prominent rufous-orange nuchal collar. Single or in pairs, rarely gathers into coveys; confirmed skulker, difficult to see; moves amidst dense, damp herbage. **Food:** seeds, insects, tender shoots. **Voice:** female has a loud drumming call. **Range:** all India, from about 1200m in the Himalaya. **Habitat:** damp grasslands, scrub, cultivation.

**(318) INDIAN BUSTARD-QUAIL** *Turnix suscitator* 15cm. Sexes alike. Female slightly larger. Distinctive white eye; dark brown crown;black speck on white sides of head; back speckled with white, black and brown. Pale buff on wing shoulders seen in flight diagnostic. **Food:** seeds, grains and small insects. **Voice:** females a loud drumming during breeding. **Range:** India, south of the Himalaya. **Habitat:** grass, scrub near cultivation, open forests.

**(320) COMMON CRANE** *Grus grus* 140cm. Sexes alike. Pale slaty-grey plumage; slight red on crown when seen from close range; black face, throat and white stripe on

*Indian Bustard-Quail*

sides of head, neck; black flight-feathers and dark, drooping tail plumes diagnostic. Gregarious in winter; feeds in mornings and evenings in cultivation; rests during day; rather shy and suspicious, ever alert; slow, but strong flight. **Food:** shoots, tubers, grain, insects; also watermelons in some areas. **Voice:** loud, strident trumpeting *krr...oohk..;* calls on ground and from high in skies; also other harsh, screeching notes. **Range:** winter visitor; commonest in NW India, progressively less towards the east, rarely straying south of S Maharashtra and N Andhra Pradesh. **Habitat:** cultivation of wheat, gram, groundnut; also riverbeds.

**(321) BLACK-NECKED CRANE** *Grus nigricollis* Sexes alike, 150cm. Female slightly smaller. Black head, neck; dull-red lores, complete crown; small white patch around eye; greyish plumage; black wing-tips, drooping plumes. Pairs or small flocks, up to 70 birds seen together in Bhutan; barely three to five pairs breeding in Indian region (Ladakh); inhabits high-altitude open marshes and lakesides, where much revered by locals; dancing displays commence around March; flies high during afternoons, calling loudly. **Food:** fallen grain, shoots, tubers, insects and possibly molluscs. **Voice:** loud, trumpet-like calls, higher-pitched than Sarus Crane's. **Range:** breeds only in Ladakh within Indian limits; possibly in parts of Arunachal Pradesh. A larger population inhabits the Tibetan plateau; up to a hundred birds winter in parts of C and E Bhutan. **Habitat:** high-altitude marshes, lakesides, open cultivation.

*Black-necked Crane*

**(323) SARUS CRANE** *Grus antigone* 165cm. Sexes alike, but female slightly smaller; grey plumage; naked red head, upper neck; young birds are brownish-grey, with rusty-brown on head. Pairs, family parties or flocks; also feeds along with other waterbirds; known to pair for life and usually well protected in northern and west-central India, but habitat loss continues to be grave threat; flies under 40 feet off ground. **Food:** fish, frogs, crustaceans, insects, grains, tubers. **Voice:** very loud, far-reaching trumpeting, often a duet between a pair; elaborate dancing rituals. **Range:** commoner in N and C India (E Rajasthan, Gujarat, N and C Madhya Pradesh, Gangetic plain). **Habitat:** marshes, jheels, well-watered cultivation, village ponds.

*Sarus Crane*

*Siberian Crane*

**(325) SIBERIAN CRANE** *Grus leucogeranus* 140cm. Sexes alike. Snow-white plumage striking; naked-red face; black in flight feathers. Young birds, which also arrive in winter, have buff-brown-cinnamon in plumage; complete head feathered. Pairs or small flocks; the flock size wintering in India (Bharatpur in Rajasthan) has been falling over the years, with barely a dozen birds arriving; spends most of its time in shallow water, feeding with head submerged; the bird is of much concern to conservationists. **Food:** shoots, tubers, aquatic seeds; perhaps also insects. **Voice:** vocal; its loud trumpeting calls may be heard in winter too; musical *koonk...koonk..* in flight. **Range:** winter visitor; rather uncommon, today restricted only to Bharatpur; sporadically recorded in parts of N India, Bihar; southernmost record is around Nagpur. **Habitat:** open marshes, jheels.

*Demoiselle Crane*

**(326) DEMOISELLE CRANE** *Anthropoides virgo* 75cm. Sexes alike. Overall plumage grey; black head and neck; prominent white ear-tufts; long black feathers of lower neck fall over breast; brownish-grey secondaries sickle-shaped and drooping over tail. Young birds have grey head and much shorter drooping secondaries over tail. Huge flocks in winter, often many thousands; feeds early mornings and early evenings in cultivation; rests during hot hours on marsh-edges and sandbanks; flies *en-masse* when disturbed. **Food:** wheat, paddy, gram; does extensive damage to winter crops. **Voice:** high-pitched, sonorous *krook...krook..* calls. **Range:** winter visitor; commonest in NW India and over E Rajasthan, Gujarat and Madhya Pradesh, though sporadically over much of the country. **Habitat:** winter crop-fields, sandy river-banks, ponds, jheel edges.

**(329) BLUEBREASTED BANDED RAIL** *Rallus striatus* 28cm. **Male:** dark-brown above, with narrow white spots and bars; chestnut head, hindneck (necksides); whitish chin, throat, ashy-blue breast, foreneck; black-and-white barred below; red beak, eyes and olive-grey legs also help identification. **Female:** duller above; whiter belly. Mostly solitary, though mate is usually nearby; unobtrusive, secretive and cautious; moves with head held high but vanishes into reeds and low growth on slightest suspicion; legs dangle behind in flight. **Food:** molluscs, insects, shoots of marsh plants. **Voice:** two-noted call sometimes heard during rains. **Range:** widespread over Indian region, though possibly absent in NW regions; commoner in SW, C and parts of E India; this is one of the several species of the family *Rallidae* that tends to be generally overlooked by bird-watchers; are in fact commoner than they appear. **Habitat:** marshes, reedbeds, paddy cultivation, ponds.

**(332) INDIAN** or **SLATYLEGGED BANDED CRAKE** *Rallina eurizonoides* 25cm. Sexes alike. Rich, cinnamon chocolate-brown head, neck and breast; white on chin and throat; darkish rufous-brown above; banded black and white below breast; slaty legs. Solitary or in pairs; semi-nocturnal; shy and elusive, sneaking into dense cover at the slightest sign of disturbance; flies into tree when suddenly flushed; walks upright, with cocked tail. **Food:** insects, molluscs, seeds and shoots of certain marshland plants. **Voice:** noisy during SW monsoon, when breeding; mix of double-noted and harsh, single-note crying calls; noisier at night. **Range:** throughout the Indian region. **Habitat:** well-watered areas, usually in and around jungle areas.

**(338) SPOTTED CRAKE** *Porzana porzana* 22cm. Sexes alike. Olive-brown above, with a rufescent wash, streaked black; grey supercilium, sides of head and neck; whitish chin, throat; greyish breast spotted white; white barring on grey-brown flanks. Solitary or pairs; crepuscular; skulks and very difficult to spot; in some areas, can be approached if one remains very quiet and still; moves amidst reed beds and jheel vegetation; gently and warily sneaks under leaf or dense growth if disturbed. The **(339) Ruddy Crake** *P fusca* has a chestnut face with upperparts dark olive-brown. **Food:** insects, worms, seeds of aquatic plants. **Voice:** unrecorded, said to be silent. **Range:** winter visitor over most of the country, south to about central Karnataka. **Habitat:** reed-covered jheels, vegetation in and around marshes.

*Ruddy Crake*

**(342) BROWN CRAKE** *Amaurornis akool* 28cm. Sexes alike, but female slightly smaller. Darkish olive-brown upperbody, wings and tail; white chin and throat fade into ashy-grey underparts; browner on breast, flanks and abdomen. Solitary or pairs; mostly crepuscular, extremely elusive and secretive; feeds in early mornings and late evenings on edges of jheels, flicking the stub tail and generally moving very suspiciously. **Food:** insects, molluscs, seeds of marshland plants. **Voice:** mostly silent, but a plaintive note and a long-drawn, vibrating whistle have been described. **Range:** resident and local migrant; south from Kashmir lowlands down through the peninsula, at least to Mysore and Orissa. **Habitat:** reed-covered marshes, irrigation channels, dense growth on jheels.

*Whitebreasted Waterhen*

**(343) WHITEBREASTED WATERHEN** *Amaurornis phoenicurus* 32cm. Sexes alike. White forehead, sides of head; dark slaty-grey above; silky white below; slaty-grey sides of breast, flanks; rufous on vent and under tail-coverts. Solitary or in small parties; often around village ponds and tanks, occasionally derelict patches in towns; jerks stumpy tail as it walks with long strides; climbs trees easily, especially when breeding. **Food:** insects, worms, molluscs, shoots of marsh plants. **Voice:** very noisy when breeding during rains, a series of loud croaks and chuckles, the commonest being a harsh *krr..khwakk...*; often calls through the night; silent during dry season. **Range:** south from Himalayan foothills through the country. **Habitat:** reed-covered marshes, ponds and tanks, monsoon cultivation and streams.

*Moorhen*

**(347) MOORHEN** *Gallinula chloropus* 32cm. Sexes alike. Dark grey head, neck; dark brownish-olive above; slaty-grey below, white centre of abdomen; fine white border to edge of wing; bright red frontal shield and base of beak with greenish-yellow tip diagnostic; greenish legs. Usually in small parties; commoner in winter; moves amidst marsh vegetation, jerking tail; good swimmer, jerks head as it swims. **Food:** seeds and tubers of water plants, insects, molluscs, small fish and frogs. **Voice:** occasional loud, harsh *prruck...*; noisy when breeding, uttering loud croaking notes. **Range:** throughout the country, from about 2400m in Himalaya; breeds commonly in Kashmir, but also in parts of the peninsula. **Habitat:** vegetation and reed covered ponds, tanks, jheels.

**(349) INDIAN PURPLE MOORHEN** *Porphyrio porphyrio*
45cm. Sexes alike. Purplish-blue plumage; long red legs
with oversized toes distinctive; thickish red beak; bald red
forehead (casque); white under stumpy tail, seen when tail
flicked up; bald red patch on forehead smaller in female.
Small parties amidst reeds and other vegetation on marsh
and jheels; sometimes large gatherings on vegetation-
covered waterbodies; walks on floating growth, swims
rarely; rather tame in some areas. **Food:** vegetable matter,
seeds, tubers; known to damage paddy crop; insects, molluscs, small frogs also eaten. **Voice:** noisy when breeding,
a mix of cackling and hooting notes. **Range:** mostly resident;
south, throughout the country, from about 1500m in Kashmir.
**Habitat:** vegetation and reed-covered jheels, tanks.

*Purple Moorhen*

**(350) COOT** *Fulica atra* 42cm. Sexes alike. Slaty-black
plumage; stout ivory-white beak and flat forehead-shield
distinctive. Almost tailless and duck-like appearance.
Gregarious; much more abundant in winter when numbers greatly augmented by winter visitors; huge gatherings on jheels, ponds and placid stretches of rivers;
wavelike sound of a huge flock of coots flying or paddling
over water, amidst much chuckling sounds; dives underwater; much hunted, especially in winter, when this
species serves as staple diet for many locals; patters along
water surface, rising with some difficulty. **Food:** seeds,
shoots of aquatic plants; paddy, insects, molluscs. **Voice:**
loud *kraw;* chuckling sounds. **Range:** all India; resident
and winter visitor. **Habitat:** reed-fringed jheels, tanks,
slow-moving rivers.

*Coot*

**(354) GREAT INDIAN BUSTARD** *Choriotis nigriceps* **Male:**
120cm. Black crown, short crest; sandy-buff upperbody, finely marked black; white below; black band on lower-breast.
**Female:** 92cm; smaller size; breast gorget broken and only
rarely full. Scattered pairs or small parties; shy, difficult to
approach; enters immediate vicinity of *Bishnoi* villages and
other rural habitation; fast runner; hides in shade of bushes;
flies low over ground. **Food:** grain, seeds, tubers; also insects, rodents, snakes and lizards. **Voice:** loud *whonk...,*
often audible for over a mile. **Range:** resident and local
migrant; distant areas of Rajasthan, Gujarat, Maharashtra,
Karnataka; numbers and erstwhile range much reduced
today. **Habitat:** open grassland and scrub; semi-desert.

*Great Indian Bustard*

*Lesser Florican*

**(357) LIKH** or **LESSER FLORICAN** *Sypheotides indica* **Male:** 45cm. Black and white plumage; narrow, upcurving plumes on head striking. **Female:** slightly larger than male; pale sandy-buff, profusely streaked, mottled with dark brown and black; black crown, with pale median stripe. Winter male like female, but more white in wings diagnostic. Solitary or in pairs; in breeding season, several males display over a wide, open grasslands; extremely difficult bird to observe, keeps to dense grass growth; tight sitters, runs through cover, but flies far and strongly when flushed; range and numbers much reduced today. **Food:** chiefly insects; also shoots, seeds. **Voice:** rattling call of displaying male, likened to sound made by rubbing tongue on palate; audible for considerable distances; calls during display jump. **Range:** moves considerably; breeds during monsoon in parts of C India; not much data for winter range. **Habitat:** tall grassland, cultivation.

*Pheasant-tailed Jacana*

**(358) PHEASANT-TAILED JACANA** *Hydrophasianus chirurgus* **Male:** 30cm, with 14cm tail when breeding; breeding plumage choco-brown and white; golden yellow on hindneck. When not breeding is dull-brown and white, also has blackish necklace and lacks long tail; very long

toes diagnostic. Solitary or pairs when breeding; small flocks in winter; purely aquatic, moving on vegetation-covered pond surface; unusually long toes enable it to trip on the lightest of floating leaves; quite confiding on village ponds. **Food:** mostly seeds, tubers, roots; also insects, molluscs. **Voice:** loud *mewing* call when breeding, two birds often calling in duet. **Range:** throughout country, from about 1500m in Kashmir; occasionally seen much higher. **Habitat:** ponds and jheels covered with floating-vegetation.

**(359) BRONZEWINGED JACANA** *Metopidius indicus* 30cm. Sexes alike. Female slightly larger. Glossy black head, neck, breast; glistening bronze-green back, wings; broad white stripe over eyes; chestnut rump, tail; long legs with massive toes distinctive. Immature birds have rufous-brown crown; black terminal band to tail and whitish underbody, tinged rufous-buff around breast. Small gatherings during winter and summer, breaking into pairs during rains; keeps to leafy, floating growth on jheel beds, village tanks, where usually difficult to see; wary, moves slowly and silently; flies low, with long legs trailing, but soon settles. **Food:** tubers, seeds of aquatic plants; also insects, crustacea, molluscs. **Voice:** loud harsh notes; also a shrill piping call. **Range:** most of India, excepting some NW regions (W Punjab and W Rajasthan). **Habitat:** vegetation-covered jheels, ponds.

*Bronzewinged Jacana*

**(360) OYSTERCATCHER** *Haematopus ostralegus* 42cm. Sexes alike. Pied plumage. Black head, upperparts, breast; white below; long orange beak and pinkish legs distinctive. White on throat in winter. White rump and broad wing-bar conspicuous in flight. Young birds are browner. Commoner on sea coasts, frequently associates with other waders, especially the larger ones; runs and probes ooze; beak highly specialised for feeding on molluscs. **Food:** molluscs, crabs, worms. **Voice:** piping *kleeeep...* in flight; also a shrill whistle, often double-noted, uttered on ground as well as in flight. **Range:** winter visitor, specially to the coastal regions; more common on western seaboard. **Habitat:** rocky and sandy coastal areas.

*Oystercatcher*

**(362) WHITETAILED LAPWING** *Vanellus leucurus* 28cm. Sexes alike. Pink-brown above, with grey-white forehead, supercilium; ash-grey chin, throat, turning dark-grey on breast; yellow legs; in flight, white rump, tail, black and white in wings diagnostic. The **(363) Sociable Lapwing** *V gregarius* has brown crown, stripe through eyes; in flight, dark sub-terminal tail-band, large white patch in dark wings. Small to medium-size flocks, often with other waders; makes short runs when feeding; less boisterous and active than the commoner Redwattled, but overall similarity in habits. **Food:** molluscs, water insects, worms. **Voice:** mostly silent in winter except for an occasional soft, double-noted whistle. **Range:** winter visitor, NW India; smaller numbers east to Uttar Pradesh, parts of Bihar, C India. **Habitat:** open marshy areas, edges of lakes and jheels.

**(366) REDWATTLED LAPWING** *Vanellus indicus* 35cm. Sexes alike. Jet-black head, neck, breast; bronze-brown upperbody; white below, continuing to broad bands up the neck-sides towards eyes; fleshy crimson facial wattles diagnostic. Solitary or pairs when breeding; often large flocks in winter; moves on open ground, feeds during mornings and evenings; vigilant species, its loud cries heralding any new activity in an area; often feeds late into evening. **Food:** insects, seeds and tubers. **Voice:** noisy; its loud, piercing *did ye do it..* calls amongst the most familiar bird-calls of India; dive-bombs at intruders when breeding, shrieking wildly. **Range:** throughout India, from about 2000m in W Himalaya. **Habitat:** open country, roadsides, village and town outskirts, edge of jheels.

*Redwattled Lapwing*

**(369) SPURWINGED LAPWING** *Vanellus spinosus* 30cm. Sexes alike. Black forehead, crown, crest drooping over back; sandy grey-brown above; black and white wings; black chin, throat, with white border; grey-brown breast band; white below with black patch on belly; black spur at bend of wing. Usually pairs in close vicinity; may collect into small parties during winter, sometimes with other waders; makes short dashes or feeds at water's edge; often remains in hunched posture, when not easy to spot; slow flight; reported to swim and dive. **Food:** crustaceans, insects, small frogs. **Voice:** rather like Redwattled, only a bit softer and less shrill; also a sharp *deed..did..did..* **Range:** breeds in parts of E and C India, including Orissa, Andhra Pradesh and eastern Madhya Pradesh; may disperse in winter. **Habitat:** stony river-beds, sandbanks; sometimes collects around jheels in winter.

**(370) YELLOW-WATTLED LAPWING** *Vanellus malabaricus* 28cm. Sexes alike. Jet black cap, bordered with white; sandy-brown upperbody; black band in white tail; in flight, white bar in black wings; black chin, throat; sandy-brown breast; black band on lower breast; white below; yellow lappets above and in front of eyes and yellow legs diagnostic. Solitary or in pairs, rarely small gatherings; sometimes with the commoner Redwattled; as a rule, prefers drier habitat; quiet and unobtrusive; feeds on ground, moving suspiciously. **Food:** mostly insects. **Voice:** short plaintive notes; on the whole a quiet bird; quick-repeated notes when nest site intruded upon. **Range:** from NW India south through country; does not occur in extreme NE. **Habitat:** dry, open country.

*Yellow-wattled Lapwing*

**(380) LITTLE RINGED PLOVER** *Charadrius dubius* 16cm. Sexes alike. Sandy-brown above; white forehead; black bands on head, breast and white neck-ring diagnostic; white chin, throat; lack of wing-bar in flight and yellow legs and ring around eye additional clues. Small numbers, often along with other waders; runs on ground, on ooze and drying jheels, walks with characteristic bobbing gait, picking food from ground; when approached close, flies rapidly, low over ground, zig-zag flight accompanied by a whistling note. **Food:** insects, worms, tiny crabs. **Voice:** a *few... few..* whistle, high-pitched but somewhat plaintive, uttered mostly on wing. **Range:** resident and local migrant; throughout country south from Himalayan foothills. **Habitat:** shingle-covered river banks, tidal mudflats, estuaries, lake edges.

*Little Ringed Plover*

**(388) CURLEW** *Numenius arquata* 58cm. Sexes alike. A large wader. Sandy-brown upperbody, scalloped fulvous and black; white rump and lower back; whitish below, streaked black; very long, down-curved beak. The very similar **(385) Whimbrel** *N phaeopus* is smaller; has a blackish crown with white stripe through centre, and white stripes on sides of head. Mostly solitary; feeds with other large waders; runs on ground, between tidemarks, occasionally venturing in very shallow water; a truly wild and wary bird, not easy to approach close. **Food:** crustaceans, insects, mudskippers. **Voice:** famed scream; a wild, rather musical *cour..lee* or *cooor..lee..* the first note longer. **Range:** winter visitor; sea coast, west to east; large inland marshes, rivers. **Habitat:** estuaries, creeks, large remote marshes.

*Curlew*

*Blacktailed Godwit*

*Redshank*

*Greenshank*

**(389) BLACKTAILED GODWIT** *Limosa limosa* 40cm. Sexes alike. Female slightly larger. Grey-brown above; whitish below; very long, straight beak; in flight, broad, white wing-bars, white rump and black tail-tip distinctive. In summer dull rufous-red on head, neck and breast, with close-barred lower breast, flanks. The **(391) Bartailed Godwit** *L lapponica* has slightly upcurved beak; in flight, lack of white wing-bars and barred black-and-white tail help identification. Gregarious, often with other large waders; quite active, probing with long beak; wades in water, often the long legs barely visible; fast and graceful, low flight. **Food:** crustaceans, worms, molluscs, aquatic insects. **Voice:** an occasional, fairly loud *kwika..kwik*. **Range:** winter visitor, fairly common over N India; lesser numbers towards E and S India. The Bartailed is commoner along the W seaboard, south to between Ratnagiri and Bombay. **Habitat:** marshes, estuaries, creeks.

**(393) REDSHANK** *Tringa totanus* 28cm. Sexes alike. Grey-brown above; whitish below, faintly marked about breast; white rump, broad band along trailing edge of wings; orange-red legs and base of beak. In summer, browner above, marked black and fulvous, and more heavily streaked below. The **(392) Spotted Redshank** *T erythropus* is very similar but lacks complete white band along trailing edge of wings in flight. Small flocks, often with other waders; makes short dashes, probing and jabbing deep in ooze; may also enter water, with long legs completely submerged; rather alert and suspicious bird. **Food:** aquatic insects, crustaceans, molluscs. **Voice:** quite musical, fairly loud and shrill *tleu.ewh.ewh*, mostly in flight or during take-off; very similar to Greenshank's call, but more shrill and high-pitched. **Range:** breeds in Kashmir, Ladakh above 3000m; winter visitor over the country; fairly common. **Habitat:** marshes, creeks, estuaries.

**(396) GREENSHANK** *Tringa nebularia* 36cm. Sexes alike. Grey-brown above; long, slightly upcurved, blackish beak; white forehead, underbody; in flight, white lower back, rump and absence of white in wings diagnostic; long, greenish legs. In summer, darker above, with blackish centres to feathers. The **(395) Marsh Sandpiper** *T stagnatilis* is very similar but smaller and has distinctly longer legs;

also has distinctive call. Either solitary or small groups of 2 to 6 birds, often with Redshanks and other waders; feeds at edge of water but may enter water to belly level. **Food:** crustaceans, molluscs, aquatic insects. **Voice:** wild, ringing *tew.tew.tew..*, much like Redshanks, but less shrill; occasionally a single note, heard when disturbed. **Range:** winter visitor, fairly common, most of India. **Habitat:** marshes, estuaries, creeks.

**(398) WOOD SANDPIPER** *Tringa glareola* 20cm. Sexes alike. Grey-brown above, closely spotted white; slender build; white rump, tail; white below; brown on breast; no wing-bar. Summer: dark olive-brown above, spotted white. The **(397) Green Sandpiper** *T ochropus* is stouter, more shy, much darker, glossy brown-olive above; in flight, white rump contrasts strikingly with dark upperbody; blackish below wings diagnostic. Small to medium-size flocks, often with others; quite active, probing deep into ooze or feeding at edge. **Food:** crustaceans, insects, molluscs. **Voice:** quite noisy; sharp, trilling notes on ground; shrill, somewhat metallic *chiff.chiff* calls when flushed; sometimes a loud, sharp *tluie..* call, *T ochropus* has distinct, wild ringing calls when flushed. **Range:** winter visitor to most of India. **Habitat:** wet cultivation, marshes, tidal creeks, mudflats.

*Green Sandpiper*

**(401) COMMON SANDPIPER** *Tringa hypoleucos* 20cm. Sexes alike. Olive-brown above, more ash-brown and streaked-brown on head, neck sides; brown rump white below, lightly streaked-brown on breast; in flight, narrow, white wing-bar and brown rump. In summer is darker above and speckled. One to three birds, either by themselves or scattered amidst mixed wader flocks; quite active, makes short dashes, bobbing, wagging short tail; usually flies low over water, the rapid wing-beats interspersed with short glides ('vibrating flight') helping identification of the species. **Food:** crustaceans, insects, molluscs. **Voice:** shrill *twee..tse.tse.tse..*note, usually when flushed; longish, trilling song. **Range:** breeds in Himalayas, Kashmir to Garhwal to about 3000m plus; winter visitor all over India. **Habitat:** freshwater marshes, lakes, tidal areas, creeks.

*Common Sandpiper*

*Solitary Snipe*

**(404) EASTERN SOLITARY SNIPE** *Gallinago solitaria* 30cm. Sexes alike. Cryptic coloured marsh-bird with plump body and very long beak. Dense plumage, brown, buff, black and fulvous, with some chestnut markings above. The various species of snipe are not easy to distinguish in field. Flight style and numbers of feathers in tail help identification. This species has 18 feathers, but this character only helpful when bird in hand. The **(405) Wood Snipe** *G nemoricola* of the Himalaya is very similar but somewhat darker and heavier and slower in flight. Usually solitary; secretive and silent; mostly seen only when flushed; short, erratic flight when flushed. **Food:** small snails, worms, aquatic insects. **Voice:** fairly loud *pench..* call in flight. **Range:** a mountain bird; breeds about 2800–4500m in Himalaya, Ladakh & Kashmir to NE India; moves lower in winter, sporadically in parts of E plains. **Habitat:** dense growth along marshy mountain streams.

**(409) COMMON** or **FANTAIL SNIPE** *Gallinago gallinago* 28cm. Sexes alike. Cryptic coloured marsh-bird, brownish-buff, heavily streaked and marked buff, rufous and black; dull-white below. Fast, erratic flight; 14 or 16 tail-feathers; whitish wing-lining distinctive, but not easily seen. The **(406) Pintail Snipe** *G stenura* is very similar and usually distinguished only in hand and with much practice. Usually several in dense marsh-growth; very difficult to see unless flushed; probes with long beak in the ooze, often in shallow water; feeds mostly during mornings and evenings, often continuing through the night. **Food:** small molluscs, worms, insects. **Voice:** loud *pench* call when flushed. **Range:** breeds in parts of W Himalaya; mostly winter visitor over the sub-continent, commoner in N and C India. **Habitat:** marshlands, paddy cultivation, jheel edges.

*Painted Snipe*

**(429) PAINTED SNIPE** *Rostratula benghalensis* 25cm. Polyandrous. **Br Female:** metallic olive above, thickly marked buff and black; buff stripe down crown-centre; chestnut throat, breast, sides of neck; white below breast. **Br Male:** duller overall; lacks chestnut. Sexes difficult to distinguish when not in breeding plumage. Crepuscular and nocturnal; solitary or a few scattered birds; feeds in squelchy mud but also moves on drier ground; runs on landing; **Food:** insects, crustaceans, molluscs and vegetable matter. **Voice:** common call a long-drawn, mellow note that can be likened to the noise made by blowing into a bottle-mouth. **Range:** resident, throughout country from about 2000m in the Himalaya. **Habitat:** wet ooze, marshes, such areas where there is a mix of open water, ooze and heavy, low cover.

**(430) BLACKWINGED STILT** *Himantopus himantopus* 25cm. **Male:** jet-black mantle, pointed wings (above and below); rest of plumage glossy white. **Female:** dark brown where male is black; black wing underside; black spots on head; duller overall in winter. Very long pink-red legs diagnostic, extend much beyond tail in flight. Gregarious; large numbers, often along with other waders on a wetland; long legs enable it to enter deeper water; clumsy walk; submerges head when feeding; characteristic flight silhouette. **Food:** aquatic insects, molluscs, vegetable matter. **Voice:** shrill notes in flight, very tern-like; noisy when breeding. **Range:** resident and local migrant over most of country, from about 1800m in W Himalaya. **Habitat:** marshes, salt-pans, tidal creeks, village ponds, also riversides.

*Blackwinged Stilt*

**(432) AVOCET** *Recurvirostra avosetta* 45cm. Sexes alike. Long legged. Black and white plumage, long bluish legs and long, slender upcurved beak diagnostic. (The Blackwinged Stilt has reddish legs, long straight beak and glossy back and wings). In flight, the long legs extend much beyond the tail. Usually gregarious, only sometimes two to three birds scattered over waterbody; either runs or moves quickly, but very gracefully on oozy ground; frequently enters shallow water; characteristic sideways movement of head when feeding, the head bent low as upcurved beak sweeps along bottom ooze; also swims and 'up-ends', ducklike. **Food:** aquatic insects, minute molluscs, crustaceans. **Voice:** loud, somewhat fluty *klooeet* or *kloeep* call, mostly on wing; also some harsh, screaming notes. **Range:** breeds in Kutch, N Buluchistan; winter visitor, sporadically over most parts of India, commoner in NW regions, including Gujarat, coastal Maharashtra. **Habitat:** freshwater marshes, coastal tidal areas, creeks.

*Avocet*

*Stone Curlew*

**(436) STONE CURLEW** *Burhinus oedicnemus* 40cm. Sexes alike. Sandy-brown plumage, streaked dark; whitish below breast; thickish head, long, bare yellow legs and large eye-goggles diagnostic; white wing-patch in flight. Solitary or in pairs; strictly a ground bird; crepuscular and nocturnal; rather quiet, sitting for long hours in same patch, where seen regularly; colouration and nature makes it difficult to spot; squats tight or runs in short steps when located and disturbed, moving suspiciously. **Food:** small reptiles, insects, slugs; also seeds. **Voice:** a plaintive, curlew-like call at dusk and thereafter; also sharp *pick...pick..* notes. **Range**: drier parts of country, from about 1200m in outer Himalaya. **Habitat:** light, dry forest, scrub, dry riverbanks, ravinous country, orchards and open *babool* clad areas.

*Great Stone Plover*

**(437) GREAT STONE PLOVER** *Esacus magnirostris* 50cm. Sexes alike. Sandy-grey above; thick-set head and enormous-looking, somewhat upturned, black and yellow beak; large goggle-eyes surrounded by white; two black bands on face; white below, washed grey on neck, breast; white in flight-feathers, visible in flight. Solitary or pairs on open barrenland, river banks or rocks in mid-river; mostly crepuscular and partly nocturnal; spends day under strong sun, resting and usually very difficult to spot; extremely wary, moving cautiously on approach. **Food:** crabs, molluscs, small insects; also lizards. **Voice:** harsh call-note, somewhat whistle-like; wild, piping calls at night, especially when breeding (February to April, sometimes till mid-May). **Range:** almost all India, south of terai; uncommon in NE regions. **Habitat:** dry, open country; barrenlands, river banks, rocky areas, islands in jheels.

*Indian Courser*

**(440) INDIAN COURSER** *Cursorius coromandelicus* 26cm. Sexes alike. Bright rufous crown; white and black stripes above and through eyes to nape; sandy brown above; chestnut throat, breast and black belly; long, whitish legs; in flight, dark underwings. Small parties in open country; strictly a ground-bird, runs in short spurts and feeds on ground, typical plover-style, suddenly dipping body;

when disturbed, flies strongly for short distance and lands; can fly very high. **Food:** black beetles, other insects. **Voice:** soft hen-like clucking call in flight, when flushed. **Range:** most of the country south of the Himalaya, but distribution rather patchy; absent in NE. **Habitat:** open scrub, fallow land, dry cultivation.

**(444) SMALL INDIAN PRATINCOLE** *Glareola lactea* 16cm. Sexes alike. Brown forehead; sandy-grey above; black stripe from eye to beak; white, squarish tail, tipped black; smoky-brown underbody has a rufous wash; whiter on lower breast and abdomen; long, narrow wings and short legs. The **(442) Collared Pratincole** *G pratincola* is larger, with forked tail and black loop on throat. Gregarious; large flocks over an open expanse, close to water; very swallow-like in demeanour; strong and graceful flight over water surface catching insects on wing; fly high in late evening. **Food:** insects, taken on wing. **Voice:** soft, but harsh call-notes in flight. **Range:** resident and local migrant; all India south of outer Himalaya, from about 1800m. **Habitat:** large, quiet riversides, sandbars, marshy expanses, coastal swamps, tidal creeks.

*Small Indian Pratincole*

**(455) BLACKHEADED GULL** *Larus ridibundus* 45cm. Sexes alike. **Winter;** when in India, greyish-white plumage; dark ear-patches; white outer flight-feathers, with black tips. **Summer Breeding:** coffee-brown head and upper neck, sometimes acquired just before emigration. The **(454) Brownheaded Gull** *L brunnicephalus* is larger and has white patches (mirrors) on black wing-tips. Highly gregarious; large flocks on sea coast, scavenging in harbour; wheels over busy seaside road or a beach; large numbers rest on rocky ground and sand; follow boats in harbour. **Food:** offal, fish, prawns, insects, earthworms. **Voice:** noisy; querulous *kree..ah...* screams. **Range:** winter visitor; commoner on western seaboard; also strays inland, both on passage and for short halts. **Habitat:** sea coast, harbours, sewage outflows, garbage dumps.

*Blackheaded Gull*

*Whiskered Tern*

**(458) WHISKERED TERN** *Chlidonias hybrida* 26cm. Sexes alike. Black markings on crown; silvery-grey-white plumage; long, narrow wings and slightly-forked, almost squarish tail; short red legs and red beak distinctive. **Summer:** jet-black cap and snow-white cheeks (whiskers); black belly. At rest, close wings extend beyond tail. Large numbers flying about a marsh or tidal creek, leisurely but methodically, beak pointed down; dive from about 5m height but turn when just about to touch the ground, perhaps picking up some insect in the process; also hunt flying insects over standing crops. **Food:** insects, crabs, small fish, tadpoles. **Voice:** sharp, wild notes. **Range:** breeds in Kashmir and Gangetic plain; common in winter over the country. **Habitat:** inland marshes, wet cultivation, coastal areas, tidal creeks.

**(462) CASPIAN TERN** *Hydroprogne caspia* 50cm. Sexes alike. A large tern. Pale-grey above; jet-black cap in summer, streaked white in winter; unmarked white below. Large size, stout, coral-red beak, black legs and feet, and slight tail-fork diagnostic. Young birds are barred brown above. Two to four birds flying over estuaries and creeks or resting on sandbanks at water's edge; rarely gathers into large flocks; when hunting, hovers over water, beak pointing down; on spotting quarry, plunges headlong. **Food:** chiefly fish; also crabs and prawns. **Voice:** loud, raucous *kreahh..krraa..* uttered in flight. **Range:** winter visitor over most of the Indian coast; breeds in Shri Lanka and W Pakistan. **Habitat:** coastal regions; lagoons, estuaries, backwaters.

*Indian River Tern*

**(463) INDIAN RIVER TERN** *Sterna aurantia* 42cm, with tail. Sexes alike. Very light grey above; jet-black cap, nape when breeding; white below; narrow, pointed wings, deeply forked tail; bright yellow, pointed beak and red legs diagnostic. In winter, black on crown and nape reduced to flecks. Solitary or small flocks, flying about erratically; keeps to riversides, calm waters, large tanks; scans over water, plunging if possible prey is sighted; rests on riverbanks, often dozens together; noisy and aggressive, especially at nesting colonies (March to mid-June). **Food:** fish, aquatic insects; also crabs, other crustaceans and molluscs. **Voice:** an occasional harsh, screeching note. **Range:** most of India; commoner in N and C India. **Habitat:** inland water bodies, rivers, tanks; almost completely absent on the seacoast.

**(479) INDIAN LESSER CRESTED TERN** *Sterna bengalensis* 45cm. Sexes alike. Greyish above, with slight lilac wash; jet black forehead, crown and nuchal crest in summer; whitish forehead and white-streaked crown diagnostic in winter. Blackish primaries, bright orange-yellow beak and black feet diagnostic. The **(478) Large Crested Tern** *S bergii* is larger and has white forehead all year round. Small parties out at sea, sometimes coming into coastal waters; flies leisurely between two and eight metres over water, hovering occasionally; dives headlong for fish. **Food:** fish, prawns. **Voice:** high-pitched *krrreeep...* scream in flight, sometimes when diving. **Range:** in winter over the entire Indian sea coast; possibly breeds in parts of W Pakistan coast, and some of the islets off the west coast of India. **Habitat:** open sea, coastal regions.

**(484) INDIAN SKIMMER** *Rynchops albicollis* 40cm. Slender, pointed-winged and tern-like. Sexes alike, but female slightly smaller. Pied plumage, blackish-brown above, contrasting with white underbody; white forehead, neck-collar, wing-bar; yellowish-orange beak, with much longer lower mandible; red legs. Solitary or loose flocks flying over water; characteristic hunting style is to skim over calm waters, beak wide open, the longer-projecting lower mandible partly submerged at an angle, to snap up fish on striking; many rest together on sandbars. **Food:** chiefly fish. **Voice:** a shrill scream; twittering cries at nest colony. **Range:** commoner in N and C India, east to Assam; less common south of Maharashtra, N Andhra Pradesh. **Habitat:** large rivers, especially fond of placid waters.

*Indian Skimmer*

*Indian Sandgrouse*

**(487) INDIAN SANDGROUSE** *Pterocles exustus* 28cm, with tail. **Male:** sandy-buff above, speckled brown and dull yellow; black gorget and choco-black belly. **Female:** buffy above, streaked and barred darker; black-spotted breast; rufous and black-barred belly, flanks. Pointed central tail feathers and black wing-underside distinctive in flight. Huge gatherings at waterholes in dry season; regularly arrives at water; strictly a ground bird, squatting tight or shuffling slowly; rises *en-masse*. **Food:** seeds of grasses and weeds. **Voice:** deep, clucking *kut...ro..* call-note, uttered mostly on wing. **Range:** all India except NE and extreme south; commoner in NW and C India. **Habitat:** open areas, semi-desert fallow land.

(489) **IMPERIAL SANDGROUSE** *Pterocles orientalis* 40cm. **Male:** mottled sandy-grey above; rufous-chestnut sides of neck, upper throat; black throat, pectoral gorget, belly and flanks; buff-brown band between gorget and belly. **Female:** mottled pink-fawn plumage; black line below yellow throat; black belly, flanks. Whitish underside of wings distinctive. Gregarious, regularly arrives at water-sites, rises almost straight from ground. **Food:** grass and weed seeds; grain. **Voice:** noisy on arrival on ground; clucking call-notes. **Range:** abundant but erratic winter visitor to NW India; sporadically in Gangetic plain and C India. **Habitat:** semi-desert areas; fallow lands.

**(492) PAINTED SANDGROUSE** *Pterocles indicus indicus*
28cm. **Male:** white and black on forehead, crown; chestnut,
fawn and black (three-coloured) breast band. **Female:**
lacks the head and breast colours of male. Both sexes have
a close-barred plumage and lack the pinlike central
feathers in tail. Pairs or half a dozen birds together; large
flocks around end-monsoon; mostly flies when almost
stepped upon; comes regularly to water in small flocks;
also runs on ground. **Food:** grass and weed seeds;
occasionally termites. **Voice:** chuckling notes in flight and
on ground; soft, clucking note when flushed. **Range:**
commoner in NW, W & C India, east to Bihar, Orissa;
absent in NE and uncommon in Gangetic plain. **Habitat:**
scrub-covered hillsides, open, dry forest.

*Painted Sandgrouse*

**(494) WEDGETAILED GREEN PIGEON** *Treron sphenura*
35cm. Yellowish green plumage and wedge-shaped tail.
**Male:** rufous-orange on crown; deep maroon on back,
scapulars; pale-orangish breast. **Female:** lacks rufous-
orange on crown and maroon on upperbody. The **(493)
Pintailed Green Pigeon** *T apicauda* is slightly larger (42cm)
and has elongated central tail feathers. Small flocks; mostly
arboreal, feeding in foliage of fruiting trees; gymnastically
reaching out to fruit; occasionally feeds at salt-licks on
ground. **Food:** fruits, berries. **Voice:** rich, mellow whistling
notes; also soft *coo...coo...* notes in summer. **Range:**
Himalaya, from Kashmir to extreme NE; foothills to about
2800m; moves altitudinally; found south of Brahmaputra
river. **Habitat:** mostly broad-leafed hill forests.

**(496) GREYFRONTED GREEN PIGEON** *Treron pompadora* 28cm. **Male:** grey crown, nape; chestnut-maroon
back, scapulars; yellow in wings; black wing-shoulder, tail
with broad, grey terminal band; bright yellowish-green
throat and orangish breast. **Female:** olive-green plumage,
without chestnut-maroon on back or orange breast; dull-
buff under tail-coverts, streaked greenish. The female **(501)
Orangebreasted Green Pigeon** *T bicincta* has slaty-grey
central tail-feathers. Arboreal; small flocks, often with
other birds on fruiting trees; occasionally large gatherings;
strong flight. **Food:** fruits, berries. **Voice:** rich whistling
notes. **Range:** restricted to the forested zones of SW and S
India, W Ghats and associated ranges; resident but also
shows some local movement. **Habitat:** forest, groves and
orchards, edges of forest.

*Greyfronted Green Pigeon*

*Yellowlegged Green Pigeon*

**(504) YELLOWLEGGED GREEN PIGEON** *Treron phoenicoptera* 33cm. Ashy olive-green above; olivish-yellow collar, band in dark slaty tail; lilac-red shoulder patch (mostly absent in female); yellow legs and underbody. Female slightly duller. The nominate (northern) race has grey lower breast and belly. Small flocks; mostly arboreal, rarely coming to salt-licks or cropland; remains well hidden in foliage but moves briskly; has favourite feeding trees. **Food:** fruits, berries. **Voice:** rich, mellow whistling notes. **Range:** south roughly of line from S Rajasthan to N Orissa; some difficulty in interpreting the exact range of this and northern races. **Habitat:** forests, orchards, city parks, cultivated village vicinities.

**(506) GREEN IMPERIAL PIGEON** *Ducula aenea* 43cm. Sexes alike. A large forest pigeon. Greyish head, neck and underbody with a distinct pinkish wash; metallic bronze-green upperbody, unbanded tail; chocolate-maroon under-tail; reddish legs. Pairs or small parties on fruiting trees, not infrequently with other species; chiefly arboreal but comes to ground, at salt-licks and water; strong flight; has favourite feeding spots. **Food:** fruit, berries. **Voice:** deep chuckling notes, quite pleasant-sounding and somewhat ventriloquistic. **Range:** forested parts of N India, from Garhwal terai eastwards; forested regions of C and

*Green Imperial Pigeon*

E India, W Ghats south of Bombay; resident in many areas but also moves considerably. **Habitat:** forests.

**(513) SNOW PIGEON** *Columba leuconota* 35cm. Sexes alike. Blackish-brown head separated from dull-brown back by whitish collar; extensive white on lower-back and three dark bands in grey wings, both these characteristic seen at rest and in flight; very dark tail has white subterminal band; black beak and red feet. Flocks of variable size gleaning on the ground, frequently around mountain habitations, freshly-sown cultivations and vicinities of melting snow; flight very strong; breeds in large colonies on cliffs and in rock-caves. **Food:** grain, bulbs, seeds. **Range:** the Himalaya, 2800–5000m, may descend to about 1000m in winter. **Habitat:** open meadows, cultivation, mountain habitation, cliff-faces.

*Snow Pigeon*

**(521) NILGIRI WOOD PIGEON** *Columba elphinstonii* 42cm. Sexes alike. Reddish-brown above; metallic purple-green on upper-back; grey head, underbody; whitish throat; black-and-white chessboard on hindneck diagnostic. Solitary or in small gatherings; arboreal but often descends to forest floor to pick fallen fruit; strong flier, wheeling and turning amidst branches at a fast speed; occasionally along with other frugivorous birds. **Food:** fruits, berries, flower buds. **Voice:** loud *who..* call, like a softer version of *Langur's* call, followed by three to five deep and eerie sounding *who...who...who....* notes; characteristic call of heavy W Ghats forest. **Range:** W Ghats south from Bombay. **Habitat:** moist evergreen forest; sholas; cardamom plantations.

**(531) RUFOUS TURTLE DOVE** *Streptopelia orientalis* 32cm. Sexes alike. Grey-and-black spotted patch on neck sides; rufous-brown back and scapulars, with black markings diagnostic; slaty-grey lower back, rump; whitish border to roundish tail, best seen when tail fanned during landing. Pairs or loose parties, occasionally solitary birds; feeds mostly on ground; rests during hot hours in leafy branches; perches on overhead wires. **Food:** seeds, crops, bamboo seeds. **Voice:** deep and grating *ghur..ghroo..goo....* **Range:** several races, resident and migratory, distributed over much of the Indian region, except the arid NW. **Habitat:** mixed forest, vicinity of cultivation, orchards.

**(534) INDIAN RING DOVE** *Streptopelia decaocto* 32cm. Sexes alike. Greyish-brown plumage; lilac wash about head and neck; black half-collar on hind-neck diagnostic; broad whitish tips to brown tail-feathers, seen as a terminal band when fanned during landing; dull lilac breast and ashy-grey underbody. Small parties when not breeding; often associates with other doves; large gatherings glean in cultivated country; strong flier, chases intruders in territory. **Food:** seeds, grain. **Voice:** characteristic *kukkoo..kook...*, almost dreamlike in quality; also a strident *koon....koon...* when male displays at onset of breeding. **Range:** most of the country, except extreme NE Himalaya; resident and local migrant; commonest in NW, W and C India. **Habitat:** cultivation, open scrub, dry forest.

**(535) RED TURTLE DOVE** *Streptopelia tranquebarica* 22cm. **Male:** deep ashy-grey head; black hindneck collar; rich wine-red back; slaty grey-brown lower back, rump and upper-tail; whitish tips to all but central tail-feathers. **Female:** much like Ring Dove, but smaller size and more brownish colouration distinctive. Solitary, in pairs or small

*Indian Ring Dove*

parties; associates with other doves but is less common; feeds on ground, gleaning on harvested croplands; perches and suns on leafless branches and overhead wires. **Food:** grass and other seeds, cereals. **Voice:** quick-repeated *gru..gurgoo...* call, with more stress on first syllable. **Range:** throughout country, south of the Himalayan foothills. **Habitat:** cultivation, scrub, deciduous country.

**(537) SPOTTED DOVE** *Streptopelia chinensis* 30cm. Sexes alike. Grey and pink-brown above, spotted white; white-spotted black hindneck collar (chessboard) diagnostic; dark tail with broad white tips to outer feathers seen in flight; vinous-brown breast, merging into white on belly. Young birds are barred above and lack chessboard. Pairs or small parties on ground; frequently settles on paths and roads, flying further on intrusion; quite tame and confiding in many areas; drinks often; at harvest times, seen along with other doves in immense gatherings. **Food:** grains, seeds. **Voice:** familiar bird-sound of India, a soft, somewhat doleful *crook..cru..croo* or *croo..croo..croo*. **Range:** all India, to about 3500m in the Himalaya. **Habitat:** open forest, scrub, habitation, cultivation.

*Spotted Dove*

*Little Brown Dove*

**(541) LITTLE BROWN** or **SENEGAL DOVE** *Streptopelia senegalensis* 26cm. Sexes alike. Pinkish-grey-brown plumage with black-and-white chessboard on sides of foreneck; white tips to outer tail-feathers and broad grey wing-patches best seen in flight; small size distinctive. Pairs or small flocks; associates freely with other doves in the huge gatherings at harvest time; feeds mostly on ground, walking about silently. **Food:** grains, grass and weed seeds. **Voice:** somewhat harsh but pleasant *cru.do.do.do.do.* **Range:** almost all India from about 1200m in the outer Himalaya; uncommon in NE states. **Habitat:** open scrub, cultivation, neighbourhood of habitation.

*Emerald Dove*

**(542) EMERALD** or **BRONZEWINGED DOVE** *Chalcophaps indica* 26cm. Sexes alike. Bronze emerald-green upperbody; white forehead, eyebrows; grey crown, neck; white on wing shoulder and across lower-back; whitish rump diagnostic in flight; rich pinkish-brown below; coral red beak and pink-red legs. Solitary or in pairs; moves on forest paths and clearings or darts almost blindly through trees, usually under 5m off ground; difficult to spot on ground. **Food:** seeds, fallen fruit; known to eat termites. **Voice:** deep, plaintive *hoo.oon..hoo.oon.*, many times at a stretch. **Range:** almost throughout country up to about 2000m. **Habitat:** forest, bamboo, clearings; foothills.

**(545) ALEXANDRINE PARAKEET** *Psittacula eupatria* 52cm, including long tail; female smaller. **Male:** rich grass-green plumage; hooked, heavy red beak; deep red shoulder patch; rose-pink collar and black stripe from lower mandible to collar distinctive. **Female:** lacks the collar and black stripe. Yellow under-tail in both sexes. Both small flocks and large gatherings; feeds on fruiting trees in orchards and on standing crop, often causing extensive damage; strong fliers; roosts along with other birds at favoured sites. **Food:** fruits, vegetables, crops, seeds. **Voice:** high-pitched *kreeak...* scream, on wing as well as on perch; popular cage-bird, learning to imitate some notes and human words. **Range:** almost throughout the country, south of Himalayan foothills. **Habitat:** forest, orchards, cultivated areas, towns.

*Alexandrine Parakeet*

**(550) ROSERINGED PARAKEET** *Psittacula krameri* 42cm, including long tail. **Male:** grass-green plumage; short, hooked, red beak; rosy-pink and black collar distinctive (obtained only during third year). **Female:** lacks the pink-and-black collar; instead, pale emerald-green around neck. Gregarious; large flocks of this species, familiar sight in India; cause extensive damage to standing crops, orchards and garden fruit-trees; also raids grain depots and markets; large roosting colonies, often along with mynas and crows. **Food:** fruit, crops, cereal. **Voice:** shrill *keeak...* screams, somewhat less grating than the larger Alexandrine's. **Range:** all India, south of Himalayan foothills. **Habitat:** light forest, orchards, towns, villages.

*Roseringed Parakeet*

**(558) BLOSSOMHEADED PARAKEET** *Psittacula cyano-cephala* 35cm including tail. **Male:** yellowish-green plumage; plum-red head; black and bluish-green collar; maroon-red wing-shoulder patch; white tips to central tail-feathers distinctive. **Female:** dull greyer head; yellow collar; almost non-existent maroon shoulder-patch. Pairs or small parties; arboreal, but descends into cultivation in forest clearings and outskirts; sometimes huge gatherings in cultivation; strong, darting flight over forest. **Food:** fruits, grain, flower nectar and petals. **Voice:** loud, interrogative *tooi....tooi...* notes in fast flight; also other chattering notes. **Range:** all India south of Himalayan foothills. **Habitat:** forest, orchards, cultivation in forest.

*Blossomheaded Parakeet*

**(562) SLATYHEADED PARAKEET** *Psittacula himalayana* 40cm including long tail. Sexes alike, but female lacks red on shoulders. Grass-green plumage; deep slaty-grey head; black chin, narrow neck-ring; blue-green hindneck collar; red shoulder-patch; long, pointed, yellow-tipped tail. The **(563) Eastern Slatyhead** *P finschii* of the NE regions is very similar but slightly smaller. Small flocks in forests; arboreal, but often feeds on standing crop; strong flier. **Food:** fruits, acorns, maize; often causes damage. **Voice:** high-pitched but pleasant double-noted *tooi..tooi..* call, somewhat interrogative in tone; calls mostly in flight; also a single-noted call. **Range:** Himalaya, to about 2800m; moves considerably, descending very low in winter. **Habitat:** forest, mountainsides, orchards, hillside cultivation.

**(564) BLUEWINGED PARAKEET** *Psittacula columboides* 38cm, including tail. Pinkish-grey head, back and breast; black chin and neck-ring, along with a blue-green collar; greenish lower-back, rump and upper-wings, middle feathers of long tail; yellow tips to tail-feathers. Blue-green collar absent in female. Pairs or small groups, rarely more than six birds together; a forest bird, chiefly arboreal but sometimes descends to cultivation; strong flight. **Food:** fruits, seeds, standing crop, flower-nectar. **Voice:** loud, high-pitched and somewhat harsh *tchoi....tchwe* call, quite like the commoner Blossomheaded's but unmistakable once heard. **Range:** restricted to W Ghats from just north of Bombay to extreme south; also some associated hill ranges. **Habitat:** forests, orchards, cultivation, clearings.

**(566) INDIAN LORIKEET** *Loriculus vernalis* 15cm. Bright grass-green plumage; short, square tail and bright crimson rump distinctive; small blue throat patch. Female like male, but lacks blue on throat. Solitary or in pairs; occasionally large flocks in flowering and fruiting trees; chiefly arboreal, difficult to locate in canopy; energetic gymnast, moving around branches or hanging upside down to feed; sleeps hanging upside-down, like bats; occasionally seen with other birds in mixed parties in canopy. **Food:** nectar, soft fruit-pulp, plant seeds. **Voice:** faint clucking note. **Range:** the Himalaya east of Nepal; peninsula mountains, chiefly the E and W Ghats. Moves a great deal locally. **Habitat:** forest, orchards.

**(570) PIED CRESTED CUCKOO** *Clamator jacobinus* 33cm. Sexes alike. Black above; noticeable crest; white in wings and white tip to long tail-feathers diagnostic in flight; white underbody. Young birds, seen in autumn, are dull sooty-brown with indistinct crests; white areas dull fulvous. Solitary or in small parties of four to six; arboreal; occasionally descends to ground to feed on insects; arrives just before SW monsoon by end-May; noisy and active, chasing one another; mobbed by crows on arrival. **Food:** insects, including hairy, noxious caterpillars. **Voice:** noisy; loud, metallic *plew...piu...* call-notes; other shrill shrieks. **Range:** chiefly SW monsoon breeding visitor; most of the country south of outer Himalaya. **Habitat:** open forest, cultivation, orchards.

*Pied Crested Cuckoo*

**(573) COMMON HAWK-CUCKOO** or **BRAINFEVER BIRD** *Cuculus varius* 35cm. Sexes alike. Ashy-grey above; dark bars on rufescent-tipped tail; dull-white below, with pale ashy-rufous on breast; barred below. Young birds broadly streaked dark below; pale rufous barrings on brown upperbody. Solitary, rarely in pairs; strictly arboreal; noisy during May–September; silent after rains. **Food:** chiefly insects; rarely wild fruit and small lizards. **Voice:** famous call-notes; interpreted as *brain-fever...*, uttered untiringly in crescendo; also described as *pipeeha..pipeeha...*; very noisy in overcast weather. **Range:** all India south of Himalayan foothills uncommon, even during rains in arid zones. **Habitat:** forests, open country, near habitation.

*Common Hawk-Cuckoo*

**(576) INDIAN CUCKOO** *Cuculus micropterus* 32cm. Slaty-brown above; greyer on head, throat and breast; whitish below, with broadly-spaced black cross-bars; broad sub-terminal tail-band (characteristic of the non-hawk cuckoos of genus *Cuculus);* the female often has rufous-brown wash on throat and breast; call-notes most important identification clue. Solitary; arboreal, not easy to see; overall appearance very hawk-like, but distinctly weaker-looking flight. The **(578) Cuckoo** *C canorus* differs from the Indian Cuckoo by lacking the subterminal black band and has the diagnostic *cuck-koo* call. **Food:** insects, with special fondness for hairy caterpillars. **Voice:** very distinct call; a four-noted mellow whistle, variously interpreted, the best known being *bo.ko.tako* and *crossword..puzzle;* the third note trailing slightly and the fourth a little more; very vocal between April–August, coinciding with the breeding of its

*Cuckoo*

principal hosts, drongos and orioles; may call for several minutes continuously, often throughout the day if overcast. **Range:** most of India south from Himalaya to about 2500m, excepting the drier and arid parts of NW India; appears to move considerably, especially just before and after the rains. **Habitat:** forest, orchards.

**(584) INDIAN PLAINTIVE CUCKOO** *Cacomantis passerinus* 23cm. Sexes alike. Grey head; grey-brown upperbody; white tail-tip and patch on wing-underside seen in flight; grey throat, upper-breast; paler, almost white below. Female also has hepatic (reddish) phase. Bright chestnut upperbody and throat, with a reddish-brown wash; cross-barred black on back; white below throat, narrowly cross-barred black. Hepatic female very similar to **(582) Baybanded Cuckoo** *C sonneratii.* Mostly solitary; keeps to foliage but often emerges to launch short sally or to move from one patch to another; active and noisy, chiefly during monsoon. **Food:** insects, specially hairy caterpillars. **Voice:** Quite noisy, with good range of calls; a mournful (plaintive) single-noted *piteeer....* call; sometimes a three-noted call, the second note shortest, the third long-drawn; also a four-noted Indian Cuckoo-like call, but distinctly higher-pitched and shrill; also a longer song of eight or nine notes. **Range:** India, south from Himalaya to about 2500m, excepting arid NW regions; widespread and commoner in forested parts; easily overlooked, thus exact status unclear; moves seasonally. **Habitat:** open forests, orchards and gardens in vicinity of habitation.

**(588) DRONGO CUCKOO** *Surniculus lugubris* 25cm including tail. Sexes alike. Glossy black plumage; appearance, including forked tail, indistinguishable from Black Drongo; white in under-tail and base of outer tail-feathers diagnostic; very distinctive calls. Young birds dull in colour, speckled white. Solitary; mostly overlooked and mistaken for drongo, but cuckoo-like flight a giveaway; strictly arboreal. **Food:** insects, wild fruit. **Voice:** diagnostic; very noisy during SW monsoon, when it disperses wide; loud, rising five to seven notes, a whistling *pee..pee..pee..pee..pee..;* ends abruptly, only to begin all over again; noisy in overcast weather. **Range:** lower Himalaya but spreads wide during the rains. **Habitat:** open forests, orchards, cultivation with trees.

*Drongo Cuckoo*

**(590) KOEL** *Eudynamys scolopacea* 42cm. **Male:** metallic black plumage; greenish beak and crimson eyes. **Female:** dark brown, thickly spotted and barred white; whitish below, dark-spotted on throat, barred below. Solitary or in pairs; arboreal; mostly silent between July and February; fast flight. **Food:** ficus and other fruits; insects, snails, eggs of smaller birds. **Voice:** familiar call of Indian countryside. Very noisy between March and June, coinciding with breeding of crows; loud *kuoo...kuooo*..whistling calls in crescendo by male; *ko.el...* call, the first syllable longish; water-bubbling call of female, and possibly male. **Range:** all India, up to about 1800m in outer Himalaya; uncommon in drier areas. **Habitat:** light forests, orchards, city parks, cultivation and open areas.

*Koel*

**(598) SIRKEER CUCKOO** *Taccocua leschenaultii* 45cm including long tail. Sexes alike. Dull olivish-brown plumage; glossy black shaft streaks on breast and head; long, graduated tail, with broad white tips to blackish outer feathers diagnostic in flight; cherry-red beak, with yellow tip. Solitary or in pairs; sometimes four or five birds in the neighbourhood; move mostly on ground, in dense growth; may clamber out on some bush-tops or low trees; flight weak and short. **Food:** insects, fallen fruit, lizards. **Voice:** fairly loud and sharp clicking notes; mostly vocal when breeding, chiefly during the rains; a non-parasitic cuckoo. **Range:** most of India, to about 1800m in the Himalaya; absent in NW India and Kashmir. **Habitat:** open jungle, scrub, ravines, dense growth around habitation.

**(600) CROW-PHEASANT** or **COUCAL** *Centropus sinensis* 50cm including tail. Sexes alike. Glossy bluish-black plumage; chestnut wings; blackish, loose-looking, long graduated tail. Female somewhat bigger. Solitary or in pairs; moves amidst dense growth, fanning and flicking tail often; clambers up into trees, but is a poor flier, lazily flying short distances. **Food:** insects, lizards, frogs, eggs and young of other birds, small snakes. **Voice:** loud and resonant *coop..coop..coop...* call familiar; occasionally a squeaky call. **Range:** all India, from outer Himalaya to about 2000m. **Habitat:** forest, scrub, cultivation, gardens, derelict patches, vicinity of habitations.

*Crow-Pheasant*

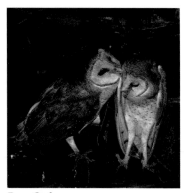

Barn Owl

Collared Scops Owl

Great Horned Owl

**(606) BARN OWL** *Tyto alba* 35cm. Sexes alike. Dull golden-buff above, finely speckled black and white; white below, often with fine, dark spots; heart-shaped, white facial disc striking. The rather similar **(608) Grass Owl** *T capensis* is dark brown above. Solitary or in pairs; nocturnal, but sometimes hunts during day; normally rests during day, mostly in a tree-cavity, dense creepers or some dark loft; perches upright; flies silently, mostly under 4m from ground; pounces on prey. **Food:** rodents, small birds, bats and large insects. **Voice:** long-drawn, wild shriek; a variety of snoring, hissing notes. **Range:** almost all India, south of Himalayan foothills. **Habitat:** grasslands, cultivation, human habitation, even town-centres.

**(623) COLLARED SCOPS OWL** *Otus bakkamoena* 25cm. Small ear-tufts and upright posture. Sexes alike. Greyish-brown above, profusely marked whitish; buffy nuchal collar diagnostic; buffy-white underbody, streaked and mottled dark. The very similar **(617) Scops Owl** *O scops* lacks nuchal collar. Solitary or in pairs; remains motionless during day in thick, leafy branches or at junctions of stems and branches; very difficult to spot; flies around dusk. **Food:** insects, small lizards and rodents; also small birds. **Voice:** a single note *wut...wut...*, rather questioning in tone; calls through the night, often for 20 minutes at stretch, a *wut..* every two to four seconds. **Range:** throughout country, from about 2400m in the Himalaya. **Habitat:** forests, cultivation, orchards, trees in vicinity of habitation.

**(627) EAGLE-OWL** or **GREAT HORNED OWL** *Bubo bubo* 56cm. Sexes alike. Brown plumage, mottled and streaked dark and light; prominent ear-tufts; orange eyes; legs fully-feathered. The **(631) Brown Fish Owl** *B zeylonensis* (56cm) is darker and has white throat patch and naked legs. Solitary or pairs; mostly nocturnal; spends day in leafy branch, rock-ledge or an old well; flies slowly but considerable distances when disturbed; emerges to feed around sunset, advertising its arrival with its characteristic call. **Food:** rodents; also reptiles, frogs and medium-sized birds. **Voice:** deep, booming *bu..boo..* call; snapping calls at nest. **Range:** throughout country, from about 1500m in the Himalaya. **Habitat:** ravines, cliffsides, riversides, scrub and open country.

**(630) DUSKY HORNED OWL** *Bubo coromandus* 58cm. Sexes alike. Pale grey-brown plumage, profusely spotted, streaked and marked with white, mostly below; dark shaft-stripes; prominent ear-tufts and dull yellow eyes diagnostic. The Brown Fish Owl is deep rufous-brown, thickly streaked, and has bright yellow eyes and naked legs. Mostly pairs, sometimes three to four scattered; has favoured roost-sites in large, leafy trees; may call and fly during daytime. **Food:** small animals, birds, frogs, insects. **Voice:** deep, hollow, somewhat eerie hoot of five to eight notes fading towards end; interpreted as *wo..wo..wo..wo..o.o.o*. **Range:** most of the country south of outer Himalaya; status in extreme south of country unclear. **Habitat:** groves, light forest, roadside leafy trees, vicinity of habitation.

**(636) BARRED JUNGLE OWLET** *Glaucidium radiatum* 20cm. Lacks ear-tufts. Sexes alike. Darkish brown above, barred rufous and white; flight-feathers barred rufous and black; white moustachial stripe, centre of breast and abdomen; remainder of underbody barred dark rufous-brown and white. The **(639) Barred Owlet** *G cuculoides* (23cm) of the Himalaya is slightly larger and has abdominal streaks. Solitary or in pairs; crepuscular, but sometimes also active and noisy by day; otherwise spends day in leafy branch; flies short distance when disturbed. **Food:** insects, small birds, lizards, rodents. **Voice:** noisy; musical *kuo.kak..kuo..kak...* call-notes, rising in crescendo for few seconds only to end abruptly; other pleasant, bubbling notes. **Range:** throughout country, from about 2000m in Himalaya; probably absent in extreme NE states. **Habitat:** forest; partial to teak and bamboo mixed forests.

**(652) SPOTTED OWLET** *Athene brama* 20cm. No ear-tufts. Sexes alike. Greyish-brown plumage, spotted white. Yellowish eyes; broken whitish-buff nuchal collar. Young birds more thickly marked white; darkish streaks below breast. Pairs or small parties; roosts during day in leafy branches, tree-cavities or cavity in wall; active in some localities during daytime; disturbed birds fly to neighbouring tree or branch and bob and stare at intruder. **Food:** insects, small rodents, lizards and birds. **Voice:** assortment of scolding and cackling notes, screeches and chuckles. **Range:** throughout country, up to about 1800m in outer Himalaya. **Habitat:** open forests, orchards, cultivation, vicinity of habitation.

*Spotted Owlet*

*Mottled Wood Owl*

**(657) MOTTLED WOOD OWL** *Strix ocellata* 48cm. Sexes alike. Tawny-grey above, profusely mottled with black, white and buff; whitish facial disc, with narrow chocolate-black barrings forming concentric circles; white spots on crown, nape; whitish throat; buffy below, barred black. The **(659) Brown Wood Owl** *S leptogrammica* (46cm) has white supercilium. The **(662) Himalayan Wood Owl** *S aluco* (45cm) has streaked underparts. Solitary or in pairs; nocturnal, spends day in dense foliage of large trees; leaves roost after sunset. **Food:** rats, mice, squirrels; also pigeons and lizards. **Voice:** loud, hooting note. **Range:** all India, from Himalayan foothills south; absent in arid NW parts and much of NE. **Habitat:** forests, orchards, vicinity of habitation, cultivation.

**(667) HODGSON'S FROGMOUTH** *Batrachostomus hodgsoni* 28cm. Unusually wide gape and broad, swollen beak diagnostic. **Male:** grey-brown plumage, boldly mottled and streaked brown, buffy, blackish and white; white patches on scapulars. **Female:** overall plumage dull rufous-brown, marked blackish-brown. Solitary and little known; nocturnal and crepuscular; spends day perched absolutely motionless on branch in thick forests; appears like a stump and extremely difficult to spot; on disturbance merely points beak towards sky. **Food:** wide gape indicates that the bird hawks insects; but also reported to catch insects on ground and from branches. **Voice:** chuckling *whoo...* has been described. **Range:** extreme NE; E Himalaya east of Nepal. Rare and unknown. **Habitat:** dense forest.

**(671) INDIAN JUNGLE NIGHTJAR** *Caprimulgus indicus* 30cm. Plumage in nightjars highly obliterative. Mottled and vermiculated grey-brown, black, buff and white; in some species, white tips to tail in male; calls highly diagnostic. Solitary or several scattered; crepuscular and nocturnal; squats during day, along a branch's length or on rocky ground amidst dry leaves; extremely difficult to spot unless almost stepped upon; flies around dusk, hawking insects in zig-zag flight; settles on cart tracks and roads, where eyes gleam in vehicle headlights. The **(675) Longtailed Nightjar** *C macrurus* is slightly larger (33cm) and has more brownish plumage. **Food:** winged insects. **Voice:** somewhat whistling *chuckoo..chuckoo*, up to seven

*Longtailed Nightjar*

minutes at a stretch, with pauses in between; a quick-repeated, mellow *tuck.tuck.tuck* call, 8 to 50 at a stretch; occasionally a pleasant *uk...kukrooo*, with a slight pause after the shorter first note; vocal between dusk and dawn. Calls help identification. **Range:** all India, up to about 3000m in the Himalaya. **Habitat:** forest clearings, broken scrubby ravines.

**(682) FRANKLIN'S** or **ALLIED NIGHTJAR** *Caprimulgus affinis* 25cm. **Male:** grey-brown plumage, mottled dark; a buffy 'V' on back, from shoulders to about centre of back; two pairs of outer tail-feathers white with pale-dusky tips; white wing-patches. **Female:** like male, but without white outer tail-feathers, which are barred; conspicuous rufous-buff wing-patches; call most important identification clue. Solitary or several scattered over an open expanse; overall behavior like other nightjars; remains motionless during day on open rocky, grass or scrub-covered ground; some-times roosts on tree, along length of a branch; flies around dusk, often flying high; drinks often. **Food:** flying insects. **Voice:** calls on wing as well as on perch, a fairly loud, penetrating *sweeesh* or *schweee...*, like whiplash cutting through air; calls every few seconds, often for hours at a stretch; if disturbed during day, may make a harsh, chuckling and faint screeching sound. **Range:** throughout country, south of outer Himalaya to about 2000m; moves considerably locally. **Habitat:** rocky hillsides, scrub and grass country, light forests, dry streams and river-beds, fallow land, cultivation.

*Franklin's Nightjar*

**(685) INDIAN EDIBLE-NEST SWIFTLET** *Collocalia unicolor* 12cm. Sexes alike. Tiny size. Blackish-brown plumage; slightly-forked tail in flight. The **(683) Himalayan Swiftlet** *C brevirostris* (14cm) is very similar except for the rump which is paler than rest of body. Gregarious and colonial; huge numbers on cliff-sides and caves; swarms leave before dawn in a rush of wings; spends day high over mountains and countryside, hawk-ing insects, often along with other swifts and martins; arrives back to caves and cliff roosts around dusk, when the bats are leaving. **Food:** winged insects. **Voice:** roosting birds keep up an incessant, faint chatter. **Range:** W Ghats, south of Ratnagiri; associated hill ranges. **Habitat:** caves, cliffs on rocky, offshore islands.

**(693) INDIAN ALPINE SWIFT** *Apus melba* 22cm. Sexes alike. Very long, sickle-shaped, pointed wings; dark sooty-brown above; white underbody; broad, brown band across breast diagnostic in flight; dark under tail-coverts. Loose parties dashing erratically at high speed in the skies; extremely strong flier; seen high in skies around dusk, many birds wheeling and tumbling, their shrill screams rending the air; drinks at ponds and puddles by skimming over water surface. **Food:** winged insects; also hawks insects disturbed by forest-fires. **Voice:** shrill *chrrrr....chee..chee...* screams in fast flight; twittering notes at roost sites. **Range:** all India, from about 2500m in Himalaya; uncommon over N Indian plains. **Habitat:** hill-country, cliffsides.

**(703) HOUSE SWIFT** *Apus affinis* 15cm. Sexes alike. Blackish plumage; white rump and throat diagnostic; short square tail and long, sickle-like swift wings. The **(699) Large Whiterumped Swift** *A pacificus* (18cm) has a deeply forked tail. Highly gregarious; on the wing during day, hawking insects, flying over human habitation, cliffs and ruins; strong fliers, exhibiting great mastery and control in fast wheeling flight; frequently utters squealing notes on wing; retires to safety of nest-colonies in overcast weather. **Food:** winged insects. **Voice:** musical squeals on the wing; very vocal at sunset, but also through the day. **Range:** throughout the country, from about 2400m in Himalaya. **Habitat:** human habitation, cliffs, ruins.

**(707) PALM SWIFT** *Cypsurus parvus* 13cm. Sooty-brown plumage; typical swift wings, long and sickle-like; deeply forked tail diagnostic, specially in flight. Sociable; small parties in open, palm-dotted country; strong in flight, and uttering lively screaming notes on the wing; hawks insects all day, occasionally rising very high; roosts on underside of palmyra frond (leaf). **Food:** winged insects. **Voice:** three-note shrill scream, uttered very fast and always on the wing. **Range:** throughout the country, south of Himalayan foothills; also in NE states. **Habitat:** open country, cultivation; this bird's life revolves around the palmyra.

**(709) CRESTED TREE SWIFT** *Hemiprocne longipennis* 23cm. **Male:** bluish-grey above, with a faint greenish wash; chestnut sides of face, throat; ashy-grey breast, whiter below. **Female:** like male, but lacks chestnut on head.

Backward curving crest and long, deeply-forked tail diagnostic. Pairs or small, scattered parties; fly during day, hawking insects; have favourite foraging areas; flight graceful, not as fast as other swifts, but displaying typical swift mastery; calls from perch and in flight; unlike other swifts, perches on bare, higher branches; drinks in flight from surface of forest pools. **Food:** winged insects. **Voice:** double-noted faint scream; also a parrot-like *kea..kea...* call. **Range:** all India, south of Himalayan foothills; absent in the arid parts of NW India. **Habitat:** open, deciduous forest.

*Crested Tree Swift*

**(710) MALABAR TROGON** *Harpactes fasciatus* 30cm. **Male:** sooty-black head, neck, breast; yellow-brown back; black wings narrowly barred white; rich crimson underbody; white breast gorget. **Female:** duller overall; lacks black on head, breast; orange-brown underbody. Long, squarish tail diagnostic. Solitary or in pairs; strictly arboreal; difficult to see because duller back mostly turned towards observer or intruder; hunts flycatcher-style or flits amongst taller branches; flicks tail and bends body when disturbed. **Food:** chiefly insects; also fruits. **Voice:** diagnostic, often a giveaway to bird's presence in a forest; 3 to 8 noted, somewhat whistling *cue..cue..* calls. **Range:** forested areas of Peninsular India; Satpuras range, W Ghats, east to Orissa and parts of E Ghats. **Habitat:** forest.

**(719) LESSER PIED KINGFISHER** *Ceryle rudis* 30cm. Speckled black-and-white plumage diagnostic; black nuchal crest; double black gorget across breast in male. The female differs in having a single, broken breast gorget. Solitary, in pairs or in small groups; always around water, either perched on poles, tree-stumps or rocks; hovers when hunting, bill pointed down as wings beat rapidly; dives fast, headlong on sighting fish; batters catch on perch; calls in flight. The **(717) Himalayan Pied Kingfisher** *C lugubris* of Himalayan streams and rivers can be identified by larger size (41cm), larger crest and white nuchal collar. **Food:** chiefly fish; occasionally tadpoles and water insects. **Voice:** piercing, twittering *chirrruk..chirruk...* cries in flight, sounding as if the bird is complaining. **Range:** all India, from about 2000m in Himalaya. **Habitat:** streams, rivers, ponds; sometimes coastal areas.

*Lesser Pied Kingfisher*

Common Kingfisher

**(722) COMMON** or **SMALL BLUE KINGFISHER** *Alcedo atthis* 18cm. Sexes alike. Bright blue above, greenish on wings; top of head finely-banded black and blue; ferruginous cheeks, ear-coverts and white patch on sides of neck; white chin and throat and deep ferruginous underbody distinctive; coral-red legs and blackish beak. Solitary or in scattered pairs; never found away from water; perches on pole or overhanging branch; flies low over water, a brilliant blue streak, uttering its shrill notes; sometimes tame and confiding; dives for fish from perch; occasionally hovers over water before diving. **Food:** fish; occasionally tadpoles and aquatic insects. **Voice:** shrill *chichee chichee* **Range:** all India, south of 2000m in Himalaya; various races differ in shade of blue-green upperbody. **Habitat:** streams, lakes, canals; also coastal areas.

**(727) INDIAN THREETOED KINGFISHER** *Ceyx erithacus* 13cm. Sexes alike. Brownish-chestnut crown; iridescent purple back, rump; deep purplish-blue of closed wings often hides the back; deep-blue and white spots on neck-sides and short, chestnut tail; orangish-yellow underbody and large, bright coral-red beak striking. Solitary or in pairs; a tiny forest bird, usually overlooked when perched on stumps or tangled roots along nullahs and mud walls, often by a forest path or road. **Food:** small fish, insects. **Voice:** sharp squeaky *chicheee* or *chcheee..* call. **Range:** apparently disjunct. From Garwal east through NE states; W Ghats south from around Bombay; Nilgiris. Appears in many areas only with the onset of SW monsoons. **Habitat:** forest streams, nullahs.

Indian Threetoed Kingfisher

**(730) STORKBILLED KINGFISHER** *Perargopis capensis* 38cm. Sexes alike. Solitary, more heard than seen. Does not normally hover. Enormous red bill diagnostic. Head dark grey-brown with yellowish collar on back of neck. Body pale green-blue above and brownish yellow below. **Food:** fish, frogs and small birds. **Voice:** Noisy *Kee..kee..kee* repeated many times. **Range:** all India except drier parts of NW. **Habitat:** Canals, streams, coastal backwaters in well wooded country.

**(735) WHITEBREASTED KINGFISHER** *Halcyon smyrnensis* 28cm. Sexes alike. Chestnut-brown head, neck and underbody below breast; bright turquoise-blue above, often with greenish tinge; black flight-feathers and white

Storkbilled Kingfisher

wing-patch in flight; white chin, throat and breast distinctive; coral-red beak and legs. Solitary or scattered pairs atop overhead wires, poles, tree-tops; frequently found far from water; drops on to ground to pick prey. **Food:** insects, frogs, lizards, small rodents; only occasionally fish. **Voice:** noisy; loud, crackling laugh, often audible over crowded urban areas; song a longish, quivering whistle, sounding as *kililililili.....* characteristic feature of hot season, when bird is breeding; fascinating courtship display. **Range:** all India, south of outer Himalaya. **Habitat:** forest, cultivation, lakes, riversides; also coastal mangroves and estuaries.

*Whitebreasted Kingfisher*

**(739) BLACKCAPPED KINGFISHER** *Halcyon pileata* 30cm. Sexes alike. Black cap, white collar and deep blue upperbody render this species unmistakable; white throat, upper breast and dull rufous below; in flight, a conspicuous white wing-patch; deep, daggerlike, coral-red beak. The **(740) Whitecollared** *H chloris* (24cm) lacks black cap; white collar bordered by black stripe and greenish-blue upperparts; white underbody, black beak and unmarked wings are further clues. Mostly solitary; a coastal bird, only sometimes wandering inland; has favoured feeding sites; dives for fish but also takes insects from ground. **Food:** fish, crabs, insects, frogs. **Voice:** shrill, fairly loud cackle, quite like the commoner Whitebreasted, but unmistakable once heard. **Range:** the coast, from around Bombay south along entire western seaboard and all along the eastern coast. **Habitat:** chiefly coastal areas, mangroves, estuaries; may wander inland, especially along rivers.

*Blackcapped Kingfisher*

**(744) CHESTNUTHEADED BEE-EATER** *Merops leschenaulti* 21cm. Sexes alike. Grass-green plumage; chestnut-cinnamon crown, hindneck, upper back; yellow chin, throat; rufous and black gorget. Small gatherings on telegraph wires or bare, upper branches of trees from where the birds launch short aerial sallies; fast, graceful flight; noisy when converging at roosting trees. **Food:** chiefly winged insects, captured in flight. **Voice:** musical twittering notes, mostly uttered on the wing, and sometimes from perch. **Range:** disjunct. Himalayan foothills country, from Dehra Dun to extreme NE; a second population exists in the W Ghats south of Goa; also Shri Lanka. Occasionally may be encountered in the peninsula, especially during the monsoon. **Habitat:** vicinity of water in forested areas.

*Chestnutheaded Bee-eater*

**(748) BLUETAILED BEE-EATER** *Merops philippinus* 30cm. Sexes alike. Elongated central tail-feathers. Greenish above, with faint blue wash on wings; bluish rump, tail diagnostic; yellow upper-throat patch with chestnut throat, upper breast; slightly curved black beak, broad black stripe through eyes. The very similar **(747) Bluecheeked Bee-eater** *M superciliosus* (31cm) has a dull-white and blue-green cheek patch. In good light, the greenish rump and tail help identification. Usually small flocks, frequently in vicinity of water; launches short, elegant flights from wire or tree perch; characteristic flight, a few quick wing-beats and a stately glide. **Food:** winged insects. **Voice:** musical, ringing notes, chiefly uttered in flight. **Range:** exact range of these species not correctly known; breeds in parts of NW and N India, and perhaps patchily through eastern and south-central India; *supercilious* possibly breeds only in NW regions, spreading wide during the rains and winter; both species frequently seen together in winter. **Habitat:** open country, light forests, vicinity of water, cultivation; may occasionally be seen in coastal areas.

*Green Bee-eater*

**(750) GREEN BEE-EATER** *Merops orientalis* 21cm including the long central tail-pins. Sexes alike. Bright green plumage; red-brown wash about head; pale blue on chin, throat, bordered below by black gorget; slender, curved black beak; rufous wash on black-tipped flight feathers; elongated central tail-feathers distinctive. Small parties; perches freely on bare branches and overhead telegraph wires; attends also to grazing cattle, along with drongos, cattle egrets and mynas; seen also in city maidans; launches graceful sorties after winged insects; batters prey against perch before swallowing. **Food:** mostly winged insects; confirmed nuisance to the honey industry. **Voice:** noisy; cheerful trilling notes, chiefly uttered on wing. **Range:** all India, south of about 1800m in outer Himalaya. **Habitat:** open country and cultivation; light forests.

**(753) BLUEBEARDED BEE-EATER** *Nyctyornis athertoni* 36cm. Sexes alike. Unmarked grass-green above, bluer on forehead; blue along centre of throat to breast appears beardlike, prominent when bird is calling; buffy-yellow below breast, streaked green; tail lacks the long central pins. Pairs or three to four birds; arboreal, rarely descending low; makes short aerial sallies after winged insects; batters prey on perch; usually not an easy bird to observe from close. **Food:** winged insects; observed on *Erythrina* and *Salmalia* flowers. **Voice:** harsh *korrr..korrr* croaking notes, often followed by softer chuckling call. **Range:** outer Himalaya to about 1800m, from Himachal to extreme east; The W Ghats and Nilgiris; forested parts of Madhya Pradesh, E Ghats through Andhra Pradesh, Orissa, Bihar and W Bengal. **Habitat:** forest edges and clearings.

*Bluebearded Bee-eater*

**(755) INDIAN ROLLER** *Coracias benghalensis* 31cm. Sexes alike. Pale greenish-brown above; rufous-brown breast; deep blue tail has light blue sub-terminal band; in flight, bright Oxford-blue wings and tail, with Cambridge-blue bands distinctive. Solitary or in pairs; perches on overhead wires, bare branches, earthen mounds, small bushtops; either glides and drops on prey or pounces suddenly; batters prey against perch before swallowing. **Food:** mostly insects; catches small lizards, frogs, small rodents and snakes. **Voice:** usually silent; occasionally harsh *khak...kak..kak..* notes; exuberant screeching notes and shrieks during courtship display, diving, tumbling and screaming wildly. **Range:** almost all India, south of outer Himalaya, where found up to about 1500m. **Habitat:** open country, cultivation, orchards; light forests.

*Indian Roller*

**(763) HOOPOE** *Upupa epops* 31cm including beak. Sexes alike. Fawn coloured plumage; black and white markings on wings, back and tail; black and white-tipped crest; longish, gently curved beak. Solitary or in scattered pairs; small loose flocks in winter; probes ground with long beak, sometimes feeding along with other birds; flits among tree branches; crest often fanned open; becomes rather aggressive with onset of breeding season. **Food:** insects caught on ground or pulled from underground. **Voice:** pleasant, mellow *hoo..po..po..*, sometimes only first two notes; calls have a slightly ventriloquistic quality; calls frequently when breeding. **Range:** all India, from about 5500m in Himalaya; several races; spreads considerably in winter. **Habitat:** meadows, open country, garden lawns, open light forests.

*Hoopoe*

*Grey Hornbill*

*Indian Pied Hornbill*

**(767) COMMON GREY HORNBILL** *Tockus birostris* 60cm. Grey-brown plumage; large, curved beak with casque diagnostic; long, graduated tail, tipped black-and-white. Casque smaller in female. The **(768) Malabar Grey Hornbill** *T griseus* (58cm), restricted to the W Ghats, south of Khandala, lacks casque on beak; dark tail tipped white, except on central feathers. Pairs or small parties; sometimes large gatherings; mostly arboreal, but descends to pick fallen fruit or a lizard; feeds along with frugivorous birds on fruiting trees; noisy, undulating flight. **Food:** fruit, lizards, insects, rodents. **Voice:** noisy; normal call a shrill squealing note; also other squeals and screams. **Range:** almost throughout India, from about 1500m in Himalaya; absent in arid NW regions and the heavy rainfall areas of southern W Ghats. **Habitat:** forests, orchards, tree-covered avenues, vicinity of habitation.

**(774) INDIAN PIED HORNBILL** *Anthracoceros malabaricus* 88cm. Sexes alike. Female slightly smaller. Black above; white face-patch, wing-tips (seen in flight), tips to outer tail-feathers; black throat, breast; white below. Black and yellow beak with large casque. The **(775) Malabar Pied Hornbill** *A coronatus* (92cm) is very similar, except for completely white outer tail feathers. Small parties, occasionally collecting into several dozen birds on favourite fruiting trees; associates with other birds; arboreal but often feeds on ground, hopping about. **Food:** fruit, lizards, snakes, young birds, insects. **Voice:** loud cackles and screams; also a rapid *pak..pak..pak.* **Range:** Haryana and Kumaon to extreme NE; E Ghats, south to Bastar and N Andhra Pradesh. The Malabar Pied is absent in NE regions, but is found over the W Ghats south of Ratnagiri. **Habitat:** forests, orchards, groves.

**(776) GREAT PIED HORNBILL** *Buceros bicornis* 130cm. Sexes alike. Black face, back and underbody; two white bars on black wings; white neck, lower abdomen and tail; broad black tail band; huge black and yellow beak with enormous concave-topped casque distinctive. Female slightly smaller. Pairs or small parties; occasionally large flocks; mostly arboreal, feeding on fruiting trees, plucking fruit with tip of bill, tossing it up, catching it in the throat and swallowing it; may settle on ground to pick fallen fruit; noisy flight, audible from over a kilometre, even when flying very high, caused by drone of air rushing through base of outer quills of wing feathers; flight alternation of flapping and gliding, less undulating than in other hornbills. **Food:** fruits, lizards, rodents, snakes. **Voice:** loud and deep barking calls; loud *tokk* at feeding sites, audible for considerable distance. **Range:** lower Himalaya east of Kumaon, up to about 1800m; another population exists in W Ghats, south of Khandala. **Habitat:** forests.

*Great Pied Hornbill*

**(777) GREAT HIMALAYAN BARBET** *Megalaima virens* 33cm. Sexes alike. Bluish-black head, throat; maroon-brown back; yellowish hind-collar; green on lower back, tail; brown upper breast; pale yellow below, with thick, greenish-blue streaks; red under-tail coverts distinctive. Large, yellowish beak. Either solitary or small bands; arboreal, but comes into low-fruiting bushes; difficult to spot and mostly heard. **Food:** fruit, flower petals. **Voice:** very noisy, especially between March and July; loud, if somewhat mournful *pi..you* or *pi..oo*, uttered continuously for several minutes; one of the most familiar bird calls in the Himalaya; often joined by the rather similar but high-pitched, more nasal calls of the **(787) Goldenthroated Barbet** *M franklinii* (23cm), of the E Himalaya. **Range:** Himalaya, 800–3200m. **Habitat:** forests, orchards.

*Great Himalayan Barbet*

**(782) LARGE GREEN BARBET** *Megalaima zeylanica* 28cm. Sexes alike. Grass-green plumage; brownish head, neck, upper back, streaked white; bare orange patch around eyes. The **(785) Small Green Barbet** *M viridis* (23cm) of S India, has a white cheek stripe. Solitary or in pairs; occasionally small parties; strictly arboreal; keeps to fruiting trees, often with other frugivorous birds; difficult to spot in the canopy; noisy in hot season; strong, undulating flight. **Food:** chiefly fruits; also flower nectar, petals, insects and small lizards. **Voice:** noisy; its *kutroo...kutroo...* or *pukrook...pukrook..* calls one of the most familiar sounds of the Indian forests; calls often begin with a guttural *kurrrr*. **Range:** most of India south of the Himalayan foothills (Himachal to Nepal). **Habitat:** forests, groves; also city gardens.

*Large Green Barbet*

*Bluethroated Barbet*

*Crimsonbreasted Barbet*

**(788) BLUETHROATED BARBET** *Megalaima asiatica* 23cm. Sexes alike. Grass-green plumage; black, crimson, yellow and blue about head; blue chin and throat diagnostic; crimson spots on sides of throat. Solitary or in pairs; sometimes small parties on fruiting trees, along with other fruit-eating birds; strictly arboreal, keeps to canopy of tall trees; difficult to spot but loud, monotonous calls an indicator of its presence. **Food:** chiefly fruits; also insects. **Voice:** calls similar to that of Large Green Barbet of the plains; on careful hearing, sounds somewhat softer and there is a short note between the two longer ones; can be interpreted as *kutt.oo.ruk...*; also a four note song when breeding. **Range:** the Himalaya east from Pakistan and Kashmir; found up to about 2250m, also found in Bengal, including Calcutta. **Habitat:** forests, groves.

**(792) CRIMSONBREASTED BARBET** or **COPPERSMITH** *Megalaima haemacephala* 17cm. Sexes alike. Grass-green plumage; yellow throat; crimson breast and forehead; dumpy appearance. The **(790) Crimsonthroated Barbet** *M rubricapilla* of the W Ghats, south of Goa, has crimson chin, throat, foreneck and upper breast. Solitary, in pairs or small parties; strictly arboreal; feeds on fruiting trees, often with other birds; visits flowering *Erythrina, Bombax* trees for flower nectar; often spends early morning sunning on bare branches. **Food:** chiefly fruits and berries; sometimes catches insects. **Voice:** noisy between December and end-April; monotonous *tuk..tuk...* calls one of the best known bird calls of India, likened to a coppersmith working on his metal. **Range:** all India, from about 1800m in outer Himalaya. **Habitat:** light forests, groves, city gardens, roadside trees.

**(794) ORANGERUMPED HONEYGUIDE** *Indicator xanthonotus* 15cm. Sexes alike. Olive-brown plumage; bright orangish-yellow forehead, cheeks and rump (lower back) diagnostic, seen also when bird is perched, with wings drooping slightly; finchlike beak; overall appearance sparrowlike. Solitary or in small scattered parties; keep to cliffs and rock faces around honeybee colonies; show marked preference for colonies where there is a mix of live and abandoned combs; clings on bee-combs or on rocks to feed on white upper wax of the combs; sometimes dive deep into forested valley; can be rather territorial and aggressive at feeding sites; no indication of guiding humans or any other mammal to honeycomb sites. **Food:** mostly beeswax; also bees and other insects. **Voice:** sharp *cheep...* call note, mostly uttered on wing, and rarely on perch. **Range:** Himalaya, from Pakistan to Bhutan, and possibly further east; optimum range 1400 to 2000m, but found over 3000m in Bhutan; overlooked species, little known. **Habitat:** rock faces and cliffs in forests; in some areas above tree-line.

**(798) SPECKLED PICULET** *Picumnus innominatus* 10cm. Sexes alike. Olive-green above (male has some orange and black on forecrown); two white stripes on sides of head, the upper one longer; dark-olive band through eyes, moustachial stripe; creamy-white below, boldly spotted with black. Usually pairs; moves around thin branches, or clings upside-down; taps with beak, probes crevices; typical woodpecker behaviour; associates in mixed hunting bands; unobtrusive, hence often overlooked; perches across branch. **Food:** chiefly ants and termites. **Voice:** sharp, rapid *tsip..tsip...;* also a loud drumming sound. **Range:** Himalaya, west to east, foothills to at least 2500m. The slightly duller southern race *malayorum* has a wide distribution over the E Ghats and the W Ghats, south of Goa; also Nilgiris, Palnis and associated mountain-ranges. **Habitat:** mixed forests, with a fondness for bamboo jungle.

*Speckled Piculet*

**(804) RUFOUS WOODPECKER** *Micropternus brachyurus* 25cm. Sexes alike. Chestnut-brown plumage; fine black crossbars on upperbody, including wings and tail; paler edges to throat feathers; crimson patch under eye in male, absent in female. Usually in pairs; sometimes four or five scattered birds close by; mostly seen around ball-shaped nests of tree ants; clings to outside of nests and digs for ants; plumage often smeared with gummy substance, especially head, breast and tail. **Food:** chiefly tree ants and their pupae; occasionally figs, other fruit; seen to suck sap from near base of banana leaves. **Voice:** rather vocal between January–April; loud, high-pitched three or four notes *ke..ke..ke..ke...,* like common myna's; drums when breeding. **Range:** all India, south of outer Himalaya, east from about Dehra Dun; found up to 1500m, but commoner at lower altitudes. **Habitat:** mixed forests.

*Rufous Woodpecker*

*Little Scalybellied Woodpecker*

**(808) LITTLE SCALYBELLIED GREEN WOODPECKER**
*Picus myrmecophoneus* 30cm. **Male:** grass-green above;
crimson crown, crest; orange and black on nape; white
supercilium and malar stripe; yellow rump; bold, black
scaly streaks on whitish underbody, with tawny-green
wash on breast; throat greyer, also streaked. **Female:** black
crown, crest. Solitary or in pairs; works up along tree-
stems; moves either straight up or in spirals; taps with beak
for insects hiding in bark; also settles on ground, hopping
clumsily to pick up ants and termites or probe dung.
**Food:** mostly insects: ants, termites, wood-boring beetle
larvae; also figs. **Voice:** occasional faint *pick*... but mostly silent; also drums on branches. **Range:** almost all
India found up to 1500m in outer Himalaya. **Habitat:**
mixed forests, plantations.

*Blacknaped Green Woodpecker*

**(809) BLACKNAPED GREEN WOODPECKER** *Picus
canus* 32cm. **Male:** darkish green above; crimson forehead;
black hindcrown, faint crest and nape; dark sides of head
and black malar stripe; yellow rump, white-barred dark
wings and blackish tail; unmarked dull greyish-olive underbody diagnostic. **Female:** black from forehead to nape;
no crimson. Solitary or in pairs; typical woodpecker,
moving on tree stems and larger branches, hunting out
insects from under bark; descends on ground, hopping
awkwardly; also digs into termite mounds. **Food:** termites,
ants, wood-boring beetle and their larvae; also feeds on
flower nectar and fruits. **Voice:** loud chattering alarm;
common call is a high-pitched *keek...keek..* of four or five
notes; drums often between March and early June. **Range:**
Himalaya from the lower foothills country to about 2700m.
**Habitat:** forests, both deciduous and temperate.

**(819) LESSER GOLDENBACKED WOODPECKER**
*Dinopium benghalense* 30cm. **Male:** shining golden-yellow
and black above; crimson crown, crest; black throat, sides
of head, with fine white streaks; white underbody,
streaked black, boldly on breast. **Female:** black crown
spotted with white; crimson crest. Usually pairs, sometimes half a dozen together; widespread and common;
moves jerkily up and around tree stems or clings on un-

derside of branches; taps out insects; often associates in mixed hunting parties; may descend to ground, picking off ants and other insects. **Food:** chiefly ants, termites; caterpillars and centipedes on ground; also figs, berries. **Voice:** noisy; loud, high-pitched cackle, like a laughter; drums often. **Range:** all India, from about 1800m in outer Himalaya; also found in drier areas of NW India. **Habitat:** forests, both dry and mixed deciduous; orchards; gardens; also neighbourhood of villages and other habitation.

**(830) INDIAN GREAT BLACK WOODPECKER** *Dryocopus javensis* 48cm. **Male:** black head, upperbody, breast; white rump and underparts below breast; bright crimson crown (including forehead), crest and cheeks. **Female:** crimson restricted to nape. Pairs, sometimes four or five birds in tall forest; move up along tree stems, jerkily and slowly, inspecting bark-crevices for lurking insects; strong, lazy flight; chuckling note in flight. **Food:** chiefly termites, ants and wood-boring beetle larvae. **Voice:** loud, metallic *chiank* note, often while clinging onto tree stems; loud drumming sound during December–March. **Range:** heavy forested areas of W Ghats, south of Tapti river; present range much reduced due to habitat destruction and the bird perhaps no longer exists in the northern parts of W Ghats; also Bastar and perhaps across C Indian hills. **Habitat:** tall evergreen forests.

*Lesser Goldenbacked Woodpecker*

**(837) HIMALAYAN PIED WOODPECKER** *Picoides himalayensis* 25cm. **Male:** black back, upperbody; white shoulder-patch; white spots and barrings on wings; crimson crown, crest; white lores, cheeks, ear-coverts; broad black moustachial stripe; yellowish-brown underbody, darker on breast; crimson under-tail. **Female:** black crown, crest. Mostly in pairs, moving about in forest; jerkily moves up and around tree-stems or clings on undersides of branches; like other woodpeckers often moves a few steps back, as if to re-examine; sometimes seen in mixed hunting parties of Himalayan birds. **Food:** mostly insects hunted from under the bark and moss; seeds of conifers; nuts and acorns. **Voice:** fairly loud calls, uttered in flight and occasionally when clinging onto stem; drums often between February and June. **Range:** Himalaya, from Kashmir to West Nepal; 1500–3200m. **Habitat:** Himalayan forests.

*Himalayan Pied Woodpecker*

*Yellowfronted Pied Woodpecker*

**(847)   YELLOWFRONTED PIED WOODPECKER** *Picoides mahrattensis* 18cm. **Male:** brownish-black above, spotted all over with white; golden-brown forehead, crown; small scarlet crest; pale fulvous below throat, streaked brown; scarlet patch in centre of abdomen distinctive. **Female:** lacks scarlet crest. Solitary or pairs, sometimes small bands of up to six birds; occasionally along with mixed hunting parties; moves in jerks along tree stems and branches; hunts in typical woodpecker manner; rather confiding in some areas; birds keep in touch with faint creaking sounds. **Food:** chiefly insects; also figs, other fruits and flower nectar. **Voice:** soft but sharp *clic..click..clickrrr...*; drums when breeding. **Range:** common and widespread; almost all India, from Himalayan foothills south; uncommon in NE regions. **Habitat:** open forests, scrub, cultivation, vicinity of habitation, gardens.

*Greycrowned Pygmy*

**(852) BROWNCROWNED PYGMY WOODPECKER** *Picoides nanus* Small woodpecker. 13cm. **Male:** barred brown and white above; paler crown with short, scarlet streak (occipital); prominent white band from just above eyes extends to neck; pale dirty-brown-white below, streaked black. **Female:** like male but lacks the scarlet streaks on sides of crown. The male **(850) Greycrowned Pygmy** *P canicapillus* (14cm) of the Himalaya has short, scarlet occipital crest; black upper back and white-barred lower back, rump. Mostly in pairs; often a part of mixed-bird parties in forest; seen more on smaller trees, branches and twigs, close to ground and also high in canopy; quite active. **Food:** small insects, grubs, obtained from crevices and under bark; also small berries. **Voice:** faint but shrill squeak, sounds like *clicck..rrr*; also drums, especially when breeding during March–May. **Range:** almost all over country, including some of the drier regions of N India. **Habitat:** light forests, cultivation, bamboos, orchards; also vicinity of habitation.

**(856)   HEARTSPOTTED WOODPECKER** *Hemicircus canente* 16cm. **Male:** black forehead (speckled white), crown and crest; black back; broad, pale-buff wing-patch (inner secondaries and wing-coverts) with heart-shaped spots; black flight-feathers; whitish-buff, olive and black below. **Female:** extensive buff-white on forehead, otherwise like male. Pairs or small parties; active and arboreal, moving up and around tree-stems and branches; perches across branch and calls often as it flies from one tree to another; often easily identifiable in flight also. **Food:** insects, mostly ants and termites. **Voice:** quite vocal, especially in flight; a somewhat harsh *churr..* note; other sharp clicking and squeaky notes. **Range:** W Ghats from Kerala north to Tapti river; east across Satpuras to SE Madhya Pradesh, Orissa, NE states. **Habitat:** Forests.

### (862) LARGE GOLDENBACKED WOODPECKER
*Chrysocolaptes lucidus* 32cm. **Male:** crimson crown, crest; golden-olive above; white and black sides of face, throat; whitish-buff below, profusely spotted black on foreneck, and speckled over rest of underbody; extensive crimson rump, black tail and flight-feathers distinctive. **Female:** white-spotted black crown, crest. The **(824) Himalayan Goldenbacked Threetoed Woodpecker** *Dinomium shorii* is very similar, but slightly smaller size, black nape, three toes and two narrow stripes down throat centre can help make the distinction. The **(825) Indian Goldenbacked Threetoed Woodpecker** *D javanense* (28cm) is also confusingly similar, but has single black malar stripe. Pairs or small bands; arboreal, moves jerkily up along tree-stems. **Food:** insects; possibly nectar. **Voice:** noisy; loud, grating scream; calls mostly in flight; loud drumming. **Range:** Garhwal to NE; parts of E Ghats, SE Madhya Pradesh; W Ghats, Kerala to Tapti river; plains to about 1500m. **Habitat:** forests.

*Large Goldenbacked Woodpecker*

### (867) INDIAN PITTA
*Pitta brachyura* 19cm. Sexes alike. A multi-coloured, stub-tailed, stoutly built bird; bright blue, green, black, white, yellowish-brown and crimson; white chin, throat and patch on wing-tips and crimson vent distinctive. Solitary or pairs; small flocks on migration, before and after monsoons; spends much time on ground, hopping about, hunting for insects amidst the leaf-litter and low herbage; quietly flies into a tree branch if disturbed; shows fondness for shaded, semi-damp areas. **Food:** chiefly insects. **Voice:** loud, lively whistle, *wheeet..peu*; very vocal when breeding (rains); also a longish single note whistle. **Range:** almost all India, with considerable seasonal movement, particularly before and after the rains; breeds commonly over northern and central India, also elsewhere. **Habitat:** forests, orchards; also cultivated country.

*Indian Pitta*

*Redwinged Bush Lark*

**(877) REDWINGED BUSH LARK** *Mirafra erythroptera* 14cm. Sexes alike. Yellowish-brown above, streaked black; rich chestnut-rufous on wings, easily seen when bird in flight; pale white chin, throat, dull yellowish-brown below; blackish, triangular spots on breast. Pairs or small flocks; moves quietly on ground, running about or perching on small stones or bush-tops; squats tight when approached but takes to wing when intruder very close; spectacular display-flight, accompanied by singing, when breeding; indulges in display flights during the night too. **Food:** seeds, tiny insects. **Voice:** faint *cheep..cheep...* call-note; song a faint but lively twittering. **Range:** almost all of N, NW and peninsular India; absent in Kerala, NE. **Habitat:** open cultivation, grass and scrub; fallow lands.

*Ashycrowned Finch Lark*

**(878) ASHYCROWNED FINCH LARK** *Eremopterix grisea* 13cm. Thickish beak. **Male:** sandy-brown above; white cheeks and sides of breast; dark chocolate-brown sides of face, most of underbody; dark brown tail with whitish outer feathers. **Female:** sandy-brown overall; dull rufous sides of face and underbody. Mostly loose flocks, scattered over an area; pairs or small parties when breeding; feed on ground; fond of dusty areas, where large numbers may squat about; sandy colouration makes it impossible to spot the birds, but when disturbed, large numbers suddenly take wing; superb display flight of male. **Food:** grass seeds, tiny insects. **Voice:** pleasant, monotonous trilling song by male; sings on wing and on ground. **Range:** almost all India, south of Himalayan foothills; moves during the rains; uncommon in heavy rainfall areas. **Habitat:** open scrub, semi-cultivation, fallow river basins, tidal mudflats.

**(882) RUFOUSTAILED FINCH LARK** *Ammomanes phoenicurus* 16cm. Sexes alike. Dark brown above; rufous-brown below, with brown streaks on throat, breast; rich rufous tail with black band across tip diagnostic. Pairs when breeding; small flocks during winter, occasionally with other larks; difficult to locate because of dull colouration; mostly keeps to ground, running about erratically, stopping every now and then; flies short distance if disturbed; as with several other larks, there is sudden appearance and disappearance of this species in many localities. **Food:** seeds of grass, paddy; small insects, especially during rains and when breeding. **Voice:** display flight of male when breeding (March–May); song a mix of rich whistling notes and chirps; sings on wing and from perch on earth mounds, stones or low bush. **Range:** commoner east from Kutch to around Delhi; east to Bengal and south to N Andhra. **Habitat:** cultivation, fallow ground, open riversides.

**(897) ELWES'S HORNED LARK** *Eremophila alpestris* 20cm. Large lark of high-mountain country. **Male:** pink-brown above, white below; black crown-band with conspicuous black 'horns' on either side; dull yellow-white face, throat; black cheeks and breast-band (gorget) separated by narrow white band distinctive; the western race *albigula* of Gilgit and Chitral has black cheeks continuous with black gorget. **Female:** crown streaked black; overall less black, duller-black cheeks, gorget; tiny 'horns'. Young birds are duller and have spotted plumage. In pairs or small parties; quiet, tame and confiding in many areas; makes short runs on ground. **Food:** seeds, grain, small insects. **Voice:** somewhat plaintive, soft *tsee..ri..* call; a high-pitched, squeaky song of breeding male (May–August). **Range:** high mountain bird. From Chitral, Gilgit east through Ladakh, Lahaul, Spiti to Bhutan and east; breeds to about 3500–5000m (up to snowline); descends somewhat in winter. **Habitat:** open barren areas, scrub, meadows.

*Horned Lark*

**(899) CRESTED LARK** *Galerida cristata* 18cm. Sexes alike. Sandy brown above, streaked blackish; pointed, upstanding crest distinctive; brown tail has dull rufous outer feathers; whitish and dull yellowish-brown below, the breast streaked dark brown. The **(901) Malabar** and **(902) Syke's Crested Larks** *G malabarica* (15cm) and *G deva* (13cm) are very similar, but overall plumage is darker, more rufous-brown; also both are birds of Peninsular and S India. Small flocks, breaking into pairs when breeding; runs briskly on ground, the pointed crest carried upstanding; also settles on bush-tops, stumps, wire fences, overhead wires. **Food:** seeds, grain, insects. **Voice:** ordinary call-note a pleasant *tee..ur.*; short song of male during soaring, display flight. **Range:** N, NW India, Gangetic plain; south to Rajasthan, Saurashtra, N Madhya Pradesh. **Habitat:** semi-desert, cultivation, dry grassy areas.

*Crested Lark*

**(907) EASTERN SKYLARK** *Alauda gulgula* 16cm. Sexes alike. Brownish above, the feathers edged yellow-brown with black centres; short, indistinct crest, not often visible; dark brown tail with pale-buff outer feathers; dull-buff below; more yellowish-brown on breast, faintly streaked and spotted darker. Pairs or small parties on ground, running in short spurts; squats when approached and usually flies low only at the last moment, with a chirping note; beautiful aerial song-flight of male when breeding. **Food:** seeds, insects. **Voice:** longish, pleasant warble of male, often imitations of other birds' calls thrown in; sings usually when soaring high, and during part of fluttering descent; occasionally sings on ground; also has chirping notes. **Range:** all India, up to about 4000m in Himalaya; half a dozen races over the subcontinent. **Habitat:** grasslands, cultivation, mudflats, fallow lands.

**(912) PLAIN SAND MARTIN** *Riparia paludicola* 12cm. Sexes alike. Long wings and slight tail-fork. Grey-brown above, slightly darker on crown; dark-brown wings, tail; dull-grey below, whiter towards abdomen. The **(910) Collared Sand Martin** *R riparia* (13cm) is white below, with a broad, grey-brown band across breast. A gregarious species, always in flocks, flying around sand-banks along water courses; individual birds occasionally stray far and high; hawks small insects in flight; flocks perch on telegraph wires. **Food:** insects captured in flight. **Voice:** a *brret...* call, rather harsh in tone, usually on the wing around nest-colony; twittering song. **Range:** NW and N India, from outer Himalaya, south at least to line from vicinity of Bombay-Nasik to C Orissa; moves considerably locally. **Habitat:** vicinity of water, sand-bank, sandy cliffsides.

*Dusky Crag Martin*

**(914) DUSKY CRAG MARTIN** *Hirundo concolor* 13cm. Sexes alike. Dark sooty-brown above; square-cut, short tail, with white spot on all but outermost and central tail-feathers; paler underbody; faintly rufous chin, throat, with indistinct black streaking. The **(913) Crag Martin** *H rupestris* is slightly larger and a paler sandy-brown, much paler below. Breeds in the NW and W Himalaya and winters in N and C India. Small parties; flies around ruins, crags, old buildings, hawking insects in flight; acrobatic, swallow-like flight and appearance; rests during hot hours on rocky ledges or some corner. **Food:** insects, captured on wing. **Voice:** faint *chip...*, uncommonly uttered. **Range:** nearly through the country, south of Himalayan foothills, to about 1500m. **Habitat:** vicinity of old forts, ruins, old stony buildings in towns.

**(921) WIRETAILED SWALLOW** *Hirundo smithii* 14cm; tail-wires nearly 15cm long, shorter in female. Sexes alike. Glistening steel-blue above; chestnut cap; unmarked, pure white underbody distinctive; two long wire-like projections (tail-wires) from outer tail-feathers diagnostic. Solitary or small parties; almost always seen around water, either perched on overhead wires or hawking insects in graceful, acrobatic flight, swooping and banking; often flies very low, drinking from the surface; roosts in reed-beds and other vegetation, often with warblers and wag-tails. **Food:** insects captured on wing. **Voice:** soft twittering note; pleasant song of breeding male. **Range:** common breeding (summer) visitor to N India, to about 1800m in the Himalaya; breeds in many other parts of country too; widespread over the country, excepting arid zones. **Habitat:** open areas, cultivation, habitation, mostly vicinity of canals, lakes, rivers.

*Wiretailed Swallow*

**(927) STRIATED** or **REDRUMPED SWALLOW** *Hirundo daurica* 19cm including tail. Sexes alike. Glossy steel-blue above; chestnut supercilium, sides of head, neck-collar and rump; dull rufous-white below, streaked brown; deeply forked-tail diagnostic. Small parties spend much of the day on the wing; the migrant, winter-visiting race *nipalensis*, is highly gregarious; hawk insects along with other birds; freely perches on overhead wires, thin branches of bushes and trees; hunt insects amongst the most crowded areas of towns, over markets and garbage heaps, flying with amazing agility, wheeling and banking and stooping with remarkable mastery. **Food:** insects caught on the wing. **Voice:** mournful chirping note; pleasant twittering song of breeding male. **Range:** six races over the subcontinent, including Shri Lanka; resident and migratory. **Habitat:** cultivation, vicinity of human habitations, town centres, rocky hilly areas.

*Grey Shrike*

**(933) GREY SHRIKE** *Lanius excubitor* 25cm. Sexes alike. Bluish-grey above; broad black stripe from beak through eyes; black wings with white mirrors; black and white tail; unmarked, white underbody. Mostly in pairs in open areas; remains perched upright on bush-tops or overhead wires or flies low, uttering a harsh scream; surveys neighbourhood from perch and pounces on prey; batters and tears prey before swallowing; said to maintain a larder, impaling surplus prey on thorns; keeps feeding territories round the year; a wild and wary bird. **Food:** insects, lizards, small birds, rodents. **Voice:** harsh, grating *khreck..* call; a mix of other harsh notes and chuckles; pleasant, ringing song of breeding male. **Range:** the drier areas of NW, W and C India, across Gangetic plain to W Bengal; south to Tamil Nadu. **Habitat:** open country, semi-desert, scrub, edges of cultivation.

*Baybacked Shrike*

**(940) BAYBACKED SHRIKE** *Lanius vittatus* 18cm. Sexes alike. Deep chestnut-maroon back; broad black forehead band, continuing through eyes to ear-coverts; grey crown, neck, separated from black by small white patch; white rump distinctive; black wings with white in outer flight feathers; white underbody, fulvous on breast and flanks. Solitary or in scattered pairs in open terrain; keeps lookout from a perch on some tree-stump, overhead wire or bush-top, usually under 4m off ground; pounces once potential prey is sighted; usually devours prey on ground, tearing it; sometimes carries it to perch; keeps to fixed territories, defended aggressively. **Food:** insects, lizards, small rodents. **Voice:** harsh *churr*; lively warble of breeding male, sometimes imitates other bird calls. **Range:** all India, from about 1800m in the Himalaya; absent in the NE. **Habitat:** open country, light forests and scrub.

*Rufousbacked Shrike*

**(946) RUFOUSBACKED SHRIKE** *Lanius schach* 25cm. Sexes alike. Pale grey from crown to middle of back; bright rufous from then on to the rump; black forehead, band through eye; white 'mirror' in black wings; whitish underbody, tinged pale rufous on lower breast, flanks. Mostly solitary; boldly defends feeding territory; keeps lookout from conspicuous perch; pounces on to ground on sighting prey; said to store surplus in 'larder', impaling prey on thorns; nick-named *Butcher-bird*. **Food:** insects, lizards, small rodents, birds. **Voice:** noisy; harsh mix of scolding notes, shrieks and yelps; excellent mimic; rather musical song of breeding male. **Range:** three races; undergo considerable seasonal movement; all India, from about 2700m in the Himalaya. The **(948) Blackheaded Shrike** *L s tricolor*, has a black head and small white patch on wings, breeds in the Himalaya east of Garhwal. **Habitat:** open country, cultivation, edges of forest, vicinity of habitation, gardens; prefers neighbourhood of water.

**(953) GOLDEN ORIOLE** *Oriolus oriolus* 25cm. **Male:** bright golden-yellow plumage; black stripe through eye; black wings and centre of tail. **Female:** yellow-green above; brownish-green wings; dirty-white below, streaked brown. Young male much like female. Solitary or in pairs; arboreal, sometimes moving with other birds in upper branches; regularly visits fruiting and flowering trees; hunts insects in leafy branches; usually heard, surprisingly not often seen, despite bright colour; seen only when it emerges on bare branch or flies across. **Food:** insects, fruit, nectar. **Voice:** fluty whistle of two or three notes, interpreted *pee.lo.lo*, the middle note lower; harsh note often heard; rich, mellow song when breeding, somewhat mournful; doesn't sing often. **Range:** summer visitor to the Himalayan foothills to about 2600m; spreads in winter to plains; breeds also in many parts of peninsula. **Habitat:** forest, orchards, gardens around habitation.

*Golden Oriole*

**(958) BLACKHEADED ORIOLE** *Oriolus xanthornus* 25cm. Sexes alike. Golden-yellow plumage; black head diagnostic; black and yellow wings, tail; deep pink-red beak seen at close quarters. Pairs or small parties; strictly arboreal, only rarely descending into lower bushes or on ground; active and lively, moves a lot in forest, chases one another, the rich colours striking against green or brown of forest; very vocal; associates with other birds in mixed parties, visits fruiting and flowering trees. **Food:** fruits, flower nectar, insects. **Voice:** assortment of melodious and harsh calls; commonest is a fluty two or three noted *tu.hee* or *tu.yow.yow..*; also a single, mellow note. **Range:** all India, from about 1000m in the Himalayan foothills. **Habitat:** forests, orchards, gardens, often amidst habitation.

*Blackheaded Oriole*

*Black Drongo*

**(963) BLACK DRONGO** or **KING CROW** *Dicrurus adsimilis* 32cm including tail. Sexes alike. Glossy black plumage; long, deeply forked tail. The **(965) Grey Drongo** *D leucophaeus* (30cm) is grey-black, and more of a forest-bird, breeding in Himalaya and a winter visitor to the peninsula. Usually solitary, sometimes small parties; keeps lookout from exposed perch; commonest bird seen on rail and road travel in India; drops on ground to capture prey, launches short aerial sallies, rides atop grazing cattle, follows cattle, tractors, grass-cutters, fires; thus consumes vast numbers of insects; bold and aggressive species, with several birds nesting in same tree. **Food:** chiefly insects; supplements with flower nectar, small lizards. **Voice:** harsh *tiu-tiu* also *cheece cheece*. **Range:** all India, up to about 1800m in outer Himalaya. **Habitat:** open country, orchards, cultivation.

*White-bellied Drongo*

**(967) WHITE-BELLIED DRONGO** *Dicrurus caerulescens* 24cm. Sexes alike. Blackish-blue above; longish, forked tail; grey-brown throat, breast; white belly, under tail-coverts. The **(971) Bronzed Drongo** *D aeneus* is of the same size, but is glossy black all over, with a bronze-green and purple sheen. Pairs or small bands of up to four birds, sometimes in association with other birds; arboreal and noisy; makes short flights after winged insects; often hunts till very late in evening. **Food:** insects, flower-nectar. **Voice:** assortment of pleasant, whistling calls and some grating notes. **Range:** most of India south and east of a line from SE Punjab to around Kutch; east to Bengal; occurs to about 1500m in the hills. **Habitat:** forests, groves, vicinity of habitation.

*Haircrested Drongo*

**(973) HAIRCRESTED** or **SPANGLED DRONGO** *Dicrurus hottentottus* 30cm including tail. Sexes alike. Glistening blue-black plumage; fine hair-like feathers on forehead; longish, downcurved, pointed beak; diagnostic tail, square-cut and inwardly-bent (curling) towards outer-ends. Solitary or scattered pairs; strictly arboreal forest-bird; small numbers may gather on favourite flowering trees like *Erythrina*, *Salmalia*, *Bombax*; rather aggressive, driving away other birds from its feeding zones; often seen in mixed hunting parties of birds. **Food:** chiefly flower-nectar; also insects, more so when there are young in nest. **Voice:** noisy; a mix of whistling, metallic calls and harsh screams. **Range:** lower Himalaya foothills, east of

Kumaon; down through NE India, along E Ghats, Orissa, Bastar, through to W Ghats, up north to Bombay, occasionally even further north. **Habitat:** forests.

**(977) GREATER RACKET-TAILED DRONGO** *Dicrurus paradiseus* 60cm, including outer-tail extensions of about 30cm. Actual size, about myna's. Sexes alike. Glossy blue-black plumage; prominent crest of longish feathers, curving backward; elongated, wire-like outer tail-feathers, ending in 'rackets' diagnostic. Solitary or in pairs, sometimes small gatherings; arboreal forest bird, but often descends into low bush; moves a lot in forest; confirmed exhibitionist, both by sight and sound; extremely noisy, often vocal long before sunrise; bold and aggressive, seen mobbing bigger birds 100m over forest. The **(972) Lesser Racket-Tailed Drongo** *D remifer* (38cm) is found in lower Himalaya, east of Garhwal. **Food:** mostly insects; also lizards, flower nectar. **Voice:** noisiest bird of forest; amazing mimic; wide variety of whistles, screams, perfect imitations of over a dozen species. **Range:** forested parts of India, roughly east and south of line from S Gujarat to Kumaon; up to about 1400m. **Habitat:** forests; also forest-edges, orchards.

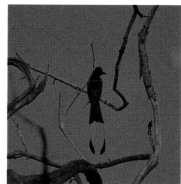

*Racket-tailed Drongo*

**(982) ASHY SWALLOW-SHRIKE** *Artamus fuscus* 19cm. Sexes alike. Slaty-grey plumage, greyer on head; paler on rump, underbody; short square tail, tipped white; white under tail coverts; somewhat heavy-looking bird, rather swallowlike in appearance, but wings much shorter and broader. Small numbers in open country; perches on leaf-stalks, overhead wires or flies characteristically, a few wingbeats and a glide; hunts flying insects; quiet during hot hours, feeds mostly in mornings and evenings. **Food:** winged insects. **Voice:** harsh *chey...chey...* or *chaek..chaek..* call, often uttered in flight; short song occasionally when breeding, a mix of harsh and melodious notes. **Range:** India, roughly east and south from west-central Gujarat to roughly Shimla; widespread but not continuously distributed; up to about 1800m in outer Himalaya. **Habitat:** open country, edges of forest; prefers palm-dotted areas.

*Whiteheaded Myna*

**(987) GREYHEADED MYNA** *Sturnus malabaricus* 21cm. Sexes alike. Silvery-grey above, with faint brownish wash; dull rufous till breast, brighter below; black and grey in wings. Sociable; noisy parties in upper branches of trees, frequently along with other birds; incessantly squabble and move about, indulging in all manners of acrobatic positions to obtain nectar or reach out to fruit; descends to ground to pick up insects. **Food:** flower nectar, fruits, insects. **Voice:** noisy; metallic, whistling call, becoming a chatter when there is a flock; warbling song when breeding. **Range:** India, roughly east and south from Mt Abu to around Dehra Dun; up to about 1800m in Himalayan foothills. The **(988) Whiteheaded** race *blythii* breeds SW India, in Mysore and Kerala, spreading north to Bombay in winter. **Habitat:** light forest, open country, gardens.

*Brahminy Myna*

**(994) BRAHMINY MYNA** *Sturnus pagodarum* 20cm. Sexes alike. A grey, black and rufous myna; black crown, head, crest; grey back; rich-buff sides of head, neck and under-body; black wings and brown tail with white sides and tip distinctive in flight. Female has a slightly smaller crest, otherwise like male. Small parties, occasionally collecting into flocks of 20 birds; associates with other birds on flowering trees or on openlands; walks typical myna-style, head held straight up, confident in looks; communal roosting-sites, with other birds. **Food:** fruits, flower nectar, insects. **Voice:** quite noisy; pleasant mix of chirping notes and whistles, sounding as conversational chatter; good mimic; pleasant warbling song of breeding males. **Range:** all India, to about 2000m in W and C Himalaya. **Habitat:** light forests, gardens, cultivation, vicinity of habitation.

*Rosy Pastor*

**(996) ROSY PASTOR** *Sturnus roseus* 24cm. Sexes alike. Rose-pink and black plumage; glossy black head, crest, neck, throat, upper-breast, wings and tail; rest of plumage rose-pink, brighter with the approach of spring emigration. Gregarious; flocks often contain young birds, crest-less, dull brown and sooty; often along with other mynas on flowering *Erythrina*, *Bombax* trees; cause enormous damage to standing crop; seen also around grazing cattle and damp openlands; overall an aggressive and extremely noisy bird; huge roosting colonies, resulting in deafening clamour before settling. **Food:** grain, insects, flower-nectar. **Voice:** very noisy; mix of guttural screams, chattering sounds and melodious whistles. **Range:** winter visitor to India, particularly common in north, west and central India; arrives as early as end-July; most birds depart around mid-April to early May; absent or uncommon east of Bihar. **Habitat:** open areas, cultivation, orchards, flowering trees amidst habitation.

**(997) STARLING** *Sturnus vulgaris* 20cm. Glossy black plumage, with iridescent purple and green; plumage spotted with buff and white; hackled feathers on head, neck and breast; yellowish beak and red-brown legs. Summer (breeding) plumage, mostly blackish. Several races winter in N India, with head purple or bronze-green, but field-identification of races not very easy in winter. Gregarious, restless birds; feeds on ground, moves hurriedly, digging with beak in soil; entire flock may often take-off from ground, flies around erratically or circles, but soon settles on trees or returns to ground. **Food:** insects, berries, grain, earthworms, small lizards. **Voice:** mix of squeaking, clicking notes; other chuckling calls. **Range:** the race *indicus* breeds in Kashmir to about 2000m; this and three other races winter over NW and N India, occasionally straying south to Gujarat; quite common in parts of N India in winter. **Habitat:** meadows, orchards, vicinity of habitation, open, fallow land.

**(1002) INDIAN PIED MYNA** *Sturnus contra* 23cm. Sexes alike. Black and white (pied) plumage distinctive; orangish-red beak and orbital skin in front of eyes confirm identity. Sociable; small parties either move on their own or associate with other birds, notably other mynas and drongos; rather common and familiar over its range but keeps a distance from man; may make its ungainly nest in garden trees, but never inside houses, nor does it enter houses; more a bird of open, cultivated areas, preferably where there is water; attends to grazing cattle; occasionally raids standing crops. **Food:** insects, flower-nectar, grain. **Voice:** noisy; a mix of pleasant whistling and screaming notes. **Range:** bird of north-central, central and eastern India, south and east of a line roughly from eastern Punjab, through east Rajasthan, west Madhya Pradesh to the Krishna delta; escaped cage birds have established themselves in several areas out of original range as in and around Bombay. **Habitat:** open cultivation, orchards, vicinity of habitation.

*Pied Myna*

*Bank Myna*

*Hill Myna*

**(1006) INDIAN MYNA** *Acridotheres tristis* 23cm. Sexes alike. Rich vinous-brown plumage; black head, neck, upper-breast; yellow beak, legs and naked wattle around eyes distinctive; large white spot in dark-brown flight feathers, best seen in flight; blackish tail, with broad, white tips to all but central feathers; whitish abdomen. Solitary, or in scattered pairs or small, loose bands; amongst our commonest, most familiar birds; hardly ever strays far from man and habitation; rather haughty and confident in looks; aggressive, curious and noisy; struts about on ground, picks out worms; attends to grazing cattle, refuse dumps; enters verandahs, kitchens, sometimes even helps itself on dining table. The slightly smaller **(1008) Bank Myna** *A ginginianus* (21cm) is pale bluish-grey and brick red naked skin behind and below eye. **Food:** omnivorous; fruits, nectar, insects, kitchen scraps, refuse. **Voice:** noisy; a great mix of chattering notes, one of India's most familiar bird sounds. **Range:** all India, up to about 3500m in the Himalaya. **Habitat:** human habitation, cultivation, light forests.

**(1015) HILL MYNA** *Gracula religiosa* 28cm. Sexes alike. Black plumage, with a purple-green gloss; white in flight feathers; orange-red beak; orange-yellow legs, facial skin and fleshy wattles on nape and sides of face. In the southern race *indica*, nape-wattles extend up along sides of crown, the eye and nape wattles distinctly separated. Small flocks in forest; extremely noisy; mostly arboreal, only occasionally descends into bush or onto ground; hops amongst branches, and on ground; large numbers gather on fruiting trees, along with barbets, hornbills, green pigeons. Such sights one of the birdwatching spectacles of the Himalayan foothills. **Food:** fruits, insects, flower-nectar, lizards. **Voice:** amazing vocalist; great assortment of whistling, warbling, shrieking notes; excellent mimic; much sought after cage-bird. **Range:** the northern race is found along lower Himalaya and terai, from Kumaon eastwards; *indica* is a bird of the W Ghats, from North Kanara to extreme south, and Shri Lanka; the race, *peninsularis* is restricted to Orissa, E Madhya Pradesh and adjoining in N Andhra Pradesh. **Habitat:** forests, clearings.

**(1020) REDCROWNED JAY** *Garrulus glandarius* 33cm. Sexes alike. Pinkish-brown plumage; velvet-black malar stripe; closely black-barred, blue wings; white rump contrasts with jet black tail. The **(1022) Blackthroated Jay**

*G lanceolatus* of the W Himalaya, east to about C Nepal, has black cap, black and white face, and white in wings. Small, noisy bands, often along with other Himalayan birds; common and familiar about Himalayan hill-stations; inquisitive and aggressive; mostly keeps to trees, but also descends into bush and onto ground; laboured flight. **Food:** insects, fruits, nuts. **Voice:** noisy; guttural chuckles, screeching notes and whistles; good mimic. **Range:** Himalaya, west to east; 1500–2800m, somewhat higher in the east; may descend low in winter. **Habitat:** mixed temperate forests.

**(1025) YELLOWBILLED BLUE MAGPIE** *Cissa flavirostris* 66cm including long tail, body size about that of pigeon. Sexes alike. Purple-blue plumage; black head; breast; white nape patch, underbody; very long, white-tipped tail; yellow beak and orange legs. The **(1027) Redbilled Blue Magpie** *C erythrorhyncha* (70cm) has more white on nape; red beak, legs; appears to be restricted to the Himalaya between Himachal and E Nepal and some parts of northeast India. Pairs or small bands, often associating with jays, laughing-thrushes, tree-pies; wanders a lot in forests, flying across clearings, entering hill-station gardens, one bird following another; arboreal, but also hunt low in bushes; even descend to ground, the long tail cocked as the bird hops about. **Food:** insects, fruit, lizards, eggs, small birds. **Voice:** noisy; great mix of metallic screams, loud whistles and raucous notes, often imitating other birds. **Range:** Himalaya, west to east; 1500–3600m; may descend low in winter. **Habitat:** forests, gardens, clearings.

*Redbilled Blue Magpie*

**(1029) WHITERUMPED MAGPIE** *Pica pica* 52cm, including long tail. Sexes alike. Pied bird. Glossy black head, neck, upper-back, wings; tail glossed bronze-green and purple-blue; white scapulars, lower-back (rump), belly; black under-tail. The Tibetan race *bottanensis* can be identified by its black rump. Usually several in vicinity; moves on ground, perches on fence-posts, trees, house-tops; frequents high-mountain villages; typical crow, bold and aggressive, but also extremely alert; flicks tail often. **Food:** almost omnivorous; refuse, insects, fruit, grain, small animals. **Voice:** loud, grating *chak..chak..* calls; also other piping notes. **Range:** high NW Himalaya, Chitral, N Kashmir, Ladakh, Himachal Pradesh; the Tibetan race is found in Bhutan and Arunachal; 1500–4700m. **Habitat:** open valleys, cultivation, habitation.

*Whiterumped Magpie*

*Indian Tree Pie*

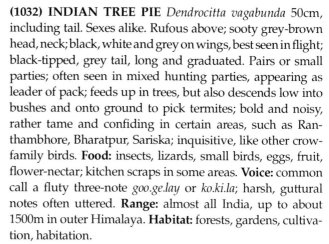

**(1032) INDIAN TREE PIE** *Dendrocitta vagabunda* 50cm, including tail. Sexes alike. Rufous above; sooty grey-brown head, neck; black, white and grey on wings, best seen in flight; black-tipped, grey tail, long and graduated. Pairs or small parties; often seen in mixed hunting parties, appearing as leader of pack; feeds up in trees, but also descends low into bushes and onto ground to pick termites; bold and noisy, rather tame and confiding in certain areas, such as Ranthambhore, Bharatpur, Sariska; inquisitive, like other crow-family birds. **Food:** insects, lizards, small birds, eggs, fruit, flower-nectar; kitchen scraps in some areas. **Voice:** common call a fluty three-note *goo.ge.lay* or *ko.ki.la*; harsh, guttural notes often uttered. **Range:** almost all India, up to about 1500m in outer Himalaya. **Habitat:** forests, gardens, cultivation, habitation.

**(1042) NUTCRACKER** *Nucifraga caryocatactes* 32cm. Sexes alike. Choco-brown plumage, thickly speckled with white; dark central tail-feathers, tipped white; white outer tail and under tail-coverts; heavy, pointed beak distinctive. The race *hemispila*, found between Kangra and CE Nepal, has smaller white spots; rump lacks white spots. The easternmost race *macella* has even smaller and less numerous white spots. Small parties in temperate forest; keeps to tree-tops but readily descends onto ground to pick nuts and acorns; rather wary; flies short distances across glades; rather noisy, usually attracting attention by its calling. **Food:** seeds of pine, spruce; nuts, acorns; occasionally insects. **Voice:** noisy; guttural *kharr..kharr.* **Range:** Himalaya; 1800–4000m, sometimes descending to about 1200m in winter. **Habitat:** coniferous, oak, rhododendron forest.

**(1046) REDBILLED CHOUGH** *Pyrrhocorax pyrrhocorax* 45cm. Sexes alike. Glossy black plumage; coral-red curved beak, legs. The **(1045) Yellowbilled** or **Alpine Chough** *P graculus* (38cm) has yellow beak and red legs. Highly gregarious; feeds in cultivation, in and around habitation, frequently in company of Yellowbilled species, finches, pigeons, magpies; probe ground and dung for insects; does not hesitate to rob corn stored in attics of upland houses; flocks often fly high into the skies, rising on thermals, playing and dancing in air currents in wild splendour; tame and confiding in some areas; cheerful

*Redbilled Chough*

companions to the high-mountain trekker. **Food:** insects, barley grain, wild-berries. **Voice:** melodious, high-pitched *cheeao..cheeao..;* also a loud *kew..kew..;* other squeaky notes. **Range:** high Himalaya; 2200–4000m; may descend to about 1500m in severe winter; the eastern race could be encountered at 6000m in summer. **Habitat:** cliffsides, alpine pastures, cultivation, vicinity of mountain habitation.

**(1049) HOUSE CROW** *Corvus splendens* 43cm. Sexes alike. Black plumage; grey collar, upper back and breast; glossy black on forehead, crown and throat. The **(1053) Jackdaw** *C monedula* (33cm) is similar to the House Crow, but is smaller, thicker-necked and white-eyed; it is common in Kashmir. An integral and conspicuous part of India, described as an extension of man's society; street-smart, sharp, swift, sociable, sinister, the crow is almost totally commensal on man; snatches food from table, shops; mobs other birds, even large raptors; performs important scavenging services; occasionally flies very high into skies, either when flying long-distance, or simply for fun; communal roost-sites. **Food:** omnivorous; robs young birds from nest; drives other birds from flowering trees. **Voice:** familiar *caw* call; occasionally a pleasant *kurrrrr* note; several other notes. **Range:** all India, reaching about 2500m in the Himalaya. **Habitat:** habitations rural and urban; cultivation, forest-edges; range of habitats very wide.

*House Crow*

**(1054) INDIAN JUNGLE CROW** *Corvus macrorhynchos* 48cm. Sexes alike. Glossy black plumage; heavy beak, with noticeable culmen-curve. The **(1058) Carrion Crow** *C corone* of NW mountains is confusingly similar, except for less curved culmen though this character not easily visible in field. Solitary or in groups of two to six; commoner around villages and only small numbers in urban areas; overall not as 'enterprising' as the familiar House Crow; in forested areas, its behaviour often indicates presence of carnivore-kills. **Food:** omnivorous. **Voice:** harsh *khaa..khaa* calls; several variations on this among the various races of this crow. **Range:** all India, to about 4500m in the Himalaya; absent in extreme W Rajasthan and parts of Punjab. **Habitat:** forests, rural habitations; small numbers in towns and cities.

*Jungle Crow*

*Common Wood Shrike*

**(1070) COMMON WOOD SHRIKE** *Tephrodornis pondicerianus* 16cm. Sexes alike. Greyish-brown plumage; broad whitish supercilium and dark stripe below eye distinctive; white outer tail-feathers seen when bird flies. Dark stripe may be slightly paler in female. The **(1068) Malabar Wood Shrike** *T gularis* is larger (23cm) and has white outer tail-feathers. Pairs or small parties; quiet for greater part of year, vocal when breeding (February–May); keeps to middle-levels of trees, hopping about, sometimes coming to ground. **Food:** insects; also flower-nectar. **Voice:** whistling *wheet..wheet...* and an interrogative, quick-repeated *whi..whi..whi..whee* thereafter; other trilling, pleasant notes when breeding. **Range:** most of the country, south of Himalayan foothills; commoner in low country. **Habitat:** light forests, edges of forest, cultivation, gardens in and around habitation.

**(1072) LARGE CUCKOO SHRIKE** *Coracina novaehollandiae* 28cm. **Male:** grey above; broad, dark stripe through eyes to ear-coverts; black wings, tail; greyish breast, whitish below. **Female:** barred grey-and-white below; paler stripe through eyes. Pairs or small bands of 4-6 birds; characteristic flight over forest, few wing-beats and a glide, often calls in flight; flicks wings on perching; keeps to upper branches, but may descend into bush; very active and noisy when breeding (March–June). **Food:** insects, larvae, flower-nectar, fruits. **Voice:** noisy; a two-noted ringing whistle, *ti..treee...*, the second note long-drawn and higher; somewhat like Blossomheaded Parakeet's call. **Range:** most of India, from about 2200m in the Himalaya; absent in the drier, semi-desert regions of Kutch, C and N Rajasthan, and much of NW India. **Habitat:** forests, gardens, tree-dotted cultivation.

**(1078) BLACKHEADED CUCKOO-SHRIKE** *Coracina melanoptera* 20cm. **Male:** grey plumage; black head, wings, tail, the latter white-tipped, except on middle feathers; pale grey below breast, whiter on abdomen, vent. **Female:** brown plumage; whitish-buff below, barred dark-brown till abdomen; lacks black head. Solitary or in pairs, only occasionally several together; often part of mixed-hunting bands; keep for most part to leafy, upper branches, probes the foliage for insects; methodically checks foliage before flying off to another grove or forest patch. **Food:** chiefly insects; also berries and flower-nectar. **Voice:** silent for

*Blackheaded Cuckoo-Shrike*

most of year; breeding male has whistling song, up to a dozen notes, frequently uttered. **Range:** all India east and south of line from Mt Abu to W Uttar Pradesh; a Himalayan race is found in parts of Punjab, Himachal and hill regions of Uttar Pradesh, to about 2000m. Undergoes considerable seasonal migration. **Habitat:** forests, gardens, groves.

**(1081) SCARLET MINIVET** *Pericrocotus flammeus* 20cm. **Male:** glistening black head, upper back; deep scarlet lower back, rump; black and scarlet wings, tail; black throat, scarlet below. **Female:** rich yellow forehead, supercilium; grey-yellow above; yellow and black wings, tail; bright yellow underbody. Pairs or small parties; sometimes several dozen together; keeps to canopy of tall trees; actively flits about to hunt for insects; also launches aerial sallies after winged insects; often seen in mixed-hunting parties of birds; spectacular sight of black, scarlet and yellow as flock flies over forest, especially when seen from above. **Food:** insects, flower-nectar. **Voice:** pleasant, two-note whistle; also a longer, whistling warble. **Range:** disjunct; several isolated races; (1) Himalaya, to about 2500m. (2) W Ghats and adjoining belt. (3) Bengal, S Bihar, W Madhya Pradesh, Orissa, N Andhra. **Habitat:** forests, gardens, groves.

*Scarlet Minivet, male (left), female (right)*

*Small Minivet*

**(1093) SMALL MINIVET** *Pericrocotus cinnamomeus* 15cm. **Male:** dark-grey head, back, throat; orange-yellow patch on black wings; black tail; flame-orange breast; orange-yellow belly, under tail. **Female:** paler above; orange rump; dusky white throat, breast tinged with yellow; yellowish belly, undertail. Pairs or small flocks; keep to tree-tops, actively moving amidst foliage; flutters and flits about in an untiring hunt for small insects, often in association with other small birds; also hunt flycatcher style. **Food:** chiefly insects; sometimes flower-nectar. **Voice:** soft, low *swee..swee..* notes uttered as birds hunt in foliage. **Range:** most of India, from about 900m in outer Himalaya; absent in arid parts of Rajasthan. **Habitat:** forests, groves, gardens, tree-dotted cultivation.

**(1098) COMMON IORA** *Aegithina tiphia* 14cm. **Male:** greenish above (rich black above, with yellowish rump, in summer breeding plumage); black wings, tail; two white wing bars; bright yellow underbody. **Female:** yellow-green plumage; white wing-bars; greenish-brown wings. Pairs keep to leafy branches, often with other small birds; moves energetically amidst branches in their hunt for insects, caterpillars; their rich call-notes often a giveaway of their presence in an area. **Food:** insects, spiders; also

*Common Iora*

flower-nectar. **Voice:** renowned vocalist; wide range of rich, whistling notes; single or two-note long-drawn *wheeeeeee* or *wheeeeeee..chu* is a common call; another common call is a three-note whistle. **Range:** all India, from about 1800m in the Himalaya; absent in arid NW, desert regions of Rajasthan, Kutch. **Habitat:** forest, gardens, orchards, tree-dotted cultivation, habitation.

**(1103) GOLDENFRONTED CHLOROPSIS** *Chloropsis aurifrons* 19cm. Leaf-green plumage; golden-orange forehead; blue shoulder patches; dark blue chin blackish in southern races; cheeks; black lores, ear-coverts, continuing as a loop around blue throat. Pairs in leafy canopy; lively birds, actively hunts in foliage; their wide range of whistling and harsh notes immediately attracting attention; owing to greenish plumage, difficult bird to see in foliage; rather aggressive, driving away other birds especially on flowering trees. **Food:** insects, spiders, flower-nectar. **Voice:** noisy; wide assortment of whistling notes, including imitations of several species; commonest call a drongo or shikra-like *che..chwe*. **Range:** from about 1600m in Garhwal Himalaya east; Bihar, Orissa, south along E Ghats and up the W Ghats and adjoining areas. **Habitat:** forests.

*Goldenfronted Chloropsis*

**(1107) GOLDMANTLED CHLOROPSIS** *Chloropsis cochinchinensis* 18cm. **Male:** green plumage; blue in wings; yellow-green forehead; black from nostrils, base of eyes to lower throat; bright purple-blue moustachial stripes; dull yellow-green band around black throat. **Female:** pale blue-green (not black) mask; greenish-blue moustachial stripe. Solitary or pairs in leafy canopy; often in mixed-hunting parties; a noisy bully on flowering trees, driving away others; important agents of pollination. The **(1106) Orangebellied Chloropsis** *C hardwickii* is found between 600–2500m along the Himalaya. **Food:** insects, flower-nectar, fruits. **Voice:** noisy; excellent mimic; a mix of its own notes and imitations of other birds' calls, notably of drongos, bulbuls, shikras and cuckoo-shrikes. **Range:** most of India, except arid NW areas of Punjab, Rajasthan, N and W Gujarat. Range of this and *aurifrons* overlaps in the forested areas of W and E Ghats. **Habitat:** light forests, gardens.

*Orangebellied Chloropsis*

*Fairy Bluebird*

*Blackheaded Bulbul*

*Redwhiskered Bulbul*

**(1109) FAIRY BLUEBIRD** *Irena puella* 28cm. **Male:** glistening blue above; deep velvet-black sides of face, underbody, wings; blue under tail-coverts. **Female:** verditer blue plumage; dull black lores, flight-feathers. Pairs or small loose bands; spends the day either in leafy, tall branches; descends into undergrowth to feed on berries or hunt insects; utter their two-noted calls while flitting amongst trees; seen along with other birds. **Food:** fruits, insects, flower-nectar. **Voice:** common call a double-noted *wit..weet..;* also a *whi..chu..;* besides, some harsh notes occasionally heard. **Range:** disjunct distribution; one population in W Ghats and associated hills south of Ratnagiri; another in E Himalaya, east of extreme SE Nepal; Kumaon foothills; Andaman & Nicobar Islands. **Habitat:** dense, evergreen forests, sholas.

**(1115) BLACKCRESTED YELLOW BULBUL** *Pycnonotus melanicterus* 18cm. Sexes alike. Glossy black head, crest and throat; olive-yellow nape, back, becoming brown on tail; yellow below throat. The ssp *gularis* has a ruby-red throat. The **(1112) Blackheaded Bulbul** *P atriceps* of NE India and Andamans lacks crest, and has black and yellow bands in tail. Pairs or small bands, sometimes with other birds; arboreal. **Food:** insects, fruit. **Voice:** cheerful whistles; also a harsh *churrr* call; four to eight-note song. **Range:** disjunct: (1) Himalaya, from Himachal eastwards; NE; foothills to about 2000m. (2) W Ghats and associated hills south of Goa (**Rubythroated** ssp *gularis*); (3) Shri Lanka. **Habitat:** forests, bamboo, clearings, orchards.

**(1120) REDWHISKERED BULBUL** *Pycnonotus jocosus* 20cm. Sexes alike. Brown above, slightly darker on wings, tail; black perky crest distinctive; crimson 'whiskers' behind eyes; white underbody with broken breast-collar; crimson-scarlet vent. Sociable; pairs or small flocks, occasionally gatherings of up to 100 birds; lively and energetic; feeds in canopy, low bush and on ground; enlivens their surroundings with cheerful whistling notes; tame and confiding in some areas; popular cage-bird. **Food:** insects, fruits, flower-nectar. **Voice:** cheerful whistling notes; also harsh, grating alarm notes. **Range:** from Garhwal east along Himalayan foothills to about 1500m commoner south of Satpura mountains in peninsular India; disjunct population in hilly areas of S, SE Rajasthan and N Gujarat. **Habitat:** forests, clearings, gardens and orchards, vicinity of human habitation.

**(1123) WHITE-EARED BULBUL** *Pycnonotus leucogenys leucotis* 20cm. Light-brown above; black head, throat; white cheeks; dark-brown tail, tipped-white; yellow vent. The **(1125) Whitecheeked Bulbul** *P l leucogenys* of the Himalaya and foothills has browner head, a front-pointed crest and a short, white superciliary stripe. Pairs or small parties; active birds on the move, attracting attention by their pleasant calls; the Himalayan bird is common in Kashmir, where quite confiding. **Food:** insects, fruits, flower-nectar. **Voice:** pleasant whistling notes. **Range:** NW and N India, south to about Bombay; the nominate race is found in the Himalaya, from the foothills to about 3400m. **Habitat:** open scrub, vicinity of habitation, edges of forest, coastal mangroves.

*Whitecheeked Bulbul*

**(1128) REDVENTED BULBUL** *Pycnonotus cafer* 20cm. Sexes alike. Dark sooty-brown plumage; pale edges of feathers on back and breast give scaly appearance; darker head, with slight crest; almost black on throat; white rump and red vent distinctive; dark tail tipped-white. Pairs or small flocks, but large numbers gather to feed; arboreal, keeps to middle levels of trees and bushes; a well-known Indian bird, rather attached to man's neighbourhood; pleasantly noisy and cheerful, lively and quarrelsome, often kept as a pet; indulges in dust-bathing; also hunts flycatcher-style. **Food:** insects, fruits, flower-nectar, kitchen-scraps. **Voice:** cheerful whistling calls; alarm calls on sighting snake, owl or some other intrusion, serving to alert other birds. **Range:** all India, to about 1800m in Himalaya. **Habitat:** light forests, gardens, haunts of man.

*Redvented Bulbul*

**(1138) WHITEBROWED BULBUL** *Pycnonotus luteolus* 20cm. Sexes alike. Olive plumage, brighter above; whitish forehead, supercilium, and explosive calls confirm identity. Pairs or small parties; not an easy bird to see; skulks in dense, low growth, from where its chattering calls suddenly explode; seen only momentarily when it emerges on bush tops, or flies low from one bush-patch to another; usually does not associate with other birds. **Food:** insects, fruits, nectar. **Voice:** loud, explosive chatter, an assortment of bubbling, whistling notes and chuckles. **Range:** peninsular India, south of a line from central Gujarat to southern W Bengal; avoids the heavy rainfall hill-zones of W Ghats. **Habitat:** dry scrub, village habitation, light forests and clearings.

*Whitebrowed Bulbul*

**(1144) YELLOWBROWED BULBUL** *Hypsipetes indicus* 20cm. Sexes alike. Bright yellowish-olive above; bright yellow forehead, sides of face, eyebrow; dark brown wings; olive-yellow tail; bright yellow underbody, olivish wash on flanks. Small parties in forest, often along with other small birds in mixed parties; a bird of the undergrowth, even entering hill-station gardens; moves energetically in the bush, works its way along the stem and leaves, sometimes ascends into the canopy of forest trees; rather vocal and active member of mixed parties. **Food:** fruits, forest berries; also insects, more so when nesting. **Voice:** pleasant, mellow whistling notes; also a harsh alarm note. **Range:** W Ghats south of Pune; Shri Lanka. **Habitat:** dense forests and edges.

Black Bulbul

**(1148) BLACK BULBUL** *Hypsipetes madagascariensis* 23cm. Sexes alike. Ashy-grey plumage; black, loose-looking crest; coral-red beak and legs diagnostic; whitish below the abdomen. Flocks in forest, often dozens together; strictly arboreal, keeps to topmost branches of tall forest-trees, rarely comes down into undergrowth; noisy and restless, hardly staying on a tree for a few minutes; feed on berries, fruits, but also hunts insects fly-catcher manner. **Food:** forest berries, fruit, insects, flower-nectar. **Voice:** very noisy; an assortment of whistles and screeches. **Range:** several races; disjunct range; Himalaya, between 800–3200m; parts of NE states; W Ghats south from near Bombay; also Shevaroy Hills in Tamil Nadu; Shri Lanka. **Habitat:** tall forests; hill-station gardens.

Spotted Babbler

**(1154) SPOTTED BABBLER** *Pellorneum ruficeps* 15cm. Sexes alike. Olivish-brown above; dark-rufous cap; whitish-buff stripe over eye; white throat; dull fulvous-white underbody, boldly streaked blackish-brown on breast and sides. Solitary or in pairs; shy, secretive bird of undergrowth; mostly heard, extremely difficult to see; rummages on ground, amidst leaf-litter; hops about, rarely ascends into upper branches. **Food:** insects. **Voice:** noisy when breeding; mellow whistle, two, three or four-noted; best-known call is a four-note whistle, interpreted *he will.beat.you.* **Range:** hilly-forest areas: Himalaya, to about 1500m, east of SE Himachal; NE states; S Bihar, Orissa, Satpura range across C India, E and W Ghats. **Habitat:** forest undergrowth, bamboo, overgrown ravines, nullahs.

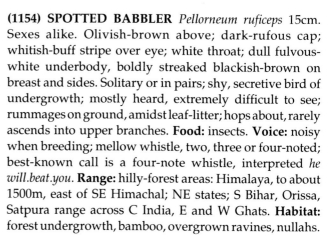

**(1173) SLATYHEADED SCIMITAR BABBLER** *Pomatorhinus horsfieldii* 22cm. Sexes alike. Deep olive-brown above; long, white supercilium; white throat, breast and belly-centre; long, curved, yellow 'scimitar' beak. Pairs or small, loose bands in forest; keep to undergrowth, where the bubbling, fluty calls are heard more often than the birds are seen; hops on jungle floor, vigorously rummaging amidst leaf-litter, digs with long beak; hop their way into leafy branches, but not for long; scattered birds keep in touch through calls. **Food:** insects, spiders, flower-nectar. **Voice:** fluty, musical whistle, often followed by a bubbling note; often calls in duet. **Range:** hilly-forest regions of the country, Himalaya to about 1500m, east of SE Himachal; NE states; Orissa, E and W Ghats; western parts of Satpura range, along Tapti and Narmada rivers. **Habitat:** mixed forest, scrub, bamboo.

**(1181) RUSTYCHEEKED SCIMITAR BABBLER** *Pomatorhinus erythrogenys* 25cm. Sexes alike. Olive-brown above; orangish-rufous (rusty) sides of face, head, thighs, flanks; remainder of underbody mostly pure white; long, curved 'scimitar' beak. Small bands in forest; a bird of undergrowth, hopping on jungle floor, turns over leaves or digs with beak; sometimes hops into leafy branches, but more at ease on ground. **Food:** insects, grubs, seeds. **Voice:** noisy; mellow, fluty whistle, two-noted *cue.pe...cue.pe*, followed by single (sometimes double) note reply by mate; guttural alarm call and a liquid contact note. **Range:** the Himalaya foothills to at least 2200m and possibly to 2600m. **Habitat:** forest undergrowth, ravines, bamboo.

**(1222) RUFOUSBELLIED BABBLER** *Dumetia hyperythra* 13cm. Sexes alike. Olivish-brown above; reddish-brown front part of crown; white throat in western and southern races; nominate race has underbody entirely fulvous. Small, noisy parties in undergrowth; rummages on floor, hopping about, always wary; hardly associates with other birds; great skulkers, difficult to see; any sign of danger and the flock disperses amidst a noisy chorus of alarm notes; soon hop and reunite. **Food:** chiefly insects, but occasionally seen on flowering silk-cotton trees; also other flower-nectar. **Voice:** faint *cheep..cheep* contact notes; also a mix of other whistling and chattering notes. **Range:** from SE Himachal, east along foothills country into peninsular India; absent in arid NW, Punjab plains, extreme NE states. **Habitat:** scrub and bamboo in and around forests.

*Rufousbellied Babbler*

**(1228) YELLOWBREASTED BABBLER** *Macronous gularis* 11cm. Sexes alike. Dull olive-brown or olive-grey above; pale rufous cap; light-yellow supercilium; pale yellow below, with fine black streaks, the streaks diminishing towards belly. Usually in small flocks, frequently in mixed-bird parties; very noisy and unusually active for a babbler; moves considerably; sometimes hunts on ground but spends most time in upper branches and tall bush. **Food:** insects. **Voice:** very noisy; variety of loud notes, a mix of harsh chuckles and whistles; a harsh *whaech..whaech.* **Range:** disjunct: (1) E Himalaya, NE; (2) E Ghats, parts of eastern peninsula (Orissa, SE Bihar and Madhya Pradesh, NE Andhra, south to Godavari river; (3) Small zone in S Mysore. **Habitat:** forests, bamboo, dense grass and bushes.

*Yelloweyed Babbler*

**(1231) YELLOWEYED BABBLER** *Chrysomma sinense* 18cm. Sexes alike. Rufous-brown above; whitish lores, short supercilium; yellow eye (iris) and orange-yellow eye-rim distinctive at close range; cinnamon wings; long, graduated tail; white below, tinged pale fulvous on flanks and abdomen. Pairs or small bands in tall grass and under-growth; noisy but skulking, suddenly clambers into view for a few seconds, before vanishing once again; works its way along stems and leaves, hunting insects; short, jerky flight. **Food:** insects, larvae; also flower-nectar. **Voice:** noisy when breeding (mostly rains); melodious, whistling notes; also a mournful *cheep..cheep* call. **Range:** all India, from the Himalayan foothills south; absent in arid parts of Rajasthan. **Habitat:** scrub, tall grass, cultivation, edges of forest.

**(1254) COMMON BABBLER** *Turdoides caudatus* 23cm. Sexes alike. Dull brown above, profusely streaked; brown wings; olivish-brown tail long and graduated, cross-rayed darker; dull-white throat; pale fulvous underbody, streaked on breast sides. Pairs or small bands in open scrub; skulker, works its way low in bush or on ground; moves with peculiar bouncing hop on the ground, the long, loose-looking tail cocked-up; extremely wary, vanishes into scrub at slightest alarm; weak flight, evident when flock moves from one scrub-patch to another, in ones and twos. **Food:** insects, flower-nectar, berries. **Voice:** noisy; pleasant, warbling whistles, several birds often in chorus; squeaky alarm-notes; calls on ground and in low flight. **Range:** most of N, NW, W and peninsular India, south of outer Himalaya to about 2000m; east to about Bengal. **Habitat:** thorn scrub, open cultivation, grass.

**(1256) STRIATED BABBLER** *Turdoides earlei* 21cm. Sexes alike. Dull brownish above, streaked darker; long, cross-barred tail; buffy-brown below, with fine dark streaks on throat, breast (the Common Babbler has white throat and lacks breast-streaks). The **(1548) Striated Marsh Warbler** *Megalurus plaustris* (25cm), with greatly overlapping range, has bolder streaking above, prominent whitish supercilium, and almost white below, streaked below breast. Sociable; parties of up to ten birds keep to tall grass and reed-beds; flies low, rarely drops down to the ground. **Food:** insects, snails. **Voice:** loud, three-noted whistle; also a quick-repeated single whistling-note. **Range:** floodplains of N and NE river systems, especially the larger rivers (Indus, Ganges, Brahmaputra). **Habitat:** tall grass, reed beds, scrub.

**(1258) LARGE GREY BABBLER** *Turdoides malcolmi* 28cm. Sexes alike. Grey-brown above; dark centres to feathers on back gives streaked look; greyer forehead; long, graduated tail cross-rayed, with white outer feathers, conspicuous in flight; fulvous-grey below. Gregarious; flocks in open country, sometimes dozens together; extremely noisy; moves on ground and in medium-sized trees; hops about, turning over leaves on ground; weak flight, never for long; at any sign of danger, the flock comes together. **Food:** insects, seeds, berries; rarely flower-nectar. **Voice:** very noisy; a chorus of squeaking chatter; short alarm-note. **Range:** from around E Uttar Pradesh, Delhi environs, south through most of peninsula; east to Bihar; abundant in the Deccan. **Habitat:** scrub, open country, gardens, vicinity of habitation.

*Jungle Babbler*

**(1265) JUNGLE BABBLER** *Turdoides striatus* 25cm. Sexes alike. Dull earth-brown above, lightly streaked on back; dark, rufous-brown tail, loose and longish, faintly cross-rayed; ashy-fulvous below, with pale markings on breast; the race *somervillei* of W coast has reddish-rufous rump, tail-coverts. Gregarious; small parties, 6 to 15 birds; also referred to as 'Satbhai' (Seven brothers); 'Seven sisters' in English, as usually there are five to seven birds in a flock; spends much time on ground, rummaging; sometimes flies into branches above, especially when alarmed, appears ruffled and agitated and breaks into a squeaking chorus; social birds, all come together if one member is in some problem. **Food:** insects, flower-nectar, figs. **Voice:** noisy; chattering chorus. **Range:** all India south of Himalayan foothills. **Habitat:** light forests, scrub, gardens, cultivation, vicinity of habitation.

**(1267) WHITEHEADED BABBLER** *Turdoides affinis* 24cm. Sexes alike. Creamy-white crown; dull-brown above, appearing scaly on centre of back; darker wings and cross-barring along tail-centre; dark brown throat, breast, the pale-grey edges to feathers giving scaled appearance; yellowish-buff below breast. Small noisy parties, feeds on ground, turning leaves; if disturbed moves about in a series of short, hopping flights; hops amongst tree-branches towards the top, from where a short flight takes the birds to an adjoining tree. **Food:** insects, nectar, figs. **Voice:** noisy; definitely more musical chatter than the commoner Jungle Babbler. **Range:** southern peninsular India–Mysore, Andhra, Tamil Nadu, Kerala; also Shri Lanka. **Habitat:** forests, dense growth, neighbourhood of cultivation and habitation, orchards.

**(1274) WHITETHROATED LAUGHING THRUSH** *Garrulax albogularis* 28cm. Sexes alike. Greyish olive-brown above, fulvous forehead, black mark in front of eye, full rounded tail with 4 outer pairs of feathers broadly tipped with white. Below rufous but with conspicuous pure white throat sharply demarcated by a line of olive brown. The white gorget stands out in the gloom of forest floor. **Food:** insects, also berries. **Voice:** continual chattering, warning *twit-tzee* alarm. **Range:** throughout Himalaya, with distinct western race, up to 3000m in summer. **Habitat:** dense forest, scrub, wooded ravines.

*Whitethroated Laughing Thrush*

**(1279) STRIATED LAUGHING THRUSH** *Garrulax striatus* 28cm. Sexes alike. Rich-brown plumage, heavily white-streaked, except on wings and rich rufous-brown tail; darkish, loose crest, streaked white towards front; heavy streaking on throat, sides of head, becoming less from breast downwards. Pairs or small parties; often along with other birds in mixed, noisy parties; feeds both in upper branches and in low bush; shows marked preference for certain sites in forest. **Food:** insects, fruits; seen eating leaves. **Voice:** very vocal; clear whistling call of 6 to 8 notes; loud, cackling chatter. **Range:** the Himalaya east of Kulu, 800–2700m parts of NE states. **Habitat:** dense forests, scrub, wooded ravines.

**(1283) WHITECRESTED LAUGHING THRUSH** *Garrulax leucolophus* 28cm. Sexes alike. Olive-brown above; pure white head, crest, throat, breast, sides of head; broad, black band through eyes to ear-coverts; rich rufous nuchal collar, continuing around breast; olive-brown below breast. Small parties in forest; moves in undergrowth but readily ascends into upper leafy branches; makes short flights between trees; very noisy; often seen along with other laughing-thrushes, tree-pies, drongos; hops on ground, rummaging in leaf-litter. **Food:** insects, berries. **Voice:** very noisy; sudden explosive chatter or 'laughter'; also pleasant two or three-note whistling calls. **Range:** the Himalaya, east of N Himachal; foothills to a height of 2400m, commonest between 600–1200m. **Habitat:** dense forest undergrowth, bamboo, wooded nullahs.

*Whitecrested Laughing Thrush*

**(1290) VARIEGATED LAUGHING THRUSH** *Garrulax variegatus* 25cm. Sexes alike. Olive-brown above; grey, black and white head, face; grey, black, white and rufous in wings, tail; black chin, throat, bordered with buffy-white; narrow white tip to tail, with grey subterminal band. Small flocks, up to a dozen and more on steep, bushy hillsides; keep to undergrowth for most part, but occasionally clambers into leafy branches; wary and secretive, not easily seen; weak flight, as in most laughing-thrushes. **Food:** insects, fruits; rarely flower-nectar. **Voice:** noisy; clear, musical whistling notes, three or four syllables; also harsh, squeaking notes. **Range:** the Himalaya, east to C Nepal; 1200–3500m; breeds between 2000–3200m. **Habitat:** forests undergrowth, bamboo; seen in hill-station gardens in winter.

**(1307) NILGIRI LAUGHING THRUSH** *Garrulax cachinnans* 20cm. Sexes alike. Olive-brown above; deep slaty-brown crown; long, white stripe over eye and much shorter streak below; black lores, stripe through and behind eye, chin and throat; rich rufous below throat. Small parties, up to a dozen birds; mostly feeds in undergrowth; also hops about actively in upper branches; often seen in mixed hunting-parties; extremely noisy, both on ground and in trees. **Food:** insects, berries and other fruit. **Voice:** extremely noisy; its chattering 'laughter' calls amongst the most familiar bird-calls of the Nilgiris; many birds call in chorus. **Range:** restricted to the Nilgiris in SW India; above 1000m. **Habitat:** dense, evergreen forests; hill-station gardens.

**(1309) WHITEBREASTED LAUGHING THRUSH** *Garrulax jerdoni* 20cm. Sexes alike. Olive-brown above; black eye-stripe; differs from *cachinnans* chiefly in having cheeks, chin, throat and breast deep grey, slightly streaked on sides; paler rufous below breast. The nominate race, restricted to a small area in Coorg has black chin, cheeks. Small flocks, a dozen or so, often with other birds; feeds in low bushes and on ground, hopping in characteristic laughing-thrush manner; extremely noisy, wary and difficult to see, as it rarely emerges in open. **Food:** insects, berries and other fruit. **Voice:** extremely noisy; whistling, chattering 'laughter'; also squeaking alarm notes. **Range:** hilly-forested parts of Kerala, W Tamil Nadu, and SW Karnataka generally above 1000m. **Habitat:** evergreen forests; sholas; undergrowth.

**(1314) STREAKED LAUGHING THRUSH** *Garrulax lineatus* 20cm. Sexes alike. Pale grey plumage, streaked dark-brown on upper back, white on lower back; rufous ear-coverts, wings; rufous-edges and grey-white tips to roundish tail; rufous streaking and white shafts on under-body. Pairs or small bands; prefers low bush and grassy areas, only rarely going into upper branches; hops, dips and bows about; flicks wings and jerks tail often; weak, short flight. **Food:** insects, berries; refuse around hillside habitation. **Voice:** fairly noisy; a near-constant chatter of a mix of whistling and squeaky notes; common call a whistle of two or three notes, *pitt..wee.er.* **Range:** the Himalaya, west to east; 1400–3800m; considerable altitudinal movement. **Habitat:** bushy hill-slopes, cultivation, edges of forest.

*Streaked Laughing Thrush*

**(1322) BLACKFACED LAUGHING THRUSH** *Garrulax affinis* 25cm. Sexes alike. Diagnostic blackish face, throat, part of head and contrasting white malar patches, neck-sides and part of eye-ring; rufous-brown above, finely scalloped on back; olivish-golden flight-feathers tipped grey; rufous-brown below throat, marked grey. Pairs or small bands, sometimes with other babblers; moves on ground and low growth, also ascends into middle levels of trees; noisy when disturbed or when snakes or other creatures arouses its curiosity. **Food:** insects, berries, seeds. **Voice:** various high-pitched notes, chuckles; a rolling *whirrr...* alarm-call; a four-noted, somewhat plaintive song. **Range:** the Himalaya, from around W Nepal eastwards; descends to about 1500m in winter, occasionally even lower. **Habitat:** undergrowth in forest; also dwarf vegetation in higher regions.

*Blackfaced Laughing Thrush*

**(1333) SILVEREARED MESIA** *Leiothrix argentauris* 15cm. Sexes alike. Brightly coloured; black crown; silver ear coverts; yellow forehead, orangish throat and breast, crimson upper and under tail-coverts, crimson patch on wing. Female has yellowish tail-coverts. Flocks of up to twenty birds flit from tree to tree; actively searches for insects and berries; tit-like acrobatic behaviour; also flycatcher like sallies. **Food:** seeds, berries and insects. **Voice:** incessant *chirrup* while feeding, also long-drawn *see..see...we..* **Range:** C Himalaya to Arunachal Pradesh. **Habitat:** scrub jungle, open clearances in evergreen forests.

*Silvereared Mesia*

**(1336) REDBILLED LEIOTHRIX** *Leiothrix lutea* 13cm. **Male:** olive-grey above; dull buffy-yellow lores, eye-ring; yellow, orange, crimson and black in wings; forked tail, with black tip and edges; yellow throat, orange-yellow breast diagnostic; scarlet beak. The red on wing is considerably reduced or absent in the western race *kumaiensis*. **Female:** like male, but yellow instead of crimson in wings. Small parties, often a part of mixed hunting-parties of small birds in forest; rummages in undergrowth but frequently moves up into leafy branches; a lively, noisy bird. **Food:** insects, berries. **Voice:** quite vocal; often utters a wistful, piping *tee.tee.tee;* a mix of sudden explosive notes; song a musical warble. **Range:** the Himalaya, from Kashmir to extreme NE; 600–2700m. **Habitat:** forest undergrowth, bushy hillsides, plantations.

*Redbilled Leiothrix*

**(1358) BARTHROATED SIVA** *Minla strigula* 14cm. Sexes alike. Grey-olive back; slightly tufted yellow-olive cap; whitish ear-coverts, black malar stripe; orange-yellow and black in wings; black tail has chestnut and yellow; dull yellow throat, with thin, black scales. Small flocks, frequently in mixed-hunting parties that so characterise the Himalaya; arboreal and active; hunts in canopy or in middle levels; when finished with a tree, the flock moves on to another, surprising the observer with the number of birds taking-off. **Food:** insects, berries, other fruits, nectar. **Voice:** mix of whistling squeaks; a loud, four-syllabled song, with accent on second syllable. **Range:** Himalaya east of Kangra (Himachal); 800–3700m; breeding mostly above 1800m. **Habitat:** forests of oak, fir, rhododendron; also bamboo.

**(1368) YELLOWNAPED YUHINA** *Yuhina flavicollis* 13cm. Sexes alike. Olive-brown above; choco-brown crown, crest; white eye-ring and black moustache seen from close; rufous-yellow nuchal collar (less distinct in western race); white underbody, streaked rufous-olive on sides of breast, flanks. Flocks, almost always in association with other small birds; active and restless, flitting about or hunting flycatcher style; moves between undergrowth and middle-levels, sometimes ascending into canopy; keeps up a constant twitter. **Food:** insects, berries, flower-nectar. **Voice:** quite vocal; a mix of soft twittering notes and fairly loud titmice-like two or three note call, *chee.chi..chew.* **Range:** the Himalaya; W Himachal to extreme NE; 800–3400m. **Habitat:** forests.

**(1380) WHITEBROWED TIT-BABBLER** *Alcippe vinipectus* 11cm. Sexes alike. Brown crown, nape; prominent white eyebrow, with black or dark-brown line above; blackish sides of face and white eye-ring; olive-brown above, washed rufous on wings, rump and tail; some grey in wings; whitish throat, breast, olive-brown below. The eastern races *chumbiensis* and *austeni* have streaked throat; 6 to 20 birds in low growth or lower branches; energetic, acrobatic birds, often seen in mixed-hunting parties. **Food:** insects, caterpillars, berries. **Voice:** fairly sharp *tsuip...* or *tship..* call; also some harsh churring notes, especially when agitated. **Range:** the Himalaya; from W Himachal, E Himalaya, NE regions; 1500–3500m but over 4000m in some parts; descends to 1200m in severe winter. **Habitat:** scrub in forest, edges of forest, ringal bamboo.

**(1389) QUAKER BABBLER** *Alcippe poioicephala* 15cm.
Sexes alike. Olive-brown above; grey crown, nape distinctive; thin, black stripe through eyes; rufescent-brown wings,
tail; dull fulvous underbody. Pairs or small parties, often
along with other birds; moves actively in undergrowth and
leafy branches, clinging sideways or springing from perch;
rather shy in most areas, but occasionally emerges in open.
**Food:** insects, spiders, flower-nectar, berries. **Voice:** best
known call is the four to eight syllabled song, interpreted as
*daddy-give-me-chocolate;* harsh *churrr..* notes serve as contact
calls. **Range:** peninsular India, south from Mt Abu across
Pachmarhi (Satpuras) to S Bihar and Orissa. **Habitat:** forests,
undergrowth, bamboo; also hill-station gardens in W Ghats.

*Quaker Babbler*

**(1396) BLACKCAPPED SIBIA** *Heterophasia capistrata*
20cm. Sexes alike. Rich-rufous plumage; grey-brown
centre of back (between wings); black crown, slight, bushy
crest, sides of head; bluish-grey wings and black shoulder
patch; grey-tipped long tail; black sub-terminal tail-band.
Small flocks, sometimes with other birds; active gymnasts,
ever on the move; have cheerful calls; hunts in canopy and
middle levels, moves amidst moss-covered branches;
springs into air after winged insects; sometimes hunts like
tree-creepers on stems, probing bark crevices. **Food:** insects,
flower-nectar, berries. **Voice:** wide range of whistling and
sharp notes; rich song of six to eight syllables during
Himalayan summer. **Range:** Himalaya; 1500–3000m sometimes up to about 3500m (Bhutan); descends to 600m in some
winters. **Habitat:** forest, both temperate and broad-leafed.

**(1409) RUFOUSTAILED FLYCATCHER** *Muscicapa
ruficauda* 14cm. Sexes alike. Dull-brown plumage; pale
eye-ring and rufous tail diagnostic; ashy throat, breast;
whitish belly. The **(1408) Brownbreasted Flycatcher** *M muttui* (13cm) which winters in SW India, has white throat and
lacks rufous tail. Mostly solitary, rarely pairs together; hunts
in leafy canopy, snapping insects as it flits about; on perch
often flicks wings and jerks body; sometimes seen with other
small birds, but even then maintains a distance and is rather
subdued. **Food:** insects. **Voice:** soft, somewhat mournful
note occasionally uttered; sings when breeding in the
Himalaya. **Range:** breeds in W Himalaya, east to C Nepal;
2100–3600m; winters in SW India, south of Kanara; erratically
in hilly-forests of C India. **Habitat:** forest edges.

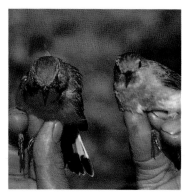

*Redbreasted Flycatcher*

**(1411) REDBREASTED FLYCATCHER** *Muscicapa parva* 13cm. **Male:** dull-brown above; white in tail conspicuous in flight or when tail is flicked; rufous-orange chin, throat; whitish below. **Female:** white throat; pale-buff breast. The adult male **(1413) Kashmir Redbreasted** *M subrubra* has black border to red throat, breast. Solitary or in scattered pairs in shaded areas; may descend to ground, but prefers low and middle branches; flicks wings and lifts tail; launches short aerial sallies; hunts till late in evening; calls often. **Food:** tiny flying insects. **Voice:** sharp clicking sound; also a double *tick..tick* call; pleasant song when breeding (extralimital). **Range:** winter visitor, arriving by early September; all India south of the Himalayan foothills. **Habitat:** forests; gardens.

*Little Pied Flycatcher*

**(1419) LITTLE PIED FLYCATCHER** *Muscicapa westermanni* 10cm. **Male:** black above; long, white supercilium and white in wings and tail; white below. **Female:** olive-brown above, with dull wing-bar; bright rufous-brown upper-tail; whitish throat, duller grey-white below. The female **(1409) Rufoustailed Flycatcher** *M ruficauda* (14cm) is quite similar, but larger. The female Slaty Blue Flycatcher lacks wing-bar; the female Whitebrowed Blue Flycather is greyer above and lacks wing-bar. Solitary or pairs, often along with other small birds; keeps to middle and upper levels of trees; active, moves from tree to tree; makes short sallies but also hunts on bark crevices. **Food:** insects. **Voice:** rather silent in winter, except for occasional utterance of longish song. **Range:** breeds in the Himalaya 1200–2500m; from around WC Nepal eastwards and in NE; winters in foothills, N India, straying to C and E India. **Habitat:** breeds in Himalayan forests; winters in forested areas, orchards, tree-dotted cultivation.

**(1421) WHITEBROWED BLUE FLYCATCHER** *Muscicapa superciliaris* 10cm. **Male:** deep blue above and sides of head, neck, breast, forming a broken breast-band; long, white eyebrow; white in tail; white below. **Female:** dull-slaty above; grey-white below. The eastern race *aestigma* lacks white over eye and in tail. The **(1423) Slaty Blue Flycatcher** *M leucomelanura* male has black on sides of head and lacks white stripe over eye. Solitary or in pairs; seen in mixed parties during winter; active, hunts in characteristic flycatcher-style; rarely ventures in open or in low growth. **Food:** insects. **Voice:** faint *tick..tick..* in winter; a *chrrr* alarm note; three-syllabled song in the Himalaya. **Range:** breeds in Himalaya, 1800–3200m; winters in N and C India, south to Mysore and N Andhra Pradesh. **Habitat:** forests, groves, gardens.

**(1427) BLACK-AND-ORANGE FLYCATCHER** *Muscicapa nigrorufa* 13cm. **Male:** rich orangish-rufous plumage; blackish crown, nape, sides of face, wings. **Female:** like male, but deep olive-brown head; pale eye-ring. Usually solitary, but pairs often close by; not often seen in mixed-hunting parties; keeps to dense, shaded undergrowth, either hopping low or making short flycatcher-sallies from low perch; in its restricted range, quite tame and confiding once spotted. **Food:** insects. **Voice:** soft, gloomy *pee..* call-note; a sharp *zit..zit* alarm call; high-pitched, metallic song when breeding. **Range:** very local; restricted to Nilgiris and associated hills in southern W Ghats, commonest above 1500m. **Habitat:** dense, evergreen forest undergrowth, bamboo.

**(1431) RUFOUSBELLIED NILTAVA** *Muscicapa sundara* 15cm. Blue patch on sides of neck. **Male:** deep purple-blue back, throat; dark-blue mask; black forehead; brilliant blue crown, shoulders, rump; chestnut-rufous underbody. **Female:** olivish-brown overall; rufescent tail; white on lower throat diagnostic. The **(1433) Rufousbellied Blue Flycatcher** *M vivida* (18cm) male lacks the blue neck-patch, is slightly larger, and is found only sporadically in the NE. The **(1440) Bluethroated Flycatcher** *M rubeculoides* (14cm) male has dark blue throat and white belly; it is duller, uniform blue above. Mostly solitary; keeps to undergrowth; highly unobtrusive, seldom seen; often flicks wings like redstart, and bobs body. **Food:** insects. **Voice:** squeaky churring note; occasionally a sharp *psi..psi;* also some harsh notes and squeaks. **Range:** the Himalaya, NE; 1500–3200m; winters in foothills, adjoining plains. **Habitat:** dense forest undergrowth, bushes.

**(1435) WHITEBELLIED BLUE FLYCATCHER** *Muscicapa pallipes* 15cm. **Male:** indigo-blue above; black lores; bright-blue forehead, supercilium; indigo-blue throat, breast; white below breast. **Female:** deep olive-brown above; chestnut tail; rufous-orange till breast, whiter below. The female Bluethroated Flycatcher has dull-rufescent (not chestnut) tail. Solitary, rarely in pairs; sometimes in mixed parties; mostly silent, un-obtrusive, hence overlooked; hunts in low growth, often flicking tail. **Food:** insects. **Voice:** soft two-noted call; longish, squeaky song when breeding; rather silent for most part of year. **Range:** W Ghats, south of Bhimashankar, around the latitude of Pune. **Habitat:** dense forest undergrowth.

*Tickell's Blue Flycatcher*

**(1442) TICKELL'S BLUE FLYCATCHER** *Muscicapa tickelliae* 14cm. **Male:** dark indigo-blue above; bright blue on forehead, supercilium; darker, almost appearing black, on sides of face; rufous-orange throat, breast; whitish below. **Female:** duller overall. The male Bluethroated Flycatcher has dark blue throat. Usually in pairs in shaded areas, often in mixed-hunting parties; vicinity of wooded streams are favoured haunts; flits about intermittently or launches short sorties; has favourite perches; often breaks into fluty song. **Food:** insects. **Voice:** clear, metallic song of six notes, sometimes extending to nine or ten; often uttered in winter too. **Range:** all India, south roughly of a line from Kutch to Dehra Dun east along terai; absent in extreme N, NW India. **Habitat:** shaded forests, bamboo, gardens.

*Verditer Flycatcher*

**(1445) VERDITER FLYCATCHER** *Muscicapa thalassina* 15cm. **Male:** verditer-blue plumage, darker in wings, tail; black lores. **Female:** duller, more grey overall. The **(1446) Nilgiri Flycatcher** *M albicaudata* of W Ghats is darker-blue with white in tail; the **(1439) Pale Blue Flycatcher** *M unicolor* (16cm) male is uniform blue, with white on belly; female is olive-brown. Solitary or in pairs in winter, sometimes with other birds; restless, flicking tail, swooping about, ever on the move, occasionally descending quite low; rather more noticeable because of its continuous movement and habit of perching in open exposed positions, like a bare twig on a tree top.

**Food:** insects. **Voice:** silent in winter, save for a rare, faint *chwe..* call; rich, trilling notes and song during Himalayan summer. **Range:** breeds in the Himalaya; 1200–3200m; winters in Indian plains, hill-forests of C, E and S India. **Habitat:** open forests, orchards.

**(1448)   GREYHEADED FLYCATCHER**   *Culicicapa ceylonensis* 9cm. Sexes alike. Ashy-grey head, throat, breast; darker crown; yellow-green back and yellow rump; yellow in browner wings, tail; yellow below breast. Some Flycatcher-Warblers (*Seicercus* spp) are superficially similar to the Greyheaded Flycatcher, but lack grey on throat and breast. Solitary or in pairs, occasionally several in vicinity, especially in mixed parties; a forest-bird, typical flycatcher, excitedly flitting about, launching aerial sallies and generally on the move; wherever this bird is, its cheerful unmistakable calls heard. **Food:** insects. **Voice:** vocal; high-pitched two or three-syllabled calls, *whi..chichee..whi..chichee;* longer, trilling song; also chattering notes. **Range:** commonly breeds in the Himalaya, 1500–3000m; possibly in some of the hill forests of C India and E Ghats; common in winter over much of the subcontinent. **Habitat:** forests, gardens, orchards.

*Greyheaded Flycatcher*

**(1451)   WHITEBROWED FANTAIL FLYCATCHER** *Rhipidura aureola* 17cm. Sexes alike, but female slightly duller. Dark brown above; black crown, sides of face; white forehead, broad stripe (brow) to nape; two white-spotted wing-bars; white edges to tail; black centre of throat, sides of breast; white, sides of throat, underbody. Solitary or in pairs; lively bird, flits about tirelessly in low growth and middle levels, fans tail, flicks wings or bursts into a whistling trill; makes short hunting dashes in air; quite tame and confiding. **Food:** insects. **Voice:** lively whistle of six to eight notes; grating *chuck...chuck..chuckrrr* note, usually when disturbed and agitated. **Range:** most of the country, south of the Himalayan foothills; absent in arid parts of NW India. **Habitat:** forests, orchards, gardens, tree-dotted cultivation.

*Whitebrowed Fantail Flycatcher*

*Whitespotted Fantail Flycatcher*

**(1454) WHITETHROATED FANTAIL FLYCATCHER** *Rhipidura albicollis* 17cm. Sexes alike. Slaty-brown plumage, including underbody; shorter, white supercilium; white throat, tips to all but central tail-feathers. The **(1458) Whitespotted Fantail Flycatcher** races *albogularis* and *vernayi* have a white-spotted slaty band across breast; also, whitish-buff belly, less white in tail-tip. Overall behaviour not appreciably different from Whitebrowed Flycatcher's. **Voice:** shorter and weaker whistling song than Whitebrowed; a harsh *chukrrr...* note. **Range:** outer Himalaya, to about 1800m; NE regions; absent through Indo-Gangetic plain west to NW parts of country; two races from Orissa to Godavari river; most widespread is the Whitespotted race *albogularis*, found all over peninsular India, south of a line from Mt Abu, across the Vindhya and south along the edge of E Ghats. **Habitat:** light forests, groves, gardens amidst habitation, scrub.

*Paradise Flycatcher*

**(1461) PARADISE FLYCATCHER** *Terpsiphone paradisi* *Adult* **Male:** 50cm including tail-streamers. Glossy blue-black head, crest, throat; black in wings; silvery-white body, long tail-streamers. In rufous phase white parts replaced by rufous-chestnut. **Female** and **Young Male:** 20cm. No tail-streamers; shorter crest; rufous above; ashy-grey throat, nuchal collar; whitish below. Solitary or pairs; makes short sallies, flits through trees, the tail streamers floating; strictly arboreal, sometimes descending into taller bushes; cheerful disposition. **Food:** insects, spiders. **Voice:** sharp, grating *chwae* or *chchwae...* call; melodious warbling song and display of breeding male. **Range:** Himalaya, foothills to about 1800m, rarely 2500m; N India, south to Bharatpur; absent in a broad belt across Gangetic Plain; widespread in peninsular India. **Habitat:** light forests, gardens, open country.

**(1465) BLACKNAPED FLYCATCHER** *Hypothymis azurea* 16cm. **Male:** lilac-blue plumage; black patch on nape, gorget on breast; slight black scaly markings on crown; sooty on wings, tail; white below breast. **Female:** ashy-blue, duller; lacks black on nape and breast. Solitary or pairs in forest, often amidst mixed-hunting parties; extremely active and fidgety, flits and flutters about, often fans tail slightly; calls often as it moves about, the calls often the first indication of its presence. **Food:** insects. **Voice:** common call a sharp, grating, high-pitched *chwich.chweech* or *chwae.chweech*, slightly interrogative in tone, the two notes quickly uttered; has short, rambling notes when breeding. **Range:** India south of outer Himalaya, to about 1200m, east of Dehra Dun; absent in arid NW, and N India. **Habitat:** forest, bamboo, gardens.

**(1478) STRONGFOOTED BUSH WARBLER** *Cettia (fortipes) montana* 11cm. Sexes alike. Rufescent olive-brown above; buffy eyebrow; dark through eyes; dull-whitish below, tinged ashy-brown on throat and buff-brown flanks, under tail. Diagnostic call. The slightly smaller **(1474) Palefooted Bush Warbler** *C pallidipes* (10cm) has yellowish or flesh-coloured legs (*fortipes* has brownish legs). Solitary, occasionally two birds close by; a loner; shy and secretive, sneaking in undergrowth; rarely seen; usually, call-notes confirm presence. **Food:** insects. **Voice:** loud three-note call; *chak...* or *suck..* note; song of breeding male loud, usually high-pitched, long-drawn whistle, beginning with an Iora-like *wheeeeeee,* and ending in an explosive, musical phrase. **Range:** the Himalaya, also NE; breeds above 2000m till about 3300m; Moves down in winter, into foothills, and possibly parts of adjacent plains. **Habitat:** undergrowth on hill-sides, edges of forest, open forest, bamboo; also tea-estates and grasslands.

**(1498) STREAKED FANTAIL WARBLER** *Cisticola juncidis* 10cm. Sexes alike. Rufous-brown above, prominently streaked darker; rufous-buff, unstreaked rump; white tips to fan-shaped tail diagnostic; buffy-white underbody, more rufous on flanks. Diagnostic calls. Pairs or several birds over open expanse; great skulker, lurking in low growth; usually seen during short, jerky flights, low over ground; soon dives into cover; most active when breeding, during rains; striking display of male, soaring erratically, falling and rising, incessantly uttering sharp, creaking note; adults arrive on nest in similar fashion. **Food:** insects, spiders; possibly some seeds. **Voice:** sharp, clicking *zit..zit* calls; continuously during display in air. **Range:** all India, south of the Himalayan foothills; absent in extreme NW Rajasthan. **Habitat:** open country, grass, cultivation, reed beds; also coastal lagoons.

*Blacknaped Flycatcher*

*Streaked Fantail Warbler*

**(1503) FRANKLIN'S WREN-WARBLER** *Prinia hodgsonii* 11cm. Sexes alike. More grey-brown, less rufous above; long, grey tail, tipped black and white; white underbody; when breeding, soft grey breast-band diagnostic. The **(1506) Rufousfronted Wren-Warbler** *P buchanani* (12cm) can be identified by the rufous head and dark brown tail, tipped black and white. Small bands ever on the move; keep to low growth but often clambers into middle levels; singing males may climb to top of trees; few nearly always present in mixed-hunting parties of small birds; nest like tailor-bird's. **Food:** insects, flower-nectar. **Voice:** noisy when breeding; longish, squeaky song; contact calls, almost continuous squeaking. **Range:** all India south of Himalayan foothills up to about 1800m; absent in arid W Rajasthan. **Habitat:** edge of forests, cultivation, gardens, scrub, often in and around habitation.

**(1508) STREAKED WREN-WARBLER** *Prinia gracilis* 13cm. Sexes alike. Dull grey-brown above, streaked darker; very pale around eyes; long, graduated tail, faintly cross-barred, tipped white; whitish underbody, buffy on belly. Plumage more rufous in winter. The **(1527) Brown Hill Warbler** *P criniger* (16cm) is larger, dark brown, streaked. **(1531) Longtailed Grass Warbler** *P burnesii* (17cm) is rufous-brown above, streaked; whitish below. Small parties moving in low growth; usually does not associate with other birds; restless, flicks wings and tail often; occasionally hunts like flycatcher. **Food:** insects. **Voice:** longish warble when breeding; wing-snapping and jumping display of male; *szeep...szip..* call-note. **Range:** NW Himalayan foothills, terai, south to Gujarat, across Gangetic Plain. **Habitat:** scrub, grass, canal-banks, semi-desert.

**(1511) PLAIN WREN-WARBLER** *Prinia subflava* 13cm. Sexes alike. Pale brown above; whitish supercilium, lores; dark wings, tail; long, graduated tail, with buff tips and white outer feathers; buff-white underbody, tawny flanks, belly. In winter, more rufous above. The **(1525) Yellowbellied Wren-Warbler** *P flaviventris* (13cm) is olivish-green above, with a slaty-grey head; yellow belly and whitish

*Plain Wren-Warbler*

throat distinctive. Pairs or several moving about in low growth; skulker, difficult to see; jerky, low flight, soon vanishing into bush; tail often flicked. **Food:** insects, flower-nectar. **Voice:** plaintive *tee..tee;* also a *krrik..krrik* sound; wheezy song, very insect-like in quality. **Range:** all India, from terai and Gangetic Plain southwards; absent in W Rajasthan. **Habitat:** tall cultivation, grass, scrub; prefers damp areas.

*Yellowbellied Wren-Warbler*

**(1517) ASHY WREN-WARBLER** *Prinia socialis* 13cm. Sexes alike. Rich, ashy-grey above, with rufous wings and long white-tipped tail; whitish lores; dull buffy-rufous below. In winter, less ashy, more rufous-brown; longer tail; whitish chin, throat. Mostly in pairs; common and familiar as tailor-bird in some areas; actively moves in undergrowth; often flicks and erects tail; typical jerky flight when flying to another bush; noisy and excited when breeding. **Food:** insects, flower-nectar. **Voice:** nasal *pee..pee..pee..;* song, a loud and lively *jivee..jivee..jivee..* or *jimmy..jimmy..*, rather like tailor-bird's in quality, but easily identifiable once heard. **Range:** all India south of Himalayan foothills, from about 1400m; absent in W Rajasthan. **Habitat:** cultivation, edges of forest, scrub, parks, vicinity of habitation.

*Ashy Wren-Warbler*

**(1535) TAILOR BIRD** *Orthotomus sutorius* 13cm. Sexes alike. Olive-green above; rust-red forecrown; buffy-white underbody; dark spot on throat-sides, best seen in calling male; long, pointed tail, often held erect; central tail-feathers about 5cm longer and pointed in breeding male. One of India's best-known birds; usually in pairs together; rather common amidst habitation, but keeps to bushes, gardens; remains unseen even when at arm's length, but very vocal; tail often cocked, carried almost to the back; clambers up into trees more than other related warblers. **Food:** insects, flower-nectar. **Voice:** very vocal; loud familiar *towit..towit;* song is a rapid version of call, with slight change, loud *chuvee..chuvee..chuvee,* uttered for up to 7 minutes at a stretch; male sings on exposed perch. **Range:** all India, to about 2000m in outer Himalaya. **Habitation:** forest, cultivation, habitation.

*Tailor Bird*

**(1550) INDIAN GREAT REED WARBLER** *Acrocephalus stentoreus* 19cm. Sexes alike. Brown above; distinct pale supercilium; whitish throat, dull buffy-white below; at close range, or in hand, salmon-coloured inside of mouth; calls diagnostic. Solitary or in pairs; difficult to see but easily heard; elusive bird, keeps to dense low reeds, mangrove and low growth, always in and around water; never associates with other species; flies low, immediately vanishes into the vegetation; occasionally emerges on reed or bush tops, warbling with throat puffed out. **Food:** insects. **Voice:** highly vocal; loud *chack, chakrrr* and *khe* notes; distinctive, loud warbling; loud, lively song. **Range:** from Kashmir valley, south through the country; sporadically breeds in many areas, migrant in others. **Habitat:** reed beds, mangrove.

**(1557) INDIAN PADDYFIED WARBLER** *Acrocephalus agricola* 13cm. Sexes alike. Rufescent-brown above; brighter on rump; whitish throat; rich buffy below. The **(1556) Blyth's Reed Warbler** *A dumetorum* (14cm), is a very common winter visitor, also has whitish throat and buffy underbody, but olive-brown upperbody is distinctive. Solitary, hopping amidst low growth; rarely seen along with other birds; damp areas, especially reed-growth and cultivation are favourite haunts; flies low, but soon vanishes into growth. **Food:** insects. **Voice:** a *chrr..chuck* or a single *chack* note, rather harsh in tone. The Blyth's Reed has a somewhat louder, quicker *tchik..* or *tchi..tchi..* call, and rarely, a warbling song before emigration, around early-April. **Range:** winter visitor; common over most of India, south of and including the terai. **Habitat:** damp areas, reed-growth, tall cultivation.

**(1563) INDIAN BOOTED TREE WARBLER** *Hippolais caligata* 12cm. Sexes alike. Dull olive-brown above; short, pale white supercilium; pale buffy-white below. The Blyth's Reed Warbler is brighter olive-brown and mostly frequents bushes. Solitary or two to four birds, sometimes in mixed bands of small birds; very active and agile, hunting amongst leaves and upper branches; overall behaviour very leaf-warbler like, but calls diagnostic. **Food:** insects. **Voice:** harsh, but low *chak..chak.. churrr..*; calls almost throughout day; soft, jingling song, sometimes heard before departure in winter grounds. **Range:** winters over peninsula south from Punjab to Bengal; breeds in NW regions, parts of W Punjab. **Habitat:** open country with *Acacias* and scrub; occasionally light forests.

**(1567) LESSER WHITETHROAT** *Sylvia curruca* 12cm. Sexes alike. Deep-grey above, washed brownish on back and wings; dark, almost blackish, ear-coverts give masked appearance; glistening white throat; white below, buff-wash on breast, belly. The **(1566) Whitethroat** *S communis* (14cm) has rusty wings and lacks the dark ear-coverts; it winters over NW India, south at least to W Gujarat. Mostly solitary; secretive, skulking; moves or creeps in dense bush-growth, including *Acacia* and *Prosopis;* jabs with beak at out of reach insect. **Food:** small insects, caterpillars, nectar of *Acacia, Prosopis* and similar flowers. **Voice:** *check* note, often uttered as it moves in bush; song a mix of soft warbling and rapid rattling outburst. **Range:** winter visitor almost all over India; the race *althaea* breeds in W Himalaya, 1500–3700m. **Habitat:** open bush country, *Acacia* and *Prosopis* growth, groves, gardens.

*Whitethroat*

**(1601) LARGEBILLED LEAF WARBLER** *Phylloscopus magnirostris* 12cm. Sexes alike. Brown-olive above; yellowish supercilium, dark eye-stripe distinctive; one or two faint wing-bars, not always easily seen; dull-yellow below. The very similar **(1602) Dull Green Leaf Warbler** *P trochiloides* (10cm) is best identifiable in field by call (squeaky, fairly loud *dhciewee* or a *cheee.ee*). Usually solitary, sometimes in mixed parties of small birds; quite active, spends most time in leafy upper branches of medium-sized trees; not easy to sight, but characteristic call-notes help in confirming its presence. **Food:** small insects. **Voice:** distinctive *dir..tee...* call, the first note slightly lower; loud, ringing, five-noted song. **Range:** breeds in the Himalaya, 1800–3600m; winters over most of the peninsula, though exact range imperfectly known. **Habitat:** forests, groves.

**(1614) BLACKBROWED FLYCATCHER-WARBLER** *Seicercus burkii* 10cm. Sexes alike. Olive-green above; greenish or grey-green eyebrow bordered above with prominent black coronal bands; greenish sides of face, yellow eye-ring; completely yellow below. The **(1613) Allied Flycatcher-Warbler** *S affinis* has grey on crown and whitish eye-ring. Small restless flocks, often in association with other small birds; keeps to the low bush and lower branches of trees. **Food:** insects. **Voice:** fairly noisy; sharp *chip..chip..* or *cheup..cheup..* notes. **Range:** breeds in the Himalaya, 2000–3500m; winters in foothills, parts of C and E peninsula, south to N Maharashtra, S Madhya Pradesh, NE Andhra Pradesh. **Habitat:** forest undergrowth.

**(1616) GREYHEADED FLYCATCHER-WARBLER** *Seicercus xanthoschistos* 10cm. Sexes alike. Grey above; prominent, long, white eyebrow; yellowish rump, wings; white in outer-tail seen in flight; completely yellow below. The **(1620) Greycheeked Flycatcher-Warbler** *S poliogenys* has dark slaty head, white eye-ring and grey chin and cheeks; it is found in Himalaya, east of Nepal. Pairs or small bands, often along with mixed-hunting parties; actively hunts and flits in canopy foliage and tall bushes; highly energetic. **Food:** insects; rarely small berries. **Voice:** quite vocal; familiar calls of Himalayan forests; loud, high-pitched double-note call; pleasant, trilling song. **Range:** the Himalaya; 900–3000m; altitudinal movement in winter. **Habitat:** Himalayan forests, gardens.

**(1629) GOLDCREST** *Regulus regulus* 8cm. **Male:** greyish-olive above; prominent golden-yellow median stripe on crown, bordered by black; two pale yellow-white wing-bars; white ring around eyes; yellow in wings, tail; whitish below. **Female:** like male, but yellow stripe on crown. Pairs or small flocks, often along with other small birds in conifer canopy; also hunts in low branches and tall growth; restless bird, moving energetically, occasionally hovers when searching insects. **Food:** insects. **Voice:** high-pitched, squeaking *tsi..tsi...* call diagnostic. **Range:** the Himalaya, breeds between 2400–4000m; considerable altitudinal movement, descending to 1500m in winter, sometimes to about 1200m. **Habitat:** coniferous forests; orchards in winter.

**(1635) GOULD'S SHORTWING** *Brachypteryx stellata* 13cm. Sexes alike. Chestnut above; blackish lores; finely barred, grey and black below, with diagnostic triangular spots on lower breast, belly; rufous wash on flanks, vent; short tail characteristic. Mostly solitary; keeps generally to ground, amidst dense undergrowth in evergreen hill forest, but occasionally ascends bush-tops and low branches; may be approached close in some localities, but on the whole a shy and silent bird. **Food:** insects, grubs; possibly also grit. **Voice:** usually silent, save an occasional, sharp *tik..tik* call. **Range:** Himalaya east of Kumaon; breeds above 3000m, to about 4200m; descends in winter to 1500m; recorded at 500m in Sikkim. **Habitat:** dense growth in forest; also boulders in alpine country.

**(1637) RUFOUSBELLIED SHORTWING** *Brachypteryx major* 15cm. Sexes alike. Deep slaty-blue above; black lores; cobalt-blue over eye (forehead); slaty-blue throat, breast; white belly-centre; rest of underbody, rusty-rufous, more olive-brown on sides. Solitary or in pairs; an unobtrusive, elusive bird of shaded areas, where it is difficult to spot; moves in dense undergrowth, hopping about; emerges late in evening on jungle paths and clearings; may ascend to low branches, especially when disturbed, but returns soon to ground. **Food:** insects. **Voice:** loud call-notes and rich whistling song-notes, uttered round the year, though more frequently when breeding (April–June). **Range:** restricted to Southern W Ghats, Palnis, Ashambu Hills. **Habitat:** sholas; evergreen forests.

*Bluethroat*

**(1644) BLUETHROAT** *Erithacus svecicus* 15cm. **Male:** pale brown above; whitish eyebrow; rufous in tail; bright blue chin, throat, with chestnut, occasionally white spot in centre; black and rufous bands below blue; whitish-buff below. **Female:** lacks blue; blackish malar stripe continues into broken gorget of brown spots across breast. Mostly solitary; great skulker, preferring damp areas with good grass and bush growth; cocks tail, straightens up a bit to look around; extremely wary; emerges in open but quickly vanishes into growth; appearing rather tame and confiding, but difficult to observe. **Food:** insects. **Voice:** harsh *tack* and a *churrr* in winter; rich song in summer, rarely before emigration, by mid-April. **Range:** breeds only in Ladakh, N Kashmir and Spiti; winter visitor over most of country. **Habitat:** damp ground, cultivation, vicinity of canals, jheels.

**(1647) HIMALAYAN RUBYTHROAT** *Erithacus pectoralis* 15cm. **Male:** slaty above; white supercilium; white in tail; scarlet chin, throat; jet black sides of throat, continuing into broad breast-band; white below, greyer on sides. **Female:** grey-brown above; white chin, throat; greyish breast. The **(1643) Rubythroat** *E calliope* male lacks black on breast; has white malar stripe; female has brown breast; winters in NE and E India. Solitary; wary, difficult to observe; cocks tail; hops on ground, or makes short dashes; ascends small bush-tops. **Food:** insects, molluscs. **Voice:** short metallic call-note; short, harsh alarm-note; rich, shrill song, occasionally in winter also. **Range:** breeds in the Himalaya, 2700-4600m; winters in N, NE India; winter range not properly known. **Habitat:** dwarf vegetation, rocky hills in summer. In winter, prefers cultivation, damp ground with grass and bush.

*Blue Chat*

**(1650) BLUE CHAT** *Erithacus brunneus* 15cm. **Male:** deep slaty-blue above; white supercilium; blackish lores, cheeks; rich-chestnut throat, breast, flanks; white belly-centre, under-tail. **Female:** brown above; white throat, belly; buffy-rufous breast, flanks. The **(1659) Whitebrowed Bush-Robin** *E indicus* male has very long, conspicuous supercilium, and completely rufous-orange underbody; it is resident in the Himalaya. Solitary, rarely in pairs; great skulker, very difficult to observe; moves amidst dense growth and hops on ground; jerks and flicks tail and wings often. **Food:** insects. **Voice:** high-pitched *churr* and harsh *tack..* in winter; trilling song of breeding male, sometimes singing from exposed perch. **Range:** breeds in the Himalaya, 1500–3300m. Winters in southern W Ghats, Ashambu Hills, and Shri Lanka. **Habitat:** dense rhododendron, ringal bamboo under-growth in summer. Evergreen forest undergrowth, cof-fee estates in winter.

**(1661) MAGPIE-ROBIN** *Copsychus saularis* 20cm. **Male:** glossy blue-black and white; white wing-patch and white in outer-tail distinctive; glossy blue-black throat, breast; white below. **Female:** rich slaty grey, where male is black. A familiar bird of India. Solitary or in pairs, sometimes with other birds in mixed parties; hops on ground, prefer-ring shaded areas; common about habitation; when per-ched, often cocks tail; flicks tail often, especially when making short sallies; active at dusk; remarkable songster, very rich voice. **Food:** insects, berries, flower-nectar. **Voice:** one of India's finest songsters; rich, clear song of varying notes and tones; male sings from exposed perches, most frequently between March and June, intermittently round the year; also has harsh *churr* and *chhek* notes; a plaintive *sweee...* is a common call. **Range:** all India, up to about 1500m in outer Himalaya; absent in extreme W Rajasthan. **Habitat:** forests, parks, towns.

*Magpie-Robin*

**(1665) SHAMA** *Copsychus malabaricus* 25cm including tail. **Male:** glossy-black head, back; white rump and sides of graduated tail distinctive; black throat, breast; orange-rufous below. **Female:** grey where male is black; slightly shorter tail and duller rufous below breast. Usually pairs; overall behaviour like Magpie-Robin's; arboreal bird of forest, hill-station gardens; keeps to shaded areas, foliage, only occasionally emerging in open; launches short sallies and hunts till late in evening. **Food:** insects; rarely flower-nectar. **Voice:** rich songster; melodious, three or four whis-tling notes very characteristic; variety of call notes, including a mix of some harsh notes. **Range:** Himalayan foothills, terai, east of Kumaon; NE India; hill-forests of Bihar, Orissa, SE Madhya Pradesh, E Maharashtra, south along E Ghats to about Cauvery river; entire W Ghats, from Kerala north to S Gujarat. **Habitat:** forests, bamboo, hill-station gardens.

*Shama*

*Black Redstart*

**(1671) BLACK REDSTART** *Phoenicurus ochruros* 15cm. **Male:** black above (marked with grey in winter); grey crown, lower back; rufous rump, sides of tail; black throat, breast; rufous below. **Female:** dull-brown above; tail as in male; dull tawny-brown below. The eastern race *rufiventris* has black crown, and is the common wintering bird of India. Mostly solitary in winter, when common all over India; easy bird to observe, in winter and in its open high-altitude summer country; perches on overhead wires, poles, rocks, stumps; characteristic shivering of tail and jerky body movements; makes short dashes to ground, soon returning to perch with catch; rather confiding in summer, breeding in houses, under roofs and in wall crevices. **Food:** insects, mostly taken on ground. **Voice:** squeaking *tictititic..* call, often beginning with faint *tsip..*note; trilling song of breeding male. **Range:** breeds in the Himalaya, 2400–5200m; winters over much of subcontinent. **Habitat:** open country, cultivation.

**(1679) PLUMBEOUS REDSTART** *Rhyacornis fuliginosus* 12cm. **Male:** slaty-blue plumage; chestnut tail diagnostic; rufous on lower belly. **Female:** darkish blue-grey-brown above; two spotted wing-bars; white in tail; whitish below, profusely mottled slaty. Young birds are brown, also with white in tail. Pairs on mountain rivers; active birds, making short dashes from boulders; move from boulder to boulder, flying low over roaring waters; tail frequently fanned open and wagged; hunts late in evening; maintains feeding territories in winter too. **Food:** insects, worms. **Voice:** sharp *kreee...* call; also a snapping *tzit..tzit*; rich, jingling song of breeding male, infrequently uttered in winter. **Range:** the Himalaya, 800–4000m, but mostly 1000–2800m; also breeds south of Brahmaputra river; in winter may descend into the foothills, terai. **Habitat:** mountain streams, rivers, rushing torrents.

**(1683) HODGSON'S GRANDALA** *Grandala coelicolor* 22cm. **Male:** glossy purplish-blue plumage; jet black lores, wings and tail. **Female:** brown above, streaked dull-white on head, neck; white in wings; blue wash on rump, upper tail-coverts; brown below, streaked as on head and neck. Gregarious, except when breeding; sometimes all male or female flocks; bird of high mountain country; strong, graceful fliers, circling and floating high in the skies, often many hundreds together; suddenly the birds rain down on to ground; hops on ground, on rocks and meadows. **Food:** insects, fruits, berries. **Voice:** *jeeu..jeeu..* call-note; more quickly and commonly uttered when breeding. **Range:** high Himalaya, from Kashmir to Arunachal; breeds 3900–5400m; descends in winter to about 2800m, rarely lower. **Habitat:** cliffs, high-altitude meadows.

**(1684) LITTLE FORKTAIL** *Enicurus scouleri* 12cm. Sexes alike. Black and white plumage. Black above, with white forehead; white band in wings extends across lower back; small, black rump patch; slightly forked, short tail with white in outer feathers; black throat, white below. Solitary or in pairs; a bird of mountain streams, waterfalls and small shaded forest puddles; energetically moves on moss-covered and wet slippery rocks; constantly wags and flicks tail; occasionally launches short sallies, but also plunges underwater, dipper-style. **Food:** aquatic insects. **Voice:** rather silent save for a rarely uttered sharp *tzittzit* call. **Range:** the Himalaya, west to east, breeding between 1200–3700m; descends to about 300m in winter. **Habitat:** rocky mountain streams, waterfalls.

**(1688) SPOTTED FORKTAIL** *Enicurus maculatus* 25cm with long tail. Sexes alike. White forehead, forecrown; black crown, nape; black back spotted white; broad, white wing-bar, rump; deeply forked, graduated black and white tail; black till breast, white below. The white-spotted back easily identifies this species from other similar sized forktails in the Himalaya. Solitary or in scattered pairs; active bird, moving on mossy boulders at water's edge or in mid-stream; long, forked tail gracefully swayed, almost always kept horizontal; flies low over streams, calling; sometimes rests in shade of forest; commonly seen bird of the Himalaya. **Food:** aquatic insects, molluscs. **Voice:** shrill, screechy *kree* call, mostly in flight; also some shrill, squeaky notes on perch. **Range:** the Himalaya; breeds mostly 1200–3600m; descends to about 600m in winter. **Habitat:** boulder-strewn torrents, forest streams, roadside canals.

*Brown Rock Chat*

*Collared Bush Chat*

*Pied Bush Chat*

**(1692) BROWN ROCK CHAT** *Cercomela fusca* 17cm. Brown above, more rufous below; dark-brown wings, almost blackish tail. Overall appearance like female Indian Robin. Usually pairs, around ruins, dusty villages, rocky hill-sides; often approaches close; tame and confiding; captures insects on ground; rather aggressive when breeding. **Food:** insects; occasionally kitchen-refuse. **Voice:** harsh *chaeck..* note; also a whistling *chee* call; melodious song of breeding male; a good mimic. **Range:** confined to parts of N and C India, from Punjab and Dehra Dun, south to about Narmada river; east to the Bihar-Bengal. **Habitat:** dry, open country, rocky hills, ravines, ruins, habitation.

**(1697) STONE CHAT** or **COLLARED BUSH CHAT** *Saxicola torquata* 13cm. **Br Male:** black above; white rump, wing-patch, sides of neck/breast (collar); black throat; orange-rufous breast. In winter, black feathers broadly edged buff-rufous-brown. **Female:** rufous-brown above, streaked darker; unmarked yellowish-brown below; white wing-patch and rufous rump. Solitary or in pairs in open country; perches on small bush-tops, fence-posts, boulders; restless, makes short trips to ground to capture insects, soon returning to perch. **Food:** insects. **Voice:** double-noted *wheet..chat* call; soft, trilling song of breeding male in Himalaya, occasionally in winter grounds. **Range:** breeds in Himalaya, 1500–3000m; winters all India except Kerala and much of Tamil Nadu. **Habitat:** dry, open areas, cultivation, tidal creeks.

**(1700) PIED BUSH CHAT** *Saxicola caprata* 13cm. **Male:** black plumage; white in wing, rump, belly. **Female:** brown above, paler on lores; darker tail; dull yellow-brown below, with a rusty wash on breast and belly. Solitary or in pairs; perches on a bush, overhead wire, pole or some earth mound; makes short sallies on to ground, either devouring prey on ground or carrying to perch; active, sometimes guards feeding territories in winter; flicks and spreads wings; fascinating display-flight of courting male (April–May). **Food:** insects. **Voice:** harsh, double-noted call serves as contact and alarm call; short, trilling song of breeding male. **Range:** all India, from outer Himalaya to about 1500m. **Habitat:** open country, scrub, cultivation, ravines.

**(1705) DARK-GREY BUSH CHAT** *Saxicola ferrea* 15cm. **Male:** dark grey above, streaked black; black mask; white supercilium, wing-patch and outer-tail; white throat, belly;

dull grey breast. **Female:** rufous-brown, streaked; rusty rump, outer-tail; white throat; yellow-brown below. Solitary or pairs; like other chats, keeps to open country and edge of forest; perches on bush-tops, poles, flirts tail often; regularly seen in an area; flies to ground on spotting insect. **Food:** insects. **Voice:** double-noted call; also a grating *praee..* call; trilling song of male. **Range:** Himalaya, 1400–3500m; descends into foothills and adjoining plains, including Gangetic Plains, in winter. **Habitat:** open scrub, forest-edges, cultivation.

**(1710) DESERT WHEATEAR** *Oenanthe deserti* 15cm. **Br Male:** sandy above, with whitish rump and black tail; black wings; white in coverts; black throat, head-sides; creamy-white below. **Female:** brown wings, tail; lacks black throat. **Winter Male:** throat feathers fringed white. The **(1706) Isabelline Chat** *O isabellina* (16cm) is larger, sandy-grey, without black throat. The male **(1708) Wheatear** *O oenanthe* is grey above, with white rump, tail-sides and black tail-centre and tip like inverted 'T'; black ear-coverts and wings. Keeps to ground or perches on low bush or small rock; has favoured haunts; colouration makes it difficult to spot; makes short sallies to capture insects. **Food:** insects. **Voice:** in winter an occasional *ch..chett* alarm note; reportedly utters its short, plaintive song in winter also. **Range:** winter visitor over N, C and W India, almost absent south of S Maharastra and Andhra Pradesh; the Tibetan race *oreophila* breeds in Kashmir, Ladakh, Lahaul and Spiti, about 3000–5000m. **Habitat:** open rocky, barren country; sandy areas; fallow lands.

**(1712) PIED CHAT** *Oenanthe picata* 17cm. A polymorphic species (occurring in various colour phases). **Male:** pied plumage; occurs in three phases, black-bellied, white-bellied and white-crowned; jet black plumage in all phases, except variation in colours of belly, crown and rump. **Female:** sooty-black, greyish-brown or earthy-brown; belly usually buff-coloured. Mostly solitary; a bird of dry, barren country; frequently bobs body on perch; flies to ground to pick insect; an aggressive bird, chasing others away from favoured feeding grounds. **Food:** insects. **Voice:** pleasant trilling notes in winter; good mimic, song of breeding male often an assortment of imitations. **Range:** mostly winter visitor to NW India, west of a line from around Delhi, through Madhya Pradesh to N Maharashtra. **Habitat:** open country, fallow lands, vicinity of villages.

*Dark-grey Bush Chat*

*Desert Wheatear*

*Guldenstadt's Redstart*

*Indian Robin*

**(1716) WHITECAPPED REDSTART** *Chaimorrornis (Thamnolaea) leucocephalus* 19cm. Sexes alike. Black back, sides of head, wings, breast; white crown diagnostic; chestnut rump, tail; black terminal tail-band; chestnut below breast. The male **(1678) Guldenstadt's Redstart** *Phoenicurus erythrogaster* (16cm) has completely chestnut tail (no black tip) and prominent white wing-patch. Solitary or pairs on Himalayan torrents; rests on rocks amidst gushing waters, flying very low over the waters to catch insects; jerks and wags tail and dips body; restless bird; interesting display of courting male. **Food:** insects. **Voice:** loud, plaintive *tseeee* call; also a *psit..psit..* call; whistling song of breeding male. **Range:** Himalaya: 2000–5000m; descends into foothills in winter. **Habitat:** rocky streams; also on canals in winter.

**(1717) INDIAN ROBIN** *Saxicoloides fulicata* 16cm. Several races in India. Males differ in having dark-brown, blackish-brown or glossy blue-back upperbody. This description concerns the race *cambaiensis* of N, NW and C India. **Male:** dark-brown above; white wing-patch glossy blue-black below; chestnut vent, undertail. **Female:** lacks white in wings; duller grey-brown below. Solitary or in pairs in open country, and often in and around habitation; rather suspicious and maintains safe distance between man and itself; hunts on ground, hopping or running in short spurts; when on ground, holds head high and often cocks tail, right up to back, flashing the chestnut vent and undertail. **Food:** insects. **Voice:** long-drawn *sweeeech* or *weeeech* call; a warbling song when breeding; also a guttural *charrr..* note. **Range:** all India, south of the Himalayan foothills; absent in extreme NE. **Habitat:** open country, edges of forest, vicinity of habitations, scrub.

**(1723) BLUEHEADED ROCK THRUSH** *Monticola cinclorhynchus* 17cm. **Male:** blue crown, nape; black back, broad stripe through eyes to ear-coverts; blue throat, shoulder patch; white wing-patch and chestnut rump distinctive; chestnut below throat. Back feathers edged fulvous in winter. **Female:** unmarked olive-brown above; buffy-white below, thickly speckled with dark-brown. The female Blue Rock Thrush is grey-brown above, has yellow-brown vent and a dull wing-bar. Solitary or in pairs; an elusive forest bird; moves in foliage in mixed parties or rummages on ground, amidst leaf-litter; best seen when it emerges in clearing. The **(1722) Rock Thrush** M *saxatilis* (19cm) lacks the black eye stripe and has a diagnostic rufous tail. **Food:** insects, flower-nectar, berries. **Voice:** mostly silent in winter, save for an occasional harsh single or double-noted call; rich song of breeding male. **Range:** breeds in the Himalaya, 1000–2500m, sometimes higher; winters in W Ghats, from Narmada river south; sporadic winter records from C Indian forests. **Habitat:** shaded forests, groves.

*Rock Thrush*

**(1726) BLUE ROCK THRUSH** *Monticola solitarius* 23cm. **Male:** blue plumage; brown wings, tail; pale fulvous and black scales more conspicuous in winter; whiter on belly in winter. **Female:** duller, grey-brown above; dark shaft-streaks; black barrings on rump; dull white below, barred brown. Solitary; has favoured sites, often around habitation; perches on rocks, stumps, roof-tops; has a rather upright posture; flies on to ground to feed, but sometimes launches short aerial sallies. **Food:** insects, berries; rarely flower-nectar. **Voice:** silent in winter; short, whistling song of breeding male. **Range:** breeds in the Himalaya, from extreme west to east Nepal; 1200–3000m, perhaps higher; winters from foothills, NE, south throughout peninsula; uncommon in Gangetic plains. **Habitat:** open rocky country, cliffs, ravines, ruins, habitation.

**(1728) MALABAR WHISTLING THRUSH** *Myiophonus horsfieldii* 25cm. Sexes alike. Deep blue-black plumage, more glistening on wings, tail; bright, cobalt-blue forehead, shoulder-patch. Solitary or in pairs; a lively bird of hilly, forested country; keeps to forest streams, waterfalls; also perches on trees; peculiar stretching of legs and raising of tail; often encountered on roadside culverts, from where it bolts into nullah or valley. **Food:** insects, crustaceans, snails, frogs, berries. **Voice:** renowned vocalist; especially vocal during the rains; begins to call very early in morning; a rich, whistling song, very human in quality, nick-named 'whistling schoolboy'; its fluty notes float over the roar of water; also, a harsh, high-pitched *kreeee* call. **Range:** hills of W India, from Mt Abu, south all along W Ghats, to about 2200m; also parts of Satpuras. **Habitat:** forest streams, waterfalls, gardens.

*Blue Whistling Thrush*

**(1729) BLUE WHISTLING THRUSH** *Myiophonus caeruleus* 34cm. Sexes alike. Deep purple-blue plumage, speckled all over with lighter but bright blue; brighter blue forehead, shoulder-patch, edge of wings and tail; whitish-blue spots on tips of median wing-coverts; yellow beak. Solitary or pairs on Himalayan streams and gorges; common all along Himalaya; hops on boulders in the middle or roaring torrent or dashes through forest; also moves on ground, far from water; seen at most hill-stations, often enters houses; remarkable songster. **Food:** aquatic insects, snails, earthworms, crabs. **Voice:** screechy *zseeet... tzee..tzee..* often audible over roar of water; loud, musical song of whistling notes; loud *kree* call. **Range:** the Himalaya, 1200–3800m, but ascending to about 4400m. **Habitat:** forest streams, gorges, hill-stations.

*Whitethroated Ground Thrush*

**(1734) WHITETHROATED GROUND THRUSH** *Zoothera citrina cyanotus* 21cm. Blue-grey above; orangish-rufous head, nape, underbody; white ear-coverts with two dark-brown vertical stripes; white throat, shoulder-patch. The **(1733) Orangeheaded** nominate race has entire head rufous-orange. Usually in pairs; feeds on ground, rummaging in leaf-litter and under thick growth; flies into leafy branch if disturbed; occasionally associates with laughing-thrushes and babblers; vocal and restless when breeding. **Food:** insects, slugs, small fruit. **Voice:** loud, rich song, often with a mix of other birds' calls thrown in; noisy in early mornings and late evenings; also a shrill, screechy *kreeee...* call. **Range:** peninsular India south of a line from S Gujarat across to Orissa; the nominate race breeds in the Himalaya, NE; winters in foothills, terai, parts of E India, Gangetic plains and south along E Ghats. **Habitat:** shaded forests, bamboo, groves, gardens.

**(1740) LONGTAILED MOUNTAIN THRUSH** *Zoothera dixoni* 27cm. Plain olive-brown above; two dull buffy wing-bars and a larger wing-patch seen best in flight; buffy throat, breast, flanks, the rest white, boldly spotted dark-brown. The confusingly similar **(1739) Plainbacked Mountain Thrush** *Z mollissima* has very indistinct wing-bars; it has a shorter tail but this character not very useful in field. The **(1741) Smallbilled Mountain Thrush** *Z dauma* (26cm) has a distinctly spotted back. Pairs or several together in winter; feeds on ground, usually difficult to spot till it takes off from somewhere close-by; flies up into branches if disturbed. **Food:** insects, snails. **Voice:** mostly silent; *mollissima* has a loud, rattling alarm-note. **Range:** the Himalaya, east of C Himachal; breeds about 2000–4000m; descends to about 1000m in winter. **Habitat:** timber-line forest, scrub in summer; heavy forests in winter.

**(1748) TICKELL'S THRUSH** *Turdus unicolor* 22cm. **Male:** light ashy-grey plumage; duller breast and whiter on belly; rufous under-wing coverts in flight. **Female:** olive-brown above; white throat, streaked on sides; tawny flanks and white belly. Small flocks on the ground, sometimes along with other thrushes; hops fast on ground, stops abruptly, as if to check some underground activity; digs worms from under soil; flies into trees when approached too close. **Food:** insects, worms, small fruit. **Voice:** rich song; double-noted alarm call; also some chattering calls. **Range:** breeds in the Himalaya, 1500–2500m, east to C Nepal, and perhaps Sikkim; winters along foothills east of Kangra, NE, and parts of C and E peninsular India. **Habitat:** open forests, groves.

**(1750) GREYWINGED BLACKBIRD** *Turdus boulboul* 28cm. **Male:** black plumage; large, grey wing-patch diagnostic; yellow eye-ring and orangish beak. **Female:** olive-brown plumage; wing-patch pale brown. The female Blackbird is darker in plumage. Solitary or small parties, sometimes with other thrushes in winter; a shy bird, taking to trees on slight suspicion; feeds on ground, picks insects or digs worms. **Food:** insects, worms, small fruit. **Voice:** distinct chuckling notes; rich, loud and fluty song; guttural *churrr...* note. **Range:** the Himalaya, breeds 1800–2700m; descends to about 1200m in winter, sometimes into foothills and adjoining plains. **Habitat:** broadleafed heavy forests; in winter, also scrub, secondary growth and vicinity of countryside habitation.

**(1755) BLACKBIRD** *Turdus merula* 25cm. **Male:** lead-grey above, more ashy-brown below; blackish cap distinctive; darker wings, tail; reddish-orange beak and yellow eye-rims distinctive. **Female:** dark ashy-brown above; browner below, with a grey wash; streaked dark-brown on chin, throat. The **(1753)** Blackcapped race *T m nigropileus* of the W Ghats, Abu and parts of Vindhyas, has a more distinct black cap; in the **(1752)** Himalayan race *T m maximus* (27cm), the male is entirely black with yellow beak; female is dark brown. Solitary or pairs, sometimes with other birds; rummages on forest floor but also moves up in leafy branches; rather confiding, especially in hill-station gardens. **Food:** insects, small fruit, earthworms. **Voice:** loud, melodious song of breeding male; sings from high tree-perch; very vocal in evening; great mimic; screechy *kreeee* during winter; also a harsh *charrr* note. **Range:** various races make this a widespread species in the Indian region; Himalaya, 2200–4000m; hills of W India, from Mt Abu southwards; E Ghats south of N Orissa. **Habitat:** forests, ravines, gardens.

**(1763) BLACKTHROATED THRUSH** *Turdus ruficollis* 25cm. **Male:** grey-brown above; black lores, malar area, sides of neck, throat, breast; white below; white streaks in winter. **Female:** browner above; dull ashy-brown breast, flanks, streaked brown; rest of underbody white, streaked blackish on sides of throat, upper-breast. The male **(1764) Redthroated Thrush** *T r ruficollis* has rufous-chestnut throat, breast and much of tail. Gregarious; often along with other thrushes; hops on ground, flies into branches only when disturbed; large gatherings seen around early April, just before departure for breeding areas. **Food:** insects, earthworms, small fruit. **Voice:** harsh but thin *schwee* call-note; chuckling *wheech..which...* **Range:** common winter visitor to Himalaya; foothills to about 4000m; may spread in plains as far south as E Rajasthan (Bharatpur). **Habitat:** forest-edges, cultivation, scrub, fallow-land.

*Blackthroated Thrush*

**(1770) KASHMIR WREN** *Troglodytes troglodytes* 9cm. Sexes alike. A tiny, skulking Himalayan bird. Short, erect, cocked tail distinctive; brown above, closely-barred; paler below, whiter on belly, also barred closely. Usually solitary; very active, but also extremely secretive; jerkily hops on boulders or moves mouselike amidst dense bush, holding tail cocked; takes to dense cover if approached close. **Food:** small insects. **Voice:** quite noisy; fairly loud *zirrr.. tzt..tzzt..* alarm-notes; shrill, rambling song, sometimes uttered in winter too, even in snow. **Range:** the Himalaya; breeds about 2700m, descends to about 1200m in winter, especially in W Himalaya. **Habitat:** thickets, dense cover, mossy growth, rocky ground, vicinity of mountain habitation.

**(1773) WHITEBREASTED DIPPER** *Cinclus cinclus* 20cm. Sexes alike. Stub-tailed, squat bird. Slaty above; choco-brown head, nape; scaly-brown markings on back, rump; white throat, breast striking; choco-brown belly. The **(1775) Brown Dipper** *C pallasii* is entirely choco-brown, with prominent white eye-ring. Solitary or pairs over a stretch of gushing, icy torrent; settles on slippery rocks amidst water; plunges and swims against current; walks on bottom; very restless and energetic, bobs and moves body from side to side; swift, fast flight, low over water; noisy. **Food:** aquatic insects. **Voice:** shrill *dzchit..dzcheet* call, audible over roaring waters; calls mostly in low flight over water; call usually heard long before bird sighted; sharp lively song. **Range:** Himalaya; 2500–4800m; sometimes to 2000m in winter. **Habitat:** rocky, icy torrents, glacial lakes.

*Whitebreasted Dipper*

**(1778) ALPINE ACCENTOR** *Prunella collaris* 17cm. Sexes alike. Grey-brown above, streaked brown/rufous-brown on back; dark-brown wings with two pale-white wing-bars; blackish-brown tail, with narrow buffy tip to feathers; whitish chin, throat, spotted black; grey throat-sides, breast, belly; flanks broadly-streaked chestnut. Pairs or up to half-dozen birds together; moves on ground, hops silently, often very close to observer; also settles on boulders, bush-tops. The **(1784) Brown Accentor** *P fulvesceus* (15cm) has a diagnostic long white supercilium. **Food:** small insects, seeds. **Voice:** silent on ground, but utters a trilling *tchirrr..ip..* when flushed; sweet-sounding, warbling song (June–July), either from ground or during short display-flight. **Range:** high-mountain bird. Found in the Himalaya; breeds above 3500m, up to about 5000m; descends to about 1800–2200m in winter. **Habitat:** rocky areas, mountain slopes, stony meadows.

*Brown Accentor*

*Robin Accentor*

**(1781) ROBIN ACCENTOR** *Prunella rubeculoides* 17cm. Sexes alike. Pale-brown above, streaked darker on back; grey head, throat; two whitish wing-bars; rufous breast and creamy-white belly; streaks on flanks. The **(1783) Rufousbreasted Accentor** *P strophiata* (15cm) has heavily streaked throat and conspicuous rufous supercilium. Flocks in winter, occasionally along with other accentors, pipits and sparrows; rather tame and confiding around high-altitude habitation; hops on ground, flies into bushes if intruded upon beyond a point. **Food:** insects, small seeds. **Voice:** a sharp trilling note; also a *tszi...tszi..*; short, chirping song. **Range:** high Himalaya; breeds 3200–5300m; descends in winter to about 2000m, rarely below 1500m. **Habitat:** Tibetan facies; damp grass, scrub; high altitude habitation.

**(1789) SULTAN TIT** *Melanochlora sultanea* 20cm. **Male:** black above; yellow crown, crest; black throat, upper-breast; yellow below. **Female:** deep olivish wash to black upperbody, throat; crest as in male; some yellow also on throat. Small bands, often along with other birds in mixed-hunting flocks; active and inquisitive, clings sideways and upside-down, checks foliage and bark-crevices; feeds in canopy but also descends to tall bush. **Food:** insects, small fruit, seeds. **Voice:** noisy; loud, whistling *cheerie..cheerie;* other shrill whistling notes, often mixed with a harsh *churr* or *chrrchuk;* varied chattering notes. **Range:** the Himalayan foothills, from C Nepal east; NE; foothills to about 1200m, sometimes ascending to 2000m. **Habitat:** mixed forests, edges of forest.

*Grey Tit*

**(1794) GREY TIT** *Parus major* 13cm. Sexes alike. Grey back; black crown continued along sides of neck to broad black band from chin along centre of underbody; white cheeks, nape-patch, wing-bar and outer feathers of black tail; ashy-white sides. The **(1798) Whitewinged Black Tit** *P nuchalis* of W India lacks black on neck-sides; has extensive white in wings and sides of body. The **(1799) Greenbacked Tit** *P monticolus* of the Himalaya has an olive back, white sides of underbody and two wing-bars. Pairs or small bands, often with other small birds; restless, clings upside down, and indulges in all sorts of acrobatic displays as it hunts amongst leaves and branches; holds food fast between feet and pecks at it noisily; tame and confiding. **Food:** insects, small fruit. **Voice:** loud, clear whistling *whee..chi.chee..;* other whistling and harsh notes. **Range:** widespread from Himalaya, foothills to about 3500m; peninsular India from Gujarat, C Rajasthan and Orissa south; absent in broad belt from NW India across Gangetic plains. **Habitat:** open forests, gardens, habitation.

**(1802) CRESTED BLACK TIT** *Parus melanolophus* 11cm. Sexes alike. Dark-grey back; black crest, sides of neck; white cheeks, nape-patch; rusty-white double, spotted wing-bars; black throat, upper-breast; slaty belly and rufous flanks, undertail. The **(1803) Coal Tit** *P ater* (10cm) also with double spotted wing-bars is yellow-brown below breast; it is found only east of C Nepal. The **(1804) Simla Black Tit** *P rubidiventris* (13cm) lacks wing-bars and has more extensive black below. Part of mixed-hunting bands of small birds, restless, forever on the move; hunts high in canopy foliage but also descends onto ground. **Food:** insects, berries. **Voice:** a double-noted *te..tui* call; faint *tzee..tzee;* also a whistling song. **Range:** W Himalaya, east to W Nepal; 2000–3600m; descends into foothills in winter. **Habitat:** coniferous forest; also mixed forest in winter.

**(1809) YELLOWCHEEKED TIT** *Parus xanthogenys* 14cm. Sexes alike. Olive-green back; black crest (faintly tipped with yellow), stripe behind eye, broad central band from chin to vent; bright yellow nape-patch, supercilium, sides of underbody. The **(1812) Blackspotted Yellow Tit** *P spilonotus* has black streaks on back, yellow lores and forehead. Pairs or small flocks, often with other small birds; arboreal, active; feeds in foliage; sometimes enters gardens. **Food:** insects, berries. **Voice:** cheerful, musical notes; loud tailor-bird like *towit..towit* calls near nest; other two- to four-noted whistling calls; whistling song; also harsh, *charrr* and some chattering notes. **Range:** the Himalaya to E Nepal; 1200–2500m, sometimes descending very low in winter; widespread in parts of C, E and W India. **Habitat:** forests, gardens.

*Yellowcheeked Tit*

*Firecapped Tit*

**(1815) FIRECAPPED TIT** *Cephalopyrus flammiceps* 9cm. **Male:** olive-yellow above; scarlet-orange cap, chin, throat; two yellow wing-bars; yellow throat, breast; whiter-buff below. In winter, no scarlet on crown; duller yellow underbody. **Female:** yellowish rump, wing-bars, edges of outer tail-feathers. Small parties, either on their own or in mixed-hunting parties; extremely active, flits about in canopy foliage, clings sideways and upside-down; overall behaviour very leaf-warbler like. **Food:** small insects, buds. **Voice:** faint, twittering song. **Range:** breeds in W Himalaya, Kashmir to Garhwal; 1800–3700m; winters in C India, mostly Madhya Pradesh and parts of NE Maharashtra, SE Uttar Pradesh. **Habitat:** forested hillsides, orchards.

**(1818) REDHEADED TIT** *Aegithalos concinnus* 10cm. Sexes alike. Grey back; chestnut-red crown; nape; black and white sides of face, throat; brown wings, tail, the latter with white tip and outer feathers; buffy-yellowish-red below throat. Highly sociable; fidgety, over-active bird, ever-curious, checking out leaves, branches, crevices; several birds together, almost always a part of mixed-hunting bands, though sometimes keep to themselves; rather tame and confiding in many areas. **Food:** insects, small fruits. **Voice:** incessant, faint *trr..trrr* and *check..check..* call-notes. **Range:** Himalaya, 500–3500m, occasionally to 4000m; optimum breeding zone about 1300–2600m. **Habitat:** open forests, gardens, secondary growth.

*Chestnutbellied Nuthatch*

**(1830) CHESTNUTBELLIED NUTHATCH** *Sitta castanea* 12cm. **Male:** blue-grey above; black stripe from lores to nape; whitish cheeks, upper throat; all but central tail-feathers black, with white markings; chestnut below. **Female:** duller chestnut below. The male **(1834) White-tailed Nuthatch** *S himalayensis* has much paler underbody and clear white patch at base of tail. Pairs or several, often with other small birds; restless climber, clings to bark and usually works up the tree-stem, hammering with beak; also moves upside-down and sideways; may visit the ground. **Food:** insects, grubs, seeds. **Voice:** loud *tzsib..* call; faint twitter; loud whistle during breeding season. **Range:** lower Himalaya east of Kumaon; to about 1800m; peninsula east of a line from C Punjab to Nasik; also the E Ghats; large gaps in distribution. **Habitat:** open forests, groves, roadside trees, habitation.

**(1838) VELVETFRONTED NUTHATCH** *Sitta frontalis* 10cm. **Male:** violet-blue above; jet-black forehead, stripe through eyes; white chin, throat, merging into vinous-grey below; coral-red beak. **Female:** lacks black stripe through eyes. Pairs or several in mixed-hunting parties; creeps about on stems and branches; fond of moss-covered trees; also clings upside-down; active and agile, quickly moves from tree to tree; calls often, till long after sunset; also checks fallen logs and felled branches. **Food:** insects. **Voice:** fairly loud, rapidly-repeated, sharp, trilling *chweet..chwit..chwit* whistles. **Range:** from around Dehra Dun east along lower Himalaya; widespread over the hilly, forested areas of C, S and E India; absent in the flat and arid regions. **Habitat:** forests; also tea and coffee plantations.

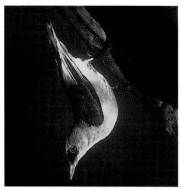

*Velvetfronted Nuthatch*

**(1839) WALL CREEPER** *Tichodroma muraria* 17cm. Sexes alike. Ashy-grey plumage; brown top of head; whitish chin, throat; large, crimson wing-patch and white spots on flight-feathers diagnostic; black tail, tipped paler, with some white in outer feathers. In summer (breeding) plumage, black chin and throat. Usually solitary, sometimes pairs; jerkily moves up on vertical cliff faces, mudbanks, boulders, flicking wings; suddenly erupts from vertical climb, either to grab some winged insect or move to another face; crimson on wings very prominent in butterfly-like flight. **Food:** insects, spiders. **Voice:** mostly silent, except for an occasional faint, cheeping note; short (four-noted) breeding song. **Range:** high Himalaya: breeds above 2800m; winters much lower, often in foothills and adjacent plains. **Habitat:** cliffs, mud-walls.

**(1841) SPOTTED GREY CREEPER** *Salpornis spilonotos* 13cm. Sexes alike. Dark brown above, spotted white; whitish supercilium; barred tail; white throat; yellowish-brown below, mottled with dark brown. Mostly solitary, though another bird is usually in vicinity; active, climbing up tree-stems and branches, especially trees that have deep-fissured bark like *khair*, *babool*; works from near-ground level to uppermost branches, probing crevices. **Food:** insects, spiders. **Voice:** whistling song, described as being of volume and timbre of sunbird's. **Range:** large part of central India, from E–SE Rajasthan, much of Gangetic plain, south to C Maharashtra. **Habitat:** open forests, groves.

**(1843) TREE CREEPER** *Certhia familiaris* 12cm. Sexes alike. Fulvous-brown above, spotted white on crown and back; white supercilium; long, pointed unbarred tail distinctive; completely white below, grey-brown on flanks. The other tree-creepers with unbarred tail are the **(1849) Sikkim Tree Creeper** *C discolor* and **(1851) Nepal Tree Creeper** *C nipalensis*; both are much darker above; *discolor* has dark throat; *nipalensis* has a buff breast and tawny flanks. Usually seen amidst other small birds; creeps up along tree-stems; probes crevices; overall very active. **Food:** insects, spiders. **Voice:** faint *tzi...* or *tsee...* note. **Range:** the Himalaya; 1500m to timber-line. **Habitat:** pine, deodar, fir forests.

**(1847) HIMALAYAN TREE CREEPER** *Certhia himalayana* 12cm. Sexes alike. Streaked blackish-brown, fulvous and grey above; pale supercilium; broad fulvous wing-band; white chin, throat; dull ash-brown below; best recognised by dark-brown barring on pointed tail. Solitary or several in mixed parties of small birds; spends almost entire life on tree-trunks; starts from near base; intermittently checks crevices and under moss, picks out insects with curved beak; usually climbs to mid-height, then moves on to another tree; sometimes creeps on moss-clothed rocks and walls. **Food:** insects, spiders. **Voice:** long-drawn squeak, somewhat ventriloquial; loud but short, monotonous song; one of the earliest bird songs, heard much before other birds have begun to sing. **Range:** the Himalaya; east to W Nepal; from about 1600m to timber-line; descends in winter. **Habitat:** Himalayan temperate forests.

**(1852) INDIAN TREE PIPIT** *Anthus hodgsoni* 15cm. Sexes alike. Olive-brown above, streaked dark-brown; dull-white supercilium, two wing-bars and in outer tail-feathers; pale buff-white below, profusely streaked dark-brown on entire breast, flanks. The **(1854) Tree Pipit** *A trivialis* is brown above, without olive wash. Gregarious in winter; spends most time on ground, running briskly; if approached close, flies with *tseep..* call into trees; descends in a few minutes. **Food:** insects, grass and other seeds. **Voice:** faint *tseep..* call; lark-like song of breeding male. **Range:** breeds in the Himalaya, east from W Himachal; above 2700m, to timber-line; winters in foothills and almost all over India, except arid NW, Kutch; *trivialis* breeds only in NW Himalaya and is commoner in winter over C India, but sporadically over range of *hodgsoni*. **Habitat:** forests, grassy slopes.

**(1858) PADDYFIELD PIPIT** *Anthus novaeseelandiae* 15cm. Sexes alike. Fulvous-brown above, with dark-brown centres of feathers, giving a distinctive appearance; dark-brown tail, with white outer-feathers, easily seen in flight; dull-fulvous below, streaked dark-brown on sides of throat, neck and entire breast. The winter-visiting **(1861) Tawny Pipit** *A campestris* usually lacks streaks on under-body while the **(1863) Blyth's Pipit** *A godlewskii* is indistin-guishable in field, except by its harsher call-note. Pairs or several scattered on ground; run in short spurts; when disturbed, utters feeble note as it takes off; singing males perch on grass-tufts and small bushes. **Food:** insects, seeds, spiders. **Voice:** thin *tsip, tseep* and *tsip..tseep..* calls; trilling song of breeding male. **Range:** from about 2000m in outer Himalaya, south throughout India. **Habitat:** grassland, marshy ground, cultivation.

*Paddyfield Pipit*

**(1874) FOREST WAGTAIL** *Motacilla indica* 17cm. Sexes alike. Olive-brown above; dark-brown wings with yellow-spotted bands; dark tail with white outer feathers; dull buffy-white below; two black bands across lower throat and breast diagnostic. Solitary or in pairs on forest-paths and below trees; characteristic sideways movement of tail and rear part of body as it runs on ground; spends considerable time up in branches also, either when disturbed or sometimes resting during day; also runs on horizontal branches, picking insects. **Food:** insects, small snails, worms. **Voice:** *pink...* or *tsif..* call note. **Range:** breeds in Assam; winters in NE India, E and W Ghats, Shri Lanka; to about 2000m. **Habitat:** forests, clearings and cultivation, stream-sides.

**(1875) GREYHEADED YELLOW WAGTAIL** *Motacilla flava* 17cm. Sexes almost alike. Olive back; slaty-grey head, ear-coverts; faint white supercilium; bright yellow below. Duller in winter. The commonest races are the Greyheaded Wagtail described above and the **(1876) Blueheaded Yellow Wagtail** *M f beema* with blue-grey head and clear white supercilium and malar streak. Small flocks on mar-shy ground; moves gently or in short runs; very active, wags tail frequently; often huge congregations, in paddy cultivation and prior to departure to breeding grounds. **Food:** insects. **Voice:** high-pitched *weeezie...* and *tssreep...* notes, uttered mostly on wing. **Range:** winter visitor throughout India, including in Himalayan valleys. **Habitat:** marshy areas, cultivation, mangroves.

*Blueheaded Yellow Wagtail*

*Yellowheaded Wagtail*

**(1881) YELLOWHEADED WAGTAIL** *Motacilla citreola* 17cm. Grey back; diagnostic yellow head, sides of face, complete underbody; white in dark wings. The **(1883) Blackbacked Yellowheaded Wagtail** *M c clacarata* has deep-black back and rump; yellow of head may be paler in female; plumage of races often confusing. Sociable, often with other wagtails; shows marked preference for damp areas, sometimes moves on floating vegetation on pond surfaces; either walks cautiously or makes short dashes. **Food:** insects, small snails. **Voice:** ordinary call-note is a wheezy *tzzeep*, quite similar in tone to Yellow Wagtail. **Range:** winter visitor over most of India; the blackbacked race breeds in Ladakh, Lahaul and Spiti and Kashmir, between 1500–4600m. **Habitat:** marshes, wet cultivation, jheel-edges.

*Grey Wagtail*

**(1884) GREY WAGTAIL** *Motacilla cinerea* 17cm. **Br Male:** grey above; white supercilium; brownish wings, with yellow-white band; yellow-green at base of tail (rump); blackish tail with white outer-feathers; black throat and white malar stripe; yellow below. **Wr Male and Female:** whitish-throat (sometimes mottled black in breeding female); paler-yellow below. Mostly solitary or in pairs; typical wagtail, feeding on ground, incessantly wagging tail; settles on house rooves and overhead wires. **Food:** insects, small molluscs. **Voice:** sharp *tzitsi..* calls, uttered on the wing; pleasant song and display flight of breeding male. **Range:** breeds in Himalaya, from N Baluchistan east to Nepal, 1200–4300m; winters from foothills south throughout India. **Habitat:** rocky mountain streams in summer; open areas, forest clearings, waterside in winter.

*Masked Wagtail*

**(1885) WHITE** or **PIED WAGTAIL** *Motacilla alba* 18cm. Ashy back, rump; white forehead, ear-coverts, large wing-patch and outer-tail feathers; black hind-crown, nape, continuous with throat and upper-breast; white below. The grey or black back and rump, white or black ear-coverts and absence of black eye-streak identify the various races. The **(1886) Masked Wagtail** *M a personata* has black ear-coverts. Usually in pairs or small bands, often two races mixing freely; associates also with other species; prefers damp areas, even entering shallow water; runs on ground, wagging tail constantly. **Food:** insects. **Voice:** sharp *cheet-sik* or *chizzit..*, uttered on the wing. **Range:** winter visitor over most of India, becoming uncommon towards extreme south; *personata* breeds sporadically in parts of NW and W Himalaya. **Habitat:** open damp areas, riverbanks, cultivation, roadside ditches, canals.

**(1891) LARGE PIED WAGTAIL** *Motacilla maderaspatensis* 21cm. Black above; prominent white supercilium, large wing-band and outer tail feathers; black throat, breast; white below. Female is usually browner where male is black. The blackbacked races of White Wagtail *M alba* have conspicuous white forehead. Mostly in pairs, though small parties may feed together in winter; a bird of flowing waters, being especially fond of rock-strewn rivers, though it may be seen on ponds or tanks; feeds at edge of water, wagging tail frequently; also rides on the ferry-boats plying on rivers. **Food:** insects. **Voice:** sharp *tzizit* or *cheezit..* call; pleasant whistling song of breeding male. **Range:** most of India south of Himalayan foothills to about 1200m; only resident wagtail in the Indian plains, breeding up to 2000m in peninsula mountains. **Habitat:** rocky streams, rivers, ponds, tanks; sometimes may enter wet cultivation.

*Large Pied Wagtail*

**(1892) INDIAN THICKBILLED FLOWERPECKER** *Dicaeum agile* 9cm. Sexes alike. Olive-grey above, greener on rump; white-tipped tail; dull whitish-grey below, streaked brown, more on breast; orange-red eyes and thick, blue-grey beak seen at close range. Solitary or in pairs in canopy foliage; arboreal, restless; flicks tail often as it hunts under leaves or along branches; frequents parasitic clumps of *Loranthus* and *Viscum*. **Food:** figs, berries of *Ficus, Lantana, Loranthus* and *Viscum*; also feeds on insects, spiders and nectar. **Voice:** loud, sharp *chik..chik*. **Range:** India south of and including the Himalayan foothills; absent over arid parts of NW India and from large tracts of Tamil Nadu. **Habitat:** forests, orchards, gardens.

*Tickell's Flowerpecker*

**(1899) TICKELL'S FLOWERPECKER** *Dicaeum erythrorhynchos* 8cm. Sexes alike. Olive-brown above; unmarked grey-white below; pinkish-flesh or yellow-brown beak seen only at close range or in good light. The **(1901) Plaincoloured Flowerpecker** *D concolor* has a dark beak and a pale supercilium. Solitary or two to three birds in canopy; frequents parasitic *Loranthus* and *Viscum*; flits from clump to clump; strictly arboreal, restless; territorial even when feeding. **Food:** causing much damage to orchards, especially mango and guava; chiefly berries, spiders and small insects. **Voice:** sharp, loud *chik..chik*; **Range:** from Kangra east along foothills to NE India; peninsular India south of a line from Baroda to S Bihar. **Habitat:** light forests, groves.

**(1905) FIREBREASTED FLOWERPECKER** *Dicaeum ignipectus* 7cm. **Male:** metallic blue-green-black above; buffy below, with scarlet breast-patch and black stripe down centre of lower breast and belly. **Female:** olive-green above, yellowish on rump; bright buff below; flanks and sides tinged olive. Mostly solitary; arboreal and active; flits about in foliage canopy, attending to *Loranthus* clumps; may be encountered in the restless mixed-hunting bands of small birds in Himalayan forests. **Food:** berries, nectar, spiders, small insects. **Voice:** sharp, metallic *chip..chip* note; high-pitched, clicking song. **Range:** the Himalaya, Kashmir to extreme east; breeds 1400–3000m; winters as low as 300m. **Habitat:** forests, orchards.

**(1906) RUBYCHEEK** *Anthreptes singalensis* 10cm. **Male:** metallic green above; deep coppery-red ear-coverts; rufous-buff throat, breast; pale yellow below. **Female:** olive-green above not metallic; paler underbody; usually some yellow on wings. Young birds similar to female, but very pale rufous (sometimes absent) on throat. Pairs or small loose bands; sometimes associates with other birds; restless bird; hunts amongst leaves and branches or attends to flowers; calls often in short jumping flights. **Food:** insects, flower-nectar. **Voice:** fairly loud chirping note. **Range:** foothills country to about 700–900m, occasionally ascending to over 1000m; E Himalaya (Nepal eastwards) and NE regions. **Habitat:** evergreen forests, bushes.

**(1907) INDIAN PURPLERUMPED SUNBIRD** *Nectarina zeylonica* 10cm. **Male:** deep chestnut-crimson back; metallic green crown, shoulder-patch; metallic-purple rump, throat; maroon collar below throat; yellow below. **Female:** ashy-brown above, with rufous in wings; whitish throat; yellow below. Usually pairs; very active, flits from flower to flower; occasionally descends into flowering garden bushes. **Food:** flower-nectar, spiders, small insects. **Voice:** *tsiswee...tsiswee..* calls; sharp, twittering song of breeding male, much lower in tone and volume than that of Purple Sunbird. **Range:** peninsular India south of a line from around Bombay, C Madhya Pradesh, S Bihar and Bengal. **Habitat:** open forests, gardens, orchards; common in towns.

*Purplerumped Sunbird*

**(1909) SMALL SUNBIRD** *Nectarina minima* 8cm. **Male:** overall appearance like Purplerumped; deep maroon back; no metallic-green shoulder patch; metallic purple throat with very broad crimson-maroon collar across lower throat and breast diagnostic; yellow belly. **Female:** olivish above; crimson on rump; pale yellow below. Solitary or pairs; typical sunbird, very active acrobat; flits and hovers in front of flowers; also seen around *Loranthus* clumps. **Food:** flower-nectar, insects, spiders. **Voice:** ordinary call-note rather similar to that of Purplerumped; short, squeaky song of breeding male. **Range:** restricted to W Ghats from S Gujarat to Kerala; also the Nilgiris, Palnis and associated hill ranges; 300–2000m. **Habitat:** evergreen forests, tea and coffee plantations, hill-station gardens.

*Small Sunbird*

**(1911) LOTEN'S SUNBIRD** *Nectarina lotenia* 13cm. **Male:** metallic purplish-black above; dull-black wings, tail; iridescent green and purple throat and purple breast; crimson-maroon breast band and yellow feather-tufts on breast-sides (armpits) diagnostic. **Female:** olive above; white tips to dark tail; pale yellow below; long, curved beak distinctive. Solitary or in pairs, spending much time in upper branches; *Loranthus* flowers are a favourite; this and other sunbirds are important pollinating agents of many flowering trees. **Food:** nectar, small insects, spiders. **Voice:** fairly loud and sharp *tchit..tchit..* call; quickish song of *chewit..chewit...* notes, somewhat tailor-bird-like in quality. **Range:** from around Bombay south along the coast and W Ghats to about 1400m; E coast and E Ghats north to Krishna river; also SC Karnataka, N Tamil Nadu. **Habitat:** forests, gardens.

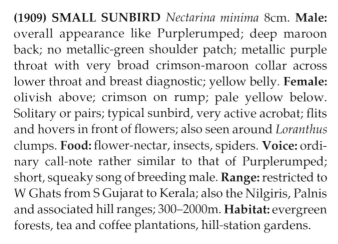

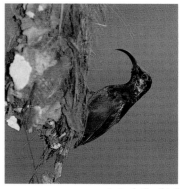

*Loten's Sunbird*

*Purple Sunbird*

**(1917) PURPLE SUNBIRD** *Nectarina asiatica* 10cm. **Br Male:** metallic purple-blue above, and on throat, breast; dark purplish-black belly; narrow chestnut-maroon band between breast and belly; yellow and scarlet pectoral tufts, normally hidden under wings. **Female:** olive-brown above; pale yellow below (*zeylonica* female has whitish throat). **Non-br Male:** much like female but with a broad purple-black stripe down centre of throat to belly. Solitary or in pairs; an important pollinating agent, almost always seen around flowering trees and bushes; displays amazing agility and acrobatic prowess when feeding; sometimes hunts flycatcher style. **Food:** nectar, small insects, spiders. **Voice:** more noisy than other sunbirds; loud *chweet..* notes. **Range:** all India, south from Himalayan foothills to about 1500m. **Habitat:** open forests, gardens, groves.

**(1927) INDIAN YELLOWBACKED SUNBIRD** *Aethopyga siparaja* 15cm. **Male:** has longer tail; metallic green crown, tail; deep crimson back, neck-sides; yellow rump not commonly seen; bright scarlet chin to breast striking; olive-yellow belly. **Female:** olive plumage, yellower below. In the W Ghats race *vigorsii*, the male's breast is streaked yellow. Solitary or in pairs; active gymnast, hanging upside-down and sideways as it probes flowers; also hovers; moves a lot in forest, between tall bushes and canopy. **Food:** nectar, small insects, spiders. **Voice:** sharp, clicking call-notes; pleasant chirping song of breeding male (June–August). **Range:** disjunct: Himalayan foothills from Kangra east; also parts of S Bihar, NE Madhya Pradesh, Bengal and Orissa; W Ghats between Narmada river and N Kanara, and possibly further south; also NE states and Nicobar Islands. **Habitat:** forests.

**(1931) LITTLE SPIDERHUNTER** *Arachnothera longirostris* 14cm. Sexes alike. Olive-green above; dark tail, tipped white; grey-white throat, merging into yellow-white below; orangish pectoral tufts. Very long, curved beak diagnostic. The much larger **(1932) Streaked Spiderhunter** *A magna* (17cm) is olive-yellow, profusely streaked. Usually solitary; sometimes two or three birds in vicinity; active, moving considerably between bush and canopy; wild banana blossoms are a favourite, the bird clinging upside-down on the bracts; long, curved beak specially adapted to nectar-diet. **Food:** nectar; also insects and spiders. **Voice:** high-pitched *chee..chee* call; loud *which..which..* song, sounding somewhat like tailorbird song. **Range:** disjunct: (1) W Ghats south of N Kanara; (2) Small zone in E Ghats (Vishakapatanam); (3) Foothills from SE Nepal eastwards, E Himalaya, much of NE states. **Habitat:** forests, secondary growth, nullahs, sholas.

*Little Spiderhunter*

*Streaked Spiderhunter*

**(1933) INDIAN WHITE-EYE** *Zosterops palpebrosa* 10cm. Sexes alike. Olive-yellow above; short blackish stripe through eyes; white eye-ring distinctive; bright yellow throat, undertail; whitish breast, belly. Small parties, occasionally up to forty birds, either by themselves or in association with other small birds; keeps to foliage and bushes; actively moves amongst leafy branches, clinging sideways and upside-down; checks through leaves and sprigs for insects and also spends considerable time at flowers; calls often, both when in branches and when flying in small bands from tree to tree. **Food:** insects, flower-nectar, berries. **Voice:** soft, plaintive *tsee..* and *tseer..* notes; short jingling song. **Range:** all India, from Himalayan foothills till about 2000m; absent in arid parts of W Rajasthan. **Habitat:** forests, gardens, groves, secondary growth.

*White-Eye*

**(1938) INDIAN HOUSE SPARROW** *Passer domesticus*
15cm. **Male:** grey crown, rump; chestnut sides of neck, nape;
black streaks on chestnut-rufous back; black chin, centre of
throat, breast; white ear-coverts. The **(1940) Spanish Sparrow** *P hispaniolensis* male has chestnut crown and black
streaks on flanks. **Female:** dull grey-brown above, streaked
darker; dull whitish-brown below. Small parties to large
gatherings; mostly commensal on man, feeding and nesting
in and around habitation, including most crowded localities;
also feeds in cultivation; hundreds roost together. **Food:**
seeds; also insects, and often omnivorous. **Voice:** noisy; a
medley of chirping notes; richer notes of breeding male;
double and triple-brooded. **Range:** all India, to about 4000m
in the Himalaya. **Habitat:** habitation, cultivation.

*Cinnamon Tree Sparrow*

**(1946) CINNAMON TREE SPARROW** *Passer rutilans*
15cm. **Male:** rufous-chestnut above, streaked black on
back; whitish wing-bars; black chin, centre of throat, bordered with dull yellow. **Female:** brown above, streaked
darker; pale supercilium, wings-bars; dull ashy-yellow
below. The **(1942) Tree Sparrow** *P montanus* male has black
patch on white ear-coverts and lacks yellow on throat
sides. Gregarious mountain bird; mostly feeds on ground,
picking seeds; may associate with other finches; often
perches on dry branches, overhead wires. **Food:** seeds,
insects. **Voice:** chirping notes; *swee..* Indian Robin-like call.
**Range:** the Himalaya; NE; breeds 1200–2600m, higher to
about 4000m in NE; descends in winter. **Habitat:** cultivation, edges of forest, mountain habitations.

*Yellowthroated Sparrow*

**(1949) INDIAN YELLOWTHROATED SPARROW**
*Petronia xanthocollis* 14cm. **Male:** dull brownish-grey
above; chestnut shoulder-patch and white wing-bars diagnostic; lemon-yellow throat patch seen in good light.
**Female:** rufous shoulder-patch and paler, often smaller,
yellow throat-patch. Gregarious during monsoon and
winter; moves considerably in some areas; keeps to tall,
leafy trees in forest; may escape notice were it not for its
characteristic, frequent chirping; feeds on ground and also
on flowering trees. **Food:** seeds, nectar, insects. **Voice:**
pleasant chirping notes, a good aid in spotting and identification. **Range:** all India south of Himalayan foothills to about
1400m. **Habitat:** forests, clearings, orchards, light habitation.

**(1957) INDIAN BAYA** *Ploceus philippinus* 15cm. **Br Male:** bright yellow crown; dark brown above, streaked yellow; dark-brown ear-coverts, throat; yellow breast. **Female:** buffy-yellow above, streaked darker; pale supercilium, throat, turning buffy-yellow on breast, streaked on sides. **Non br Male:** bolder streaking than female; male of eastern race *burmanicus* has yellow restricted to crown. Gregarious; one of the most familiar and common birds of India, best known for its nest; keeps to cultivated areas, interspersed with trees; feeds on ground and in standing crop. **Food:** grain, seeds, insects, nectar. **Voice:** chirping and high-pitched wheezy notes of breeding male; very noisy at nest-colony (monsoons). **Range:** most of India from about 1000m in outer Himalaya; evidently absent in Kashmir. **Habitat:** open country, tree and palm-dotted cultivation.

*Indian Baya*

**(1962) INDIAN STREAKED WEAVER-BIRD** *Ploceus manyar* 15cm. **Br Male:** yellow crown; blackish head-sides; fulvous streaks on dark brown back; heavily streaked lower throat, breast. **Female and Non br Male:** streaked above; yellow stripe over eye continues to behind ear-coverts; very pale below, boldly streaked on throat, breast. The **(1961) Blackthroated Weaver** *P benghalensis* male has dark breast-band. Gregarious; prefers tall grass, reed beds in well-watered areas; active, as a rule not flying into trees; often nests close to other weavers. **Food:** seeds, grain, insects. **Voice:** high-pitched chirping, wheezy notes and chatter, much like Baya's. **Range:** most of India south of the Himalaya; absent in parts of Rajasthan and NW regions; the eastern race *peguensis* is darker, much more rufous above. **Habitat:** reed beds, tall grass in well-watered areas, marshes.

*Streaked Weaver-Bird*

**(1964) RED MUNIA** or **AVADAVAT** *Estrilda amandava* 10cm. **Br Male:** crimson and brown, spotted white on wings, flanks; white-tipped tail. **Female:** brown above, spotted on wings; crimson rump; dull white throat; buffy-grey breast, yellow-brown below. **Non br Male:** like female, but greyer throat, upper breast distinctive. Small flocks, often with other munias; partial to tall grass and scrub, preferably around well-watered areas; active and vibrant birds, rather confiding also; large numbers captured for bird markets. **Food:** grass seeds; also insects when breeding. **Voice:** shrill and high-pitched notes, uttered in flight also. **Range:** all India, south of Himalayan foothills. **Habitat:** tall grass, reeds, sugarcane, scrub, gardens.

*Red Munia*

*Green Munia*

**(1965) GREEN MUNIA** *Estrilda formosa* 10cm. **Male:** olive-green above, with blackish tail; yellow below, paler on throat; prominent dark and white barrings on flanks diagnostic. **Female:** more brown above, paler below, with fewer barrings on flanks. Small flocks, sometimes gathering into several dozen birds; does not usually associate with other munias; like others of family, feeds on ground, picking up grass seeds; sometimes raids standing crops; when disturbed, the flock flies off into grass or bush, occasionally uttering faint *scheep..* calls. **Food:** mostly small seeds. **Voice:** faint *swee...swee...* notes; when disturbed, a variation on this note. **Range:** broad belt across C India, from around Mt Abu to C Orissa and south to N Andhra Pradesh and around Mahabaleshwar; evidently absent in the coastal regions. **Habitat:** sugarcane, scrub and grass.

*Whitethroated Munia*

**(1966) WHITETHROATED MUNIA** *Lonchura malabarica* 10cm. Sexes alike. Dull-brown above, with white rump; very dark, almost black, wings, pointed tail; pale buffy-white below, with some brown on flanks; thick, grey-blue or slaty beak striking. Gregarious, mostly keeps to scrub in open country; feeds on ground and on standing crop, especially millet; overall a rather 'dull' bird, both in colour and demeanour. **Food:** small seeds, millet. **Voice:** faint *tee..tee..* notes; sometimes also a whistling note. **Range:** all India; to about 1500m in Himalaya, chiefly the outer ranges. **Habitat:** prefers dry areas; cultivation, scrub and grass; sometimes light, open forests.

**(1968) WHITEBACKED MUNIA** *Lonchura striata* 10cm. Sexes alike. Blackish-brown above, with conspicuous white rump; at close range, pale (shaft) streaks visible on back; dark wings and pointed tail; dark-brown throat; whitish-cream below. The race *acuticauda* of Himalayan foothills and NE regions has a grey belly with fine streaks. Small to medium-sized flocks, often seen along with other munias; quite active, feeds on ground and also on standing crops and grasses; sometimes large, mixed gatherings can cause damage to standing crops. **Food:** grass seeds, crops; also feeds on insects, especially when breeding (chiefly during rains). **Range:** peninsular India, south of line from S Gujarat, across C Madhya Pradesh to S Bihar and Orissa. **Habitat:** scrub, cultivation, grass; forests and orchards.

**(1974) INDIAN SPOTTED MUNIA** *Lonchura punctulata*
10cm. Sexes alike. Choco-brown above; olivish-yellow,
pointed tail; white bars on rump; chestnut sides of face,
chin, throat; white below, thickly speckled with very
dark brown on breast, flanks and part of belly (speckles
may be absent during winter and much of summer).
Sociable, moving in flocks of six to several dozen birds,
often with other munias, weaver birds; feeds on ground
and low bush, but rests in trees. **Food:** seeds, small
berries; also insects. **Voice:** common call a double-noted
*ki.tee....ki.tee.* **Range:** most of India, to about 1500m in parts
of the Himalaya; absent in much of Punjab, NW regions
and W Rajasthan. **Habitat:** open scrub, cultivation, especially where interspersed with trees; also gardens.

*Spotted Munia*

**(1978) SOUTHERN BLACKHEADED MUNIA** *Lonchura*
*malacca* 10cm. Sexes alike. Black head, throat, breast, belly-
centre and thighs; rufous-chestnut back, deeper chestnut
on rump; white upper belly, sides of underbody. The races
*rubroniger* and *atricapilla* of N and NE India have white of
lower parts replaced by chestnut. Gregarious, except when
breeding, as in other munias; prefers reed beds and cultivation, especially where flooded; during breeding season
(rains), often seen along with Streaked Weaver birds; feeds
on ground. **Food:** grass seeds, paddy; occasionally insects.
**Voice:** faint, *pee...pee...* calls. **Range:** foothills and terai from
SE Punjab eastwards; most of NE, N Orissa; peninsular
India south of line from Bombay to S Madhya Pradesh.
**Habitat:** reed beds, paddy, grass and scrub.

*Blackheaded Munia*

**(1982) BLACK-AND-YELLOW GROSBEAK** *Mycerobas*
*icterioides* 22cm. **Male:** black head, throat, wings, tail and
thighs; yellow collar, back, underbody below breast; thick,
finchbill. *Female:* Grey above; buffy rump, belly. The very
similar male **(1983) Allied Grosbeak** *M affinis* is brighter
yellow (often with orangish wash), with yellow thighs.
Small parties in tall coniferous forest; also feeds on ground
and bushes, but spends much time in higher branches,
where difficult to see; rather noisy. **Food:** conifer seeds,
shoots; also berries and insects. **Voice:** loud two- or three-
noted whistle is familiar birdcall of W Himalaya; loud
*chuck...chuck* note when feeding; rich song of male. **Range:** the
Himalaya, extreme west to around C Nepal; 1500–3500m;
may winter lower. *M affinis* occurs throughout the Himalaya,
from west to extreme east. **Habitat:** mountain forests.

*Black-and-Yellow Grosbeak*

**(1985) WHITEWINGED GROSBEAK** *Mycerobas carnipes* 22cm. **Male:** black above, on throat and breast; olive-yellow rump, belly and wing-spots; larger, white wing-patch. **Female:** brownish-grey where male is black; streaks on ear-coverts. The **(1986) Spottedwinged Grosbeak** M *melanozanthos* male is uniformly black above, with more white in wings; less black below, more bright yellow; female is boldly streaked black and yellow. Small flocks, often with other grosbeaks; active and noisy; mostly feeds in higher branches. **Food:** chiefly seeds of juniper; also other seeds, fruit; insects, especially when breeding. **Voice:** loud three- or four-noted calls, usually from tree-top; sometimes a harsh note. **Range:** the Himalaya, extreme west to east; 1500–4000m, but mostly above 2500m, even in winter. *M melanozanthos* descends much lower in winter. **Habitat:** dwarf juniper above timberline; high forest; may be seen in bamboo and pine during winter.

**(1989) GREYHEADED GOLDFINCH** *Carduelis carduelis* 14cm. Sexes alike. Crimson forehead; greyish-brown above, with large, white rump-patch and black and white; black and yellow wings striking, at rest and in flight. Young birds have streaked upperparts. Sociable; flock-size ranges from four to several dozen together, sometimes along with other finches; forages on ground; also attends to flower-heads; undulating, somewhat dancing flight. **Food:** seeds of flowers, especially thistle and sunflowers. **Voice:** ordinary call-note a somewhat liquid *witwit..witwit..*; pleasant, twittering song; also a *chhrrik* call. **Range:** the Himalaya, extreme west to around C Nepal; breeds mostly 2000–4000m, ascending somewhat more; descends into foothills in winter. **Habitat:** open coniferous forests, orchards, cultivation, scrub.

*Himalayan Greenfinch*

**(1990) HIMALAYAN GREENFINCH** *Carduelis spinoides* 14cm. **Male:** blackish-brown crown, ear-coverts, malar stripe; yellow forehead, supercilium, sides of neck; greenish-brown back, streaked dark; wings have yellow, black-brown and some white; yellow rump, sides of tail; yellow below. **Female:** duller, with less yellow in wings. The male **(1993) Tibetan Siskin** *C tibetana* (12cm) of NE

lacks dark-brown above. Usually small flocks; keeps to low growth, feeding on flower-heads; moves considerably. **Food:** flower and other seeds; also insects. **Voice:** twittering *dwit.it.it..* notes; also a long-drawn *weeeee.chu* call, rather Iora-like; liquid song. **Range:** the Himalaya; foothills to about 4400m; breeds mostly about 1800–3000m. **Habitat:** forest slopes, meadows, gardens, scrub.

**(1998) GOLDFRONTED FINCH** *Serinus pusillus* 12cm. Sexes alike. Scarlet-orange forehead; blackish-grey crown; buffy back, streaked dark; yellow-orange rump, shoulder; yellow wing-edges and whitish wing-bars; sooty-brown below, with grey and buff; dull yellow-buff belly and flanks, streaked brown. Gregarious; quite active and on the move; feeds on flower-heads and on ground; drinks and bathes often; spend considerable time in bushes and low trees. **Food:** flower and grass seeds; small berries. **Voice:** pleasant twittering *chrr..chrr;* a faint *tree...tree...* call-note. **Range:** W Himalaya, extreme west to Garhwal; 750–4500m; breeds mostly 2400–4000m. **Habitat:** rocky, bush-covered mountainsides.

*Goldfronted Finch*

**(1999) HODGSON'S** or **PLAINCOLOURED MOUNTAIN FINCH** *Leucosticte nemoricola* 15cm. Sexes alike. Grey-brown above, streaked dark-brown; greyer on rump; pale buffy bar and markings in dark-brown wings; dull grey-brown below, streaked browner on breast-sides and flanks. The **(2003) Brandt's Mountain Finch** *L brandti* (18cm) is darker above, with rosy-pink rump and white in outer-tail. The finches with plenty of white in wings, and generally found in the high Tibetan country of the Himalaya are snow finches. Gregarious; good-sized flocks on ground, amidst stones; sometimes associates with other finches, buntings; calls often when feeding. **Food:** grass and other seeds; small insects. **Voice:** twittering and chattering notes, rather sparrowlike in tone; call frequently. **Range:** high Himalaya, breeds about 3200–4800m (above timber-line); descends in winter, occasionally to as low as 1000m. **Habitat:** open meadows, dwarf scrub, cultivation.

*Common Rosefinch*

**(2013) COMMON ROSEFINCH** or **SCARLET GROS-BEAK** *Carpodacus erythrinus* 15cm. **Male:** crimson above, tinged brown; dark eye-stripe; crimson rump, underbody, fading into dull rose-white belly. **Female:** buff-brown above, streaked dark; two pale wing-bars; dull-buff below, streaked, except on belly. The male **(2016) Blanford's Rosefinch** *C rubescens* lacks dark eye-stripe and has two crimson wing-bars. Small flocks; feeds in bush, on crops and ground; associates with other birds. **Food:** crop seeds, fruit, buds, nectar. **Voice:** rather quiet in winter; pleasant song of up to eight notes; may sing before departure from wintering grounds; also a double-noted, questioning, *twee..ee* call. **Range:** breeds in the Himalaya, 2700–4000m; winters over most of India. **Habitat:** cultivation, open forests, gardens, bushes.

**(2015) NEPAL DARK ROSEFINCH** *Carpodacus nipalensis* 15cm. **Male:** crimson-rose forehead; rose-red supercilium and dark, broad eye-stripe; deep crimson-brown above; pinkish throat and dark crimson-maroon breast-band. **Female:** buff-brown above; two buffy wing-bars; unstreaked below. Absence of crimson on rump identifies male from Common and Blanford's; female Blanford's is unstreaked below, but grey belly and white undertail distinctive. Small parties, sometimes with others; feeds on ground and bush. **Food:** seeds, berries. **Voice:** plaintive, two-note whistle. **Range:** the Himalaya, east of W Nepal; breeds about 3000–4400m; descends in winter. **Habitat:** rhododendron, fir forests; bushy, rocky slopes; clearings.

**(2017) PINKBROWED ROSEFINCH** *Carpodacus rhodochrous* 15cm. **Male:** rosy-pink forehead, broad supercilium; crimson-brown, unstreaked crown, eye-stripe; streaked back and pinkish rump, underbody. **Female:** streaked throughout; pale yellowish supercilium. The **(2018) Redmantled Rosefinch** *C rhodochlamys* (18cm) is similar, but larger. The **(2023) Beautiful Rosefinch** *C pulcherrimus* has streaked crown. Usually small flocks, sometimes with others; feeds on ground, on paths and clearings; perches on trees and in bush; undergoes considerable altitudinal movement. **Food:** seeds, berries. **Voice:** single-noted, *sweet..* call; song of breeding male. **Range:** the Himalaya, less common in E Himalaya; breeds about

2800–4000m; winters low, sometimes to 600m. **Habitat:** open forests, dwarf junipers, upland habitation.

**(2021) WHITEBROWED ROSEFINCH** *Carpodacus thura* 17cm. **Male:** brown above, streaked blackish; pink and white forehead, supercilium; dark eye-stripe; rose-pink rump and double wing-bar. **Female:** streaked brown; broad, whitish supercilium and single wing-bar; yellow rump; buffy below, streaked. The white in supercilium easily identifies this species. Small flocks, either by themselves or with other finches; mostly feeds on ground, but settles on bushes and small trees. **Food:** seeds, berries. **Voice:** calls often when feeding on ground, a fairly loud *pupuepipi...* call. **Range:** the Himalaya, breeds 3000–4000m; winters to about 1800m. **Habitat:** tree-line forests, fir, juniper, rhododendron; open mountainsides and bushes in winter.

**(2028) EASTERN GREAT ROSEFINCH** *Carpodacus rubicilloides* 19cm. **Male:** crimson-red head, sides, under-body, spotted white; grey-brown back, washed pink and streaked brown; pinkish rump. **Female:** grey-brown, streaked; pale-buff below, streaked dark. The **(2027) Great Rosefinch** *C rubicilla* is paler, with fewer streaks on back. The **(2031) Redbreasted Rosefinch** *C puniceus* (20cm) is more scarlet. Small parties, occasionally several dozens together; may associate with others; feeds on ground and in bushes; a bird of higher regions, even in winter. **Food:** seeds, berries. **Voice:** loud, single-note call. **Range:** high Himalaya, Ladakh to Bhutan; breeds above 3500m, till about 4800m; usually does not descend below 2000m in winter. **Habitat:** high-altitude barren areas, scrub.

*Great Rosefinch*

**(2032) CROSSBILL** *Loxia curvirostra* 15cm. **Male:** dull-red above, lightly marked brown; dark stripe through eyes; blackish wings, short, forked tail; unmarked dull-red below. **Female:** olivish above, lightly marked brown; yellower on rump; dark brown wings, tail; olive-yellow below. The crossed mandibles are seen at close range. Small, active parties; keep to conifer-tops; unique beak helps feed on conifer seeds; clings sideways and upside-down to extract seeds from cones; also descends on ground. **Food:** chiefly conifer seeds. **Voice:** fairly loud *chip..chip..chip..* call, both when feeding and during flight; creaky, trilling song. **Range:** the Himalaya, east of Himachal; 2700–4000m; may descend in winter. **Habitat:** coniferous forests.

**(2035) GOLDHEADED BLACK FINCH** *Pyrrhoplectes epauletta* 15cm. **Male:** orange-yellow hindcrown, nape; blackish plumage; white on tertiaries seen as conspicuous 'V' on wing/lower-back. **Female:** greenish crown, grey nape; rufous-brown above; grey-black wing-tips, tail; dull-brown below; white wing-lining as in male. Small parties of eight to ten birds; associates with other finches; feeds mostly on ground and low bushes. **Food:** seeds, berries. **Voice:** high-pitched *pew..pew..* call. **Range:** the Himalaya; Himachal eastwards; breeds about 2800–4000m; descends in winter to 1400m, sometimes lower. **Habitat:** rhododendron and ringal bamboo in summer; dense bushes, scrub in winter.

**(2039) REDHEADED BULLFINCH** *Pyrrhula erythrocephala* 17cm. **Male:** black around base of beak, eyes; brick-red crown; grey back; white rump; glossy purple-black wings, forked tail; black chin; rust-red below; ashy-white belly. **Female:** like male, but olive-yellow on crown; grey brown back, underbody. The male **(2040) Orange Bullfinch** *P aurantiaca* (14cm) of W Himalaya has orange-yellow back and underbody; female is yellow-brown. Small parties, occasionally with other birds; feed in low bushes, sometimes on ground; a bird of cover, rather quiet and secretive. **Food:** seeds, buds, berries; also flower-nectar. **Voice:** single or double-noted *pheu..pheu..* call. **Range:** the Himalaya, Kashmir to extreme east; breeds 2400–4000m; descends in winter to about 1200m. **Habitat:** forests, bushes.

**(2043) BLACKHEADED BUNTING** *Emberiza melanocephala* 18cm. **Male:** black head; thin yellow collar and rufous-chestnut back; unmarked yellow below, with some rufous on breast-sides; wing-bars. **Female:** dull fulvous-brown above, streaked; yellowish rump; pale buff-yellow below; very similar to female Redheaded Bunting. Gregarious; winter visitor, often great numbers with other buntings, notably the Redheaded; feeds on crops and ground; does considerable damage to standing crop; bold, not easily driven away from croplands; in most areas, the yellow males are in greater numbers. **Food:** seeds, grain. **Voice:** musical *tzeett...* call-note; a faint *chip...* occasionally: **Range:** common in winter (mid-September to April) over wide part in W and C India; Gujarat, Rajasthan, W and C Madhya Pradesh, Maharashtra, parts of Karnataka. **Habitat:** open cultivation.

**(2044) REDHEADED BUNTING** *Emberiza bruniceps* 17cm. **Male:** rufous-chestnut crown, throat, breast; olive-yellow back, streaked blackish; unmarked yellow rump; whitish wing-bars; yellow neck-sides, underbody below breast. **Female:** pale-brown above, streaked; yellowish rump. The male **(2045) Chestnut Bunting** *E rutila* (14cm) is completely chestnut above and on throat. Highly gregarious winter visitor; huge numbers, frequently along with Blackheaded; cause considerable damage to crops. **Food:** seeds, grain. **Voice:** high-pitched *tzeett..* call. **Range:** common winter visitor over most of country south of the Himalaya; absent in extreme south and along eastern coastal regions. **Habitat:** open cultivated areas.

**(2046) YELLOWBREASTED BUNTING** *Emberiza aureola* 15cm. **Br Male:** blackish forehead, sides of face, chin, throat; deep chestnut above; yellow throat, neck-sides; chestnut upper-breast-band; yellow below, streaked flanks. Black mask absent in winter, when dark ear-coverts and yellow supercilium distinctive. **Female:** brown above, streaked; pale crown stripe, supercilium, edged by dark stripes; pale-chestnut rump; yellow below; streaked flanks. Winter visitor; small flocks, up to forty birds; associates with other buntings, finches; mostly feeds on ground. **Food:** seeds, grain; catches insects. **Voice:** a *tzip...tzip...* note; also a soft *trrssit.* **Range:** quite common in winter from Nepal eastwards, in plains and terai. **Habitat:** cultivation, scrub; enters habitation, gardens.

**(2048) WHITECAPPED BUNTING** *Emberiza stewarti* 15cm. **Male:** grey-white top of head; black eye-stripe, whitish cheeks, black chin, upper-throat distinctive; chestnut back, rump; white outer-tail; white breast with chestnut gorget below; dull-fulvous below, chestnut flanks. **Female:** lacks black and white head pattern of male; brown above, streaked; rufous-chestnut rump; fulvous-buff below, with rufous breast. The male **(2057) Striolated Bunting** *E striolata* (14cm), with more or less overlapping range, has grey-white head, completely streaked black. Small flocks, often with other buntings, finches; feeds on ground; rests in bushes, trees. **Food:** chiefly grass seeds. **Voice:** faint but sharp *tsit..* or *chit..* note. **Range:** breeds in W Himalaya, extreme west to Garhwal, 1500–3500m; winters in W Himalayan foothills, and over extensive parts of W and C India, south to Maharashtra. **Habitat:** open, grass-covered, rocky hillsides, scrub.

**(2050) GREYNECKED BUNTING** *Emberiza buchanani*
15cm. **Male:** grey head with white eye-ring; brown back, with
faint rufous wash and dark streaks; white edges of dark
tail; whitish throat, mottled rufous; dark moustachial
stripe, not easily visible; pale rufous-chestnut below.
**Female:** somewhat duller than male; more prominent
moustachial stripe. Winter visitor; small flocks, feeds
mostly on ground, sometimes along with other birds;
quite active. **Food:** grass seeds, sometimes grain. **Voice:** a
faint single note. **Range:** winter visitor; quite common
over W and C India—Gujarat, S and W Rajasthan, SW
Uttar Pradesh, south through W and C Madhya Pradesh,
Maharashtra and parts of Karnataka. **Habitat:** open rocky
grassy country, scrub.

*Rock Bunting*

**(2052) ROCK BUNTING** *Emberiza cia* 15cm. **Male:** blue-
grey head with black coronal stripe, eye-stripe, malar
stripe, the latter curled and meeting eye-stripe diagnostic; whitish supercilium, cheeks; pale chestnut-brown
back, streaked dark; unmarked rump; white outersides
of dark tail distinctive; blue-grey throat, breast; rufous-
chestnut below. **Female:** slightly duller. The male **(2055)
Greyheaded Bunting** *E fucata* has black-streaked grey
head, white throat, breast and chestnut ear-coverts.
Solitary or in small parties; active and restless; mostly
feeds on ground, meadows, paths and roads; flicks tail
often; regularly settles on bushes and trees. **Food:** seeds,
small insects. **Voice:** squeaky *tsip...tsip..* note; calls often;
common bird-call of W Himalaya; has squeaky song of
several notes. **Range:** the Himalaya, west to east; 1500–
4200m; commoner in W Himalaya; winters in foothills
and plains of N India, coming as far south as Delhi.
**Habitat:** grassy, rocky hillsides in open forests; cultivation, scrub.

**(2060) CRESTED BUNTING** *Melophus lathami* 15cm.
**Male:** striking glossy black plumage, with long, pointed
crest and chestnut wings, tail. **Female:** crested; olive-
brown above, streaked darker; rufous in wings distinctive; buffy-yellow below, streaked dark on breast;

darkish moustachial stripe. Small flocks, often spread wide over an area; feeds on ground, on paths, meadows and on tar roads, especially along mountainsides; perches on ruins, walls, stones and low bushes; on ground, an active and upright bird. **Food:** grass seeds; presumably also insects. **Voice:** faint *chip..* call; pleasant, though somewhat monotonous song of breeding male (May–August). **Range:** resident over wide part of India, from outer Himalaya to about 1800m south to SW Maharashtra and N Andhra; appears to move considerably after the rains. **Habitat:** open, bush and rock-covered mountainsides, open country; sometimes also cultivation.

*Crested Bunting*

# Glossary

| | |
|---|---|
| **adult** | Mature, capable of breeding. Final plumage. |
| **aquatic** | Living on or in water. |
| **arboreal** | Living in trees. |
| **banyan** | A fig tree *(Ficus bengalensis)*. |
| **bund** | Man-made embankment. |
| **cap** | Upper head. |
| **carpal** | The forward pointing area on a closed wing. |
| **casque** | Growth above bill of hornbills. |
| **cere** | Patch of bare skin at base of bill of raptors. |
| **crepuscular** | Active at dusk. |
| **crown** | Upper part of head. |
| **deciduous** | Forests that shed leaves seasonally. |
| **dimorphic** | Having more than one form of plumage. |
| **diurnal** | Active during daytime. |
| **duars** | Forested areas, south of eastern Himalaya. |
| **eclipse** | Changed plumage after breeding season. |
| **endemic** | Indigenous and confined. |
| **evergreen** | Forests that retain their leaves. |
| **family** | Specific group of genera. |
| **fledglings** | Phase in chicks. |
| **fulvous** | Brownish-yellow. |
| **genus** | Group of related species. |
| **ghats** | Hills parallel to the east and west coasts of India. |
| **gorget** | Band across upper chest. |
| **hawking** | Capturing insects in flight. |
| **immature** | Plumage phases prior to adult. |
| **jheel** | Shallow lake or wetland. |
| **juvenile** | Immature bird immediately after leaving nest. |
| **lores** | Area in front of eye. |
| **mandible** | Bill or beak. |
| **malar** | Stripe on side of throat. |
| **mantle** | Back and adjoining areas. |
| **migration** | Seasonal movement. |
| **monsoon** | Rainy season. |
| **moult** | Seasonal shedding of plumage. |

| | |
|---|---|
| **nape** | Back of neck. |
| **nocturnal** | Active at night. |
| **nullah** | Ditch or stream bed. |
| **passerines** | Perching and song birds. |
| **pectoral** | The breast area. |
| **pipal** | A tree of the fig family *(Ficus religiosa)*. |
| **primaries** | Main flight feathers. |
| **raptors** | Birds of prey, excluding owls. |
| **resident** | Non-migratory. |
| **rump** | Lower back and base of tail. |
| **sholas** | Small forests in valleys. |
| **speculum** | Area of colour on wings. |
| **submontane** | Low foothills. |
| **supercilium** | Streak above eye. |
| **terai** | Alluvial stretch of land, south of Himalaya. |
| **terrestrial** | Ground living. |
| **vinaceous** | Red wine coloured. |
| **wattle** | Bare skin, often coloured on part of head. |

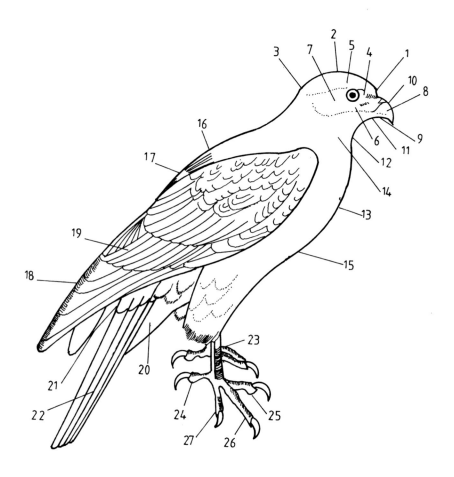

| 1. | Forehead | 10. | Culmen or bill ridge | 19. | Secondaries |
|---|---|---|---|---|---|
| 2. | Crown | 11. | Chin | 20. | Under tail coverts |
| 3. | Nape | 12. | Throat | 21. | Upper tail coverts |
| 4. | Lores | 13. | Breast | 22. | Tail feathers |
| 5. | Supercilium | 14. | Neck | 23. | Tarsus |
| 6. | Cheeks | 15. | Belly | 24. | Hind toe |
| 7. | Bar-coverts | 16. | Back | 25. | Inner toe |
| 8. | Upper mandible | 17. | Wing coverts | 26. | Middle toe |
| 9. | Lower mandible | 18. | Primaries | 27. | Outer toe |

# Bibliography

Ali, Salim. *The Book of Indian Birds*. Bombay: Bombay Natural History Society (BNHS) 1941. Many editions and recently revised and expanded with new plates. Excellent descriptions.

*Birds of Kerala*. Bombay: Oxford University Press (OUP). Excellent coverage of Southwest India. reprint 1986.

*Birds of Kutch*. Bombay: OUP 1945.

*Birds of Sikkim*. Bombay: OUP 1962, reprint 1989.

*Indian Hill Birds*. Bombay: OUP 1949, 1979.

*Bird Study in India: its history and its importance*. New Delhi: ICCR 1979. A printed version of the 1978 Azad Memorial Lecture.

*The Fall of a Sparrow*. Bombay: OUP 1984. Fascinating autobiography of one of the world's greatest ornithologists.

*Field Guide to the Birds of the Eastern Himalayas*. Bombay: OUP 1977. Combines plates and information from *Birds of Sikkim* with new material to give excellent coverage of Bhutan and Arunachal Pradesh.

Ali, Salim & S Dillon Ripley. *The Handbook of the Birds of India and Pakistan*. 10 vols. Bombay: OUP 1968–74. The ultimate and definitive work now available in a single volume (1984) covers all the birds in South Asia with maps, illustrations and plates.

Baker, EC Stuart. *Fauna of British India—Birds*. 8 vols: 1922–30. An interesting early study to which Ali & Ripley refer for detailed plumage descriptions.

*Indian Ducks and Their Allies*. Bombay: BNHS 1908.

*Indian Pigeons and Doves*. Bombay: 1913.

*The Gamebirds of India, Burma and Ceylon*. 3 vols. Bombay: BNHS 1921.

Bates, RSP & EHN Lowther. *Breeding Birds of Kashmir*. New Delhi, OUP 1952, reprint 1991. A useful book with excellent photographs.

Bates, RSP. *Birds in India*. 1931.

Choudhury, Anwaruddin. *Checklist of the Birds of Assam*. Guwahati: Sofia Press. 1990.

Cronin, EW. *The Arun: a natural history of the world's deepest valley*. Boston: Houghton Mifflin. 1979.

Delacour, J. *The Pheasants of the World*. London: 1957, 1977. Detailed descriptions of all Galliforms, many of which are found in eastern India and the Himalaya.

Dewar, Douglas. *Glimpse of Indian Birds*. 1913.

*Himalayan and Kashmir Birds*. London: 1923.

Dharamkumarsinjhi. RS. *The Birds of Saurashtra*. Bombay: 1957. An excellent book specific to parts of Gujarat but relevant to much of western India.

Dick, John Henry. *A Pictorial Guide to the Birds of the Indian Sub-continent*. Bombay: OUP/BNHS 1983. A unique guide giving illustrations for all the bird species. A companion to Ali and Ripley's *Handbook*.

EHA. *The Common Birds of Bombay*. Bombay, Thacker & Co. *c*.1920. A collection of detailed, anecdotal papers first published in the Times of India at the turn of the century.

Ewans, Martin. *Bharatpur—Bird Paradise*. New Delhi: Lustre Press. 1989.

Fleming, RL Snr. & Jnr & J. Bangdel. *Birds of Nepal*. Kathmandu. 1976. A good field guide with over 700 colour illustrations facing the text on each species.

Fleming, Robert L. Jr. *Comments on the endemic Birds of Sri Lanka*: Colombo 1977.

Finn, F. *How To Know the Indian Waders*. Calcutta: 1920. Interesting line drawings of various species with head details.

   *Indian Sporting Birds*. London: 1915. With over 100 colour plates.

   *The Water Fowl of India and Asia*. Calcutta: 1909.

Ganguli, Usha. *A Guide to the birds of the Delhi Area*. New Delhi:1975.

Glenister, AG. *Birds of the Malay Peninsula*. Singapore: OUP 1971, 1985. Includes species in the Andaman and Nicobar islands, Burma and parts of eastern India.

Henry, GM. *A Guide to the Birds of Ceylon*. OUP: 1955, 1971.

Hutson, HPW. *The Birds about Delhi*. 1954.

Hume, Allan O. *The Nests and Eggs of Indian Birds*. 3 vols. 1889-90.

Inskipp, Carol. *A Birdwatchers Guide to Nepal*. UK: Prion. 1988.

   *Nepal's Forest Birds, their status and conservation*. Cambridge: ICPB. 1989.

   *The Birds and Mammals of the Annapurna Conservation Area*. Kathmandu: ACAP. 1989.

Inskipp, Carol & Tim. *A Guide to the Birds of Nepal*. London: Christopher Helm. 1985, 2nd edition, 1992.

Inskipp, Carol and Cocker, PM. *A Himalayan Ornithologist: The Life and Work of Brian Hodgson*. London: OUP 1989.

Jerdon, TC. *The Birds of India*. 3 vols 1862–64. The first comprehensive work.

Kalpavriksh. *What's that bird?* New Delhi. 1991.

King, Ben, EC Dickinson & Martin Woodcock. *The Birds of South-East Asia*. London: Collins 1975. A well-illustrated and comprehensive guide to continental South East Asia with many references to eastern India and the Himalaya.

Lekagul, Boonsong & EW Cronin. *Bird Guide of Thailand*. Bangkok. 1974, revised edition 1990. Good illustrations; covers many species common to eastern India.

Lowther, EHM. *A Bird Photographer in India*. OUP. 1949.

Macdonald, Malcolm. *Birds in My Indian Garden*. London: Cape 1960. A general text illustrated with excellent photographs by Christina Loke.

Osmaston, BB. *Birds of Dehra Dun and Adjacent Hills*. 1935. Reprinted in 1989 by Natraj, Dehra Dun as part of *Wildlife of Dehra Dun*.

Phillips, WWA. *Checklist of the birds of Ceylon*. Colombo. 1977.

    *Birds of Ceylon*. 4 vols. 1949, 1952, 1955 & 1961.

Rahmani, Asad R. *Bustard Sanctuaries of India*. Bombay: BNHS 1988.

Ranasinghe, Douglas. *A Guide to Bird-watching in Sri Lanka*. Colombo, 1977.

'Raoul'. *Small Game Shooting in Bengal*. Calcutta: W Newman & Co 1899. An interesting account of game birds (including Floricans and waders) and their habitat ending with a section on "how to cook the game"!

Ripley, S Dillon. *Search for the Spiny Babbler*. Boston. 1952.

    *A Synopsis of the Birds of India and Pakistan*. Bombay: BNHS. 1961, revised 1982. The basis of the *Handbook*.

    *A Bundle of Feathers*. Delhi: OUP 1978. A festschrift proffered to Salim Ali on his 75th birthday.

Roberts, T. *The Birds of Pakistan*. 2 vols. Karachi: OUP. 1991 & 1992.

Sankhala, Kailash. *Gardens of Eden: The Waterbird Sanctuary at Bharatpur*. New Delhi: Vikas. 1990. A detailed and affectionate account of the sanctuary by one of India's leading conservationists.

Saxena, VS. *Bharatpur Bird Sanctuary*. Jaipur. 1975. An introductory study of the flora and fauna of this important national park.

Smythies, BE. *The Birds of Burma*. London. 1953. Reprint 1988.

Tikader, BK. *Birds of the Andaman & Nicobar Islands*. Calcutta: Z.S.I. 1984.

Vaurie, Charles. *Tibet and its Birds*. London: Witherby. 1972. Covers the trans-Himalayan areas of India and Nepal. An excellent study of the history of ornithological exploration and the zoogeography of this little known area.

Whistler, Hugh. *The Popular Hand Book of Indian Birds*. London. 1949 (4th edition), reprinted Dehra Dun: Natraj. 1989.

Woodcock, Martin. *Handguide to the Birds of the Indian Sub-continent*. London: Collins 1980. Excellent illustrations and useful text.

Woodcock, MW & M Gallagher. *The Birds of Oman*. London: Quartet 1980. Definitive volume with excellent illustrations. Many species common to western India and Pakistan.

# Systematic Index of Families and Species

☐ 74.    LESSER FLAMINGO *Phoeniconaias minor*

Family ***ANATIDAE***: Ducks, Geese, Swans

☐ 75.    SIBERIAN REDBREASTED GOOSE *Branta ruficollis*
☐ 76.    BEAN GOOSE *Anser fabalis*
☐ 79.    WHITEFRONTED GOOSE *Anser albifrons*
☐ 80.    LESSER WHITEFRONTED GOOSE *Anser erythropus*
☐ 81.    GREYLAG GOOSE *Anser anser*
☐ 82.    BARHEADED GOOSE *Anser indicus*
☐ 84.    BEWICK'S SWAN *Cygnus cygnus bewickii*
☐ 86.    WHOOPER SWAN *Cygnus cygnus*
☐ 87.    MUTE SWAN *Cygnus olor*
☐ 88.    LESSER WHISTLING TEAL or TREE DUCK *Dendrocygna javanica*
☐ 89.    LARGE WHISTLING TEAL *Dendrocygna bicolor*
☐ 90.    RUDDY SHELDUCK *Tadorna ferruginea*
☐ 91.    COMMON SHELDUCK *Tadorna tadorna*
☐ 92.    MARBLED TEAL *Marmaronetta angustirostris*
☐ 93.    PINTAIL *Anas acuta*
☐ 94.    COMMON TEAL *Anas crecca*
☐ 95.    BAIKAL TEAL *Anas formosa*
☐ 96.    GREY TEAL *Anas gibberifrons*
☐ 97.    SPOTBILLED DUCK *Anas poecilorhyncha*
☐ 100.   MALLARD *Anas platyrhynchos*
☐ 101.   GADWALL *Anas strepera*
☐ 102.   FALCATED TEAL *Anas falcata*
☐ 103.   WIGEON *Anas penelope*
☐ 104.   GARGANEY *Anas querquedula*
☐ 105.   SHOVELLER *Anas clypeata*
☐ 106.   PINKHEADED DUCK *Rhodonessa caryophyllacea*
☐ 107.   REDCRESTED POCHARD *Netta rufina*
☐ 108.   COMMON POCHARD *Aythya ferina*
☐ 109.   WHITE-EYED POCHARD or FERRUGINOUS DUCK *Aythya nyroca*
☐ 110.   BAER'S POCHARD *Aythya baeri*
☐ 111.   TUFTED DUCK *Aythya fuligula*
☐ 112.   SCAUP DUCK *Aythya marila*
☐ 114.   COTTON TEAL or QUACKY-DUCK *Nettapus coromandelianus*
☐ 115.   COMB DUCK *Sarkidiornis melanotos*
☐ 116.   WHITEWINGED WOOD DUCK *Cairina scutulata*
☐ 117.   LONGTAIL or OLD SQUAW DUCK *Clangula hyemalis*
☐ 118.   GOLDENEYE DUCK *Bucephala clangula*
☐ 119.   SMEW *Mergus albellus*
☐ 120,121 GOOSANDER, COMMON MERGANSER *Mergus merganser*
☐ 123.   WHITEHEADED STIFFTAILED DUCK *Oxyura leucocephala*

Family ***ACCIPITRIDAE***: Hawks, Vultures, etc.

☐ 124.   BLACKWINGED KITE *Elanus caeruleus*
☐ 125.   BLYTH'S BAZA *Aviceda jerdoni*
☐ 127.   BLACKCRESTED BAZA *Aviceda leuphotes*
☐ 130.   HONEY BUZZARD *Pernis ptilorhyncus*
☐ 131.   RED KITE *Milvus milvus*

☐ 132.   BLACK KITE *Milvus migrans migrans*
☐ 133.   PARIAH KITE *Milvus migrans govinda*
☐ 134.   BLACKEARED or LARGE INDIAN KITE *Milvus migrans lineatus*
☐ 135.   BRAHMINY KITE *Haliastur indus*
☐ 136.   GOSHAWK *Accipiter gentilis*
☐ 139.   SHIKRA *Accipiter badius*
☐ 141.   CAR NICOBAR SHIKRA *Accipiter badius butleri*
☐ 143.   HORSFIELD'S GOSHAWK *Accipiter soloensis*
☐ 144.   CRESTED GOSHAWK *Accipiter trivirgatus*
☐ 147.   SPARROW-HAWK *Accipiter nisus melaschistos*
☐ 148.   SPARROW-HAWK *Accipiter nisus nisosimilis*
☐ 151.   BESRA SPARROW-HAWK *Accipiter virgatus besra*
☐ 152.   EASTERN BESRA SPARROW-HAWK *Accipiter virgatus gularis*
☐ 153.   LONGLEGGED BUZZARD *Buteo rufinus*
☐ 154.   UPLAND BUZZARD *Buteo hemilasius*
☐ 155.   DESERT BUZZARD *Buteo buteo vulpinus*
☐ 156.   JAPANESE BUZZARD *Buteo buteo japonicus*
☐ 157.   WHITE-EYED BUZZARD-EAGLE *Butastur teesa*
☐ 158.   HODGSON'S HAWK-EAGLE *Spizaetus nipalensis*
☐ 160.   CHANGEABLE HAWK-EAGLE *Spizaetus cirrhatus limnaeetus*
☐ 161.   CRESTED HAWK-EAGLE *Spizaetus cirrhatus cirrhatus*
☐ 163.   BONELLI'S EAGLE *Hieraaetus fasciatus*
☐ 164.   BOOTED HAWK-EAGLE *Hieraaetus pennatus*
☐ 165.   RUFOUSBELLIED HAWK-EAGLE *Hieraaetus kienerii*
☐ 166.   GOLDEN EAGLE *Aquila chrysaetos*
☐ 167.   IMPERIAL EAGLE *Aquila heliaca*
☐ 168.   TAWNY EAGLE *Aquila rapax vindhiana*
☐ 169.   EASTERN STEPPE EAGLE *Aquila rapax nipalensis*
☐ 170.   GREATER SPOTTED EAGLE *Aquila clanga*
☐ 171.   LESSER SPOTTED EAGLE *Aquila pomarina*
☐ 172.   BLACK EAGLE *Ictinaetus malayensis*
☐ 172a.  WHITETAILED EAGLE *Haliaeetus albicilla*
☐ 173.   WHITEBELLIED SEA EAGLE *Haliaeetus leucogaster*
☐ 174.   PALLAS'S FISHING EAGLE *Haliaeetus leucoryphus*
☐ 175.   GREYHEADED FISHING EAGLE *Ichthyophaga ichthyaetus*
☐ 177.   HIMALAYAN GREYHEADED FISHING EAGLE *Ichthyophaga nana*
☐ 178.   BLACK or KING VULTURE *Sarcogyps calvus*
☐ 179.   CINEREOUS VULTURE *Aegypius monachus*
☐ 180.   GRIFFON VULTURE *Gyps fulvus*
☐ 181.   HIMALAYAN GRIFFON *Gyps himalayensis*
☐ 182.   INDIAN LONGBILLED VULTURE *Gyps indicus*
☐ 185.   INDIAN WHITEBACKED VULTURE *Gyps bengalensis*
☐ 186.   EGYPTIAN or SCAVENGER VULTURE *Neophron percnopterus*

☐ 188.  BEARDED VULTURE or LAMMERGEIER *Gypaetus barbatus*
☐ 189.  HEN-HARRIER *Circus cyaneus*
☐ 190.  PALE-HARRIER *Circus macrourus*
☐ 191.  MONTAGU'S HARRIER *Circus pygargus*
☐ 192.  PIED HARRIER *Circus melanoleucos*
☐ 193.  MARSH HARRIER *Circus aeruginosus*
☐ 194.  EASTERN MARSH HARRIER (or STRIPED HARRIER) *Cirucs aeruginosus spilonotus*
☐ 195.  SHORT-TOED EAGLE *Circaetus gallicus*
☐ 196.  CRESTED SERPENT EAGLE *Spilornis cheela*
☐ 200.  ANDAMAN PALE SERPENT EAGLE *Spilornis cheela davisoni*
☐ 201.  NICOBAR CRESTED SERPENT EAGLE *Spilornis cheela minimus*
☐ 202.  GREAT NICOBAR SERPENT EAGLE *Spilornis klossi*
☐ 202a. ANDAMAN DARK SERPENT EAGLE *Spilornis elgini*
☐ 203.  OSPREY *Pandion haliaetus*

Family *FALCONIDAE*: Falcons

☐ 204.  REDBREASTED FALCONET *Microhierax caerulescens*
☐ 205.  WHITELEGGED FALCONET *Microhierax melanoleucos*
☐ 206.  SAKER or CHERRUG FALCON *Falco biarmicus cherrug*
☐ 207.  SHANGHAR FALCON *Falco biarmicus milvipes*
☐ 209.  PEREGRINE FALCON *Falco peregrinus japonensis*
☐ 211.  SHAHEEN FALCON *Falco peregrinus peregrinator*
☐ 212.  HOBBY *Falco subbuteo*
☐ 215.  ORIENTAL HOBBY *Falco severus*
☐ 216.  SOOTY FALCON *Falco concolor*
☐ 217.  MERLIN *Falco columbarius*
☐ 219.  REDHEADED MERLIN *Falco chicquera*
☐ 220.  REDLEGGED FALCON *Falco vespertinus*
☐ 221.  LESSER KESTREL *Falco naumanni*
☐ 222.  KESTREL *Falco tinnunculus*

Family *MEGAPODIIDAE*: Megapodes

☐ 225.  MEGAPODE *Megapodius freycinet*

Family *PHASIANIDAE*: Pheasants, Partridges, Quails, etc.

☐ 227.  SNOW PARTRIDGE *Lerwa lerwa*
☐ 228.  SEESEE PARTRIDGE *Ammoperdix griseogularis*
☐ 229.  TIBETAN SNOWCOCK *Tetraogallus tibetanus*
☐ 232.  HIMALAYAN SNOWCOCK *Tetraogallus himalayensis*
☐ 233.  PHEASANT-GROUSE *Tetraophasis szechenyii*
☐ 236.  CHUKAR PARTRIDGE *Alectoris chukar*
☐ 238.  BLACK PARTRIDGE *Francolinus francolinus*
☐ 241.  PAINTED PARTRIDGE *Francolinus pictus*
☐ 243.  CHINESE FRANCOLIN *Francolinus pintadeanus*

☐ 246.  GREY PARTRIDGE *Francolinus pondicerianus*
☐ 247.  SWAMP PARTRIDGE or KYAH *Francolinus gularis*
☐ 249.  TIBETAN PARTRIDGE *Perdix hodgsoniae*
☐ 250.  GREY QUAIL *Coturnix coturnix*
☐ 252.  BLACKBREASTED or RAIN QUAIL *Coturnix coromandelica*
☐ 253.  BLUEBREASTED QUAIL *Coturnix chinensis*
☐ 255.  JUNGLE BUSH QUAIL *Perdicula asiatica*
☐ 261.  ROCK BUSH QUAIL *Perdicula argoondah*
☐ 263.  PAINTED BUSH QUAIL *Perdicula erythrorhycha*
☐ 265.  MANIPUR BUSH QUAIL *Perdicula manipurensis*
☐ 267.  COMMON HILL PARTRRIDGE *Arborophila torqueola*
☐ 270.  RUFOUSTHROATED HILL PARTRIDGE *Arborophila rufogularis*
☐ 272.  WHITECHEEKED HILL PARTRIDGE *Arborophila atroguaris*
☐ 273.  REDBREASTED HILL PARTRIDGE *Arborophila mandellii*
☐ 274.  BAMBOO PARTRIDGE *Bambusicola fytchii*
☐ 275.  RED SPURFOWL *Galloperdix spadicea*
☐ 278.  PAINTED SPURFOWL *Galloperdix lunulata*
☐ 279.  CEYLON SPURFOWL *Galloperdix bicalcarata*
☐ 280.  MOUNTAIN QUAIL *Ophrysia superciliosa*
☐ 282.  BLOOD PHEASANT *Ithaginis cruentus*
☐ 285.  WESTERN TRAGOPAN *Tragopan melanocephalus*
☐ 286.  CRIMSON or SATYR TRAGOPAN *Tragopan satyra*
☐ 288.  BLYTH'S or GREYBELLIED TRAGOPAN *Tragopan blythii*
☐ 289.  TEMMINCK'S TRAGOPAN *Tragopan temminckii*
☐ 290.  IMPEYAN or MONAL PHEASANT *Lophophorus impejanus*
☐ 291.  SCLATER'S MONAL *Lophophorus sclateri*
☐ 292.  EARED PHEASANT *Crossoptilon crossoptilon*
☐ 294.  KALEEJ PHEASANT *Lophura leucomelana*
☐ 299.  RED JUNGLEFOWL *Gallus gallus*
☐ 301.  GREY or SONNERAT'S JUNGLEFOWL *Gallus sonneratii*
☐ 302.  CEYLON JUNGLEFOWL *Gallus lafayettii*
☐ 304.  KOKLAS PHEASANT *Pucrasia macrolopha*
☐ 307.  CHIR PHEASANT *Catreus wallichii*
☐ 308.  MRS HUME'S BARREDBACK PHEASANT *Syrmaticus humiae*
☐ 310.  PEACOCK-PHEASANT *Polyplectron bicalcaratum*
☐ 311.  COMMON PEAFOWL *Pavo cristatus*
☐ 312.  BURMESE PEAFOWL *Pavo muticus*

Family *TURNICIDAE*: Bustard-Quails

☐ 313.  LITTLE BUSTARD-QUAIL *Turnix sylvatica*
☐ 314.  YELLOWLEGGED BUTTON QUAIL *Turnix tanki*
☐ 318.  COMMON BUSTARD-QUAIL *Turnix suscitator*

Family *GRUIDAE*: Cranes

- [ ] 320.  COMMON CRANE *Grus grus*
- [ ] 321.  BLACK-NECKED CRANE *Grus nigricollis*
- [ ] 322.  HOODED CRANE *Grus monacha*
- [ ] 323.  SARUS CRANE *Grus antigone*
- [ ] 325.  SIBERIAN CRANE *Grus leucogeranus*
- [ ] 326.  DEMOISELLE CRANE *Anthropoides virgo*

Family *RALLIDAE*: Rails, Coots

- [ ] 327.  WATER RAIL *Rallus aquaticus*
- [ ] 329.  BLUEBREASTED BANDED RAIL *Rallus striatus*
- [ ] 331.  REDLEGGED BANDED CRAKE *Rallina fasciata*
- [ ] 332.  BANDED CRAKE *Rallina eurizonoides*
- [ ] 333.  ANDAMAN BANDED CRAKE *Rallina canningi*
- [ ] 334.  CORN CRAKE *Crex crex*
- [ ] 335.  LITTLE CRAKE *Porzana parva*
- [ ] 337.  BAILLON'S CRAKE *Porzana pusilla*
- [ ] 338.  SPOTTED CRAKE *Prozana prozana*
- [ ] 339.  RUDDY CRAKE *Prozana fusca*
- [ ] 341.  ELWES'S CRAKE *Amaurornis bicolor*
- [ ] 342.  BROWN CRAKE *Amaurornis akool*
- [ ] 343.  WHITEBREASTED WATERHEN *Amaurornis phoenicurus*
- [ ] 346.  WATER COCK *Gallicrex cinerea*
- [ ] 347.  MOORHEN *Gallinula chloropus*
- [ ] 349.  PURPLE MOORHEN *Porphyrio porphyrio*
- [ ] 350.  COOT *Fulica atra*

Family *HELIORNITHIDAE*: Finfoots

- [ ] 351.  MASKED FINFOOT *Heliopais personata*

Family *OTIDIDAE*: Bustards

- [ ] 352.  GREAT BUSTARD *Otis tarda*
- [ ] 353.  LITTLE BUSTARD *Otis tetrax*
- [ ] 354.  GREAT INDIAN BUSTARD *Choriotis nigriceps*
- [ ] 355.  HOUBARA *Chlamydotis undulata*
- [ ] 356.  BENGAL FLORICAN *Eupodotis bengalensis*
- [ ] 357.  LIKH or LESSER FLORICAN *Sypheotides indica*

Family *JACANIDAE*: Jacanas

- [ ] 358.  PHEASANT-TAILED JACANA *Hydrophasianus chirurgus*
- [ ] 359.  BRONZEWINGED JACANA *Metopidius indicus*

Family *HAEMATOPODIDAE*: Oystercatchers

- [ ] 360.  OYSTERCATCHER *Haematopus ostralegus*

Family *ROSTRATULIDAE*: Painted Snipe

- [ ] 429.  PAINTED SNIPE *Rostratula benghalensis*

Family *RECURVIROSTRIDAE*: Stilts, Avocets

- [ ] 430.  BLACKWINGED STILT *Himantopus himantopus*

- [ ] 432.  AVOCET *Recurvirostra avosetta*

Family *IBIDORHYNCHIDAE*: Ibisbill

- [ ] 433.  IBISBILL *Ibidorhyncha struthersii*

Family *DROMADIDAE*: Crab Plovers

- [ ] 434.  CRAB PLOVER *Dromas ardeola*

Family *BURHINIDAE*: Stone Curlews, Thick-knees

- [ ] 436.  STONE CURLEW *Burhinus oedicnemus*
- [ ] 437.  GREAT STONE PLOVER *Esacus magnirostris*

Family *GLAREOLIDAE*: Coursers, Pratincoles

- [ ] 439.  CREAMCOLOURED COURSER *Cursorius cursor*
- [ ] 440.  INDIAN COURSER *Cursorius coromandelicus*
- [ ] 441.  JERDON'S or DOUBLEBANDED COURSER *Cursorius bitorquatus*
- [ ] 442.  COLLARED PRACTINCOLE *Glareola pratincola pratincola*
- [ ] 443.  LARGE INDIAN PRATINCOLE *Glareola pratincola maldivarum*
- [ ] 444.  SMALL INDIAN PRATINCOLE *Glareola lactea*

Family *CHARADRIIDAE*: Plovers, Sandpipers, Snipe

- [ ] 362.  WHITETAILED LAPWING *Vanellus leucurus*
- [ ] 363.  SOCIABLE LAPWING *Vanellus gregarius*
- [ ] 364.  LAPWING *Vanellus vanellus*
- [ ] 365.  GREYHEADED LAPWING *Vanellus cinereus*
- [ ] 366.  REDWATTLED LAPWING *Vanellus indiucs*
- [ ] 369.  SPURWINGED LAPWING *Vanellus spinosus*
- [ ] 370.  YELLOW-WATTLED LAPWING *Vanellus malabaricus*
- [ ] 371.  GREY or BLACKBELLIED PLOVER *Pluvialis squatarola*
- [ ] 372.  GOLDEN PLOVER *Pluvialis apricaria*
- [ ] 373.  EASTERN GOLDEN PLOVER *Pluvialis dominica*
- [ ] 374.  LARGE SAND PLOVER *Charadrius leschenaultii*
- [ ] 376.  CASPIAN SAND PLOVER *Charadrius asiaticus*
- [ ] 378.  RINGED PLOVER *Charadrius hiaticula*
- [ ] 380.  LITTLE RINGED PLOVER *Charadrius dubius*
- [ ] 383.  LONGBILLED RINGED PLOVER *Charadrius placidus*
- [ ] 384.  LESSER SAND PLOVER *Charadrius mongolus*
- [ ] 385.  WHIMBREL *Numenius phaeopus*
- [ ] 388.  CURLEW *Numenius arquata*
- [ ] 389.  BLACKTAILED GODWIT *Limosa limosa*
- [ ] 391.  BARTAILED GODWIT *Limosa lapponica*
- [ ] 392.  SPOTTED or DUSKY REDSHANK *Tringa erythropus*
- [ ] 393.  REDSHANK *Tringa totanus*
- [ ] 395.  MARSH SANDPIPER *Tringa stagnatilis*
- [ ] 396.  GREENSHANK *Tringa nebularia*
- [ ] 397.  GREEN SANDPIPER *Tringa ochropus*
- [ ] 398.  WOOD SANDPIPER *Tringa glareola*

☐ 399.   SPOTTED GREENSHANK *Tringa guttifer*
☐ 400.   TEREK SANDPIPER *Tringa terek*
☐ 401.   COMMON SANDPIPER *Tringa hypoleucos*
☐ 402.   TURNSTONE *Arenaria interpres*
☐ 403.   SNIPEBILLED GODWIT or ASIAN DOWITCHER *Limnodromus semipalmatus*
☐ 404.   SOLITARY SNIPE *Gallinago solitaria*
☐ 405.   WOOD SNIPE *Gallinago nemoricola*
☐ 406.   PINTAIL SNIPE *Gallinago stenura*
☐ 407.   SWINHOE'S SNIPE *Gallinago megala*
☐ 408.   GREAT SNIPE *Gallinago media*
☐ 409.   FANTAIL SNIPE *Gallinago gallinago*
☐ 410.   JACK SNIPE *Gallinago media*
☐ 411.   WOODCOCK *Scolopax rusticola*
☐ 412.   KNOT *Calidris canuta*
☐ 413.   EASTERN KNOT *Calidris tenuirostris*
☐ 414.   SANDERLING *Calidris alba*
☐ 416.   LITTLE STINT *Calidris minuta*
☐ 417.   TEMMINCK'S STINT *Calidris temminckii*
☐ 418.   LONGTOED STINT *Calidris subminuta*
☐ 419.   ASIAN PECTORAL SANDPIPER *Calidris acuminata*
☐ 420.   DUNLIN *Calidris alpina*
☐ 422.   CURLEW-SANDPIPER *Calidris testacea*
☐ 423.   SPOONBILLED SANDPIPER *Eurynorhychus pygmeus*
☐ 424.   BROADBILLED SANDPIPER *Limicola falcinellus*
☐ 426.   RUFF and REEVE *Philomachus pugnax*
☐ 428.   REDNECKED PHALAROPE *Phalaropus lobatus*

Family ***STERCORARIIDARE***: Skuas, Jaegers

☐ 445.   ANTARCTIC SKUA *Catharacta skua antarctica*
☐ 446a.  ANTARCTIC SKUA (MACCORMICK'S SKUA) *Catharacta skua maccormicki*
☐ 447.   POMATORHINE SKUA or JAEGER *Stercorarius pomarinus*
☐ 448.   PARASITIC or RICHARDSON'S SKUA or JAEGER *Stercorarius arasiticus*

Family ***LARIDAE***: Gulls, Terns

☐ 449.   SOOTY GULL *Larus hemprichii*
☐ 450.   HERRING GULL *Larus argentatus*
☐ 452.   LESSER BLACKBACKED GULL *Larus fuscus*
☐ 453.   GREAT BLACKHEADED GULL *Larus ichthyaetus*
☐ 454.   BROWNHEADED GULL *Larus brunnicephalus*
☐ 455.   BLACKHEADED GULL *Larus ridibundus*
☐ 456.   SLENDERBILLED GULL *Larus genei*
☐ 457.   LITTLE GULL *Larus minutus*
☐ 458.   WHISHKERED TERN *Childonias hybrida*
☐ 459.   WHITEWINGED BLACK TERN *Childonias leucopterus*
☐ 459a.  BLACK TERN *Childonias niger*
☐ 460.   GULLBILLED TERN *Gelochelidon nilotica*
☐ 462.   CASPIAN TERN *Hydroprogne caspia*
☐ 463.   INDIAN RIVER TERN *Sterna aurantia*
☐ 464.   COMMON TERN *Sterna hirundo*
☐ 466.   ROSEATE or ROSY TERN *Sterna dougallii*

☐ 467.   WHITE CHEEKED TERN *Sterna represa*
☐ 468.   BLACKNAPED TERN *Sterna sumatrana*
☐ 470.   BLACKBELLIED TERN *Stern acuticauda*
☐ 471.   BROWNWINGED TERN *Sterna anaethetus*
☐ 474.   SOOTY TERN *Sterna fuscata*
☐ 475.   LITTLE TERN *Sterna albifrons*
☐ 478.   LARGE CRESTED TERN *Sterna bergii*
☐ 479.   INDIAN LESSER CRESTED TERN *Sterna bengalensis*
☐ 480.   SANDWICH TERN *Sterna sandvicensis*
☐ 481.   NOODY TERN *Anous stolidus*
☐ 483.   INDIAN OCEAN WHITE TERN, FAIRY TERN *Gygis alba*
☐ 484.   INDIAN SKIMMER *Rynchops albicollis*

Family ***PTEROCLIDIDAE***: Sandgrouse

☐ 485.   TIBETAN SANDGROUSE *Syrrhaptes tibetanus*
☐ 485a.  PALLAS'S SANDGROUSE *Syrrhaptes paradoxus*
☐ 486.   LARGE PINTAIL SANDGROUSE *Pterocles alchata*
☐ 487.   INDIAN SANDGROUSSE *Pterocles exustus*
☐ 488.   SPOTTED SANDGROUSE *Pterocles senegallus*
☐ 489.   IMPERIAL SANDGROUSE *Pterocles orientalis*
☐ 490.   CORONETTED SANDGROUSE *Pterocles coronatus*
☐ 491.   CLOSEBARRED SANDGROUSE *Pterocles indicus arabicus*
☐ 492.   PAINTED SANDGROUSE   *Pterocles indicus indicus*

Family ***COLUMBIDAE***: Pigeons, Doves

☐ 493.   PINTAILED GREEN PIGEON *Treron apicauda*
☐ 494.   WEDGETAILED GREEN PIGEON *Treron sphenura*
☐ 495.   THICKBILLED GREEN PIGEON *Treron curvirostra*
☐ 496.   POMPADOUR or GREYFRONTED GREEN PIGEON *Treron pompadora*
☐ 501.   ORANGEBREASTED GREEN PIGEON *Treron bicincta*
☐ 503.   YELLOWLEGGED GREEN PIGEON *Treron phoenicoptera*
☐ 506.   GREEN IMPERIAL PIGEON *Ducula aenea*
☐ 509.   PIED IMPERIAL PIGEON *Ducula bicolor*
☐ 510.   IMPERIAL PIGEON *Ducula badia*
☐ 513.   SNOW PIGEON *Columba leuconota*
☐ 515.   HILL PIGEON *Columba rupestris*
☐ 516.   BLUE ROCK PIGEON *Columba livia*
☐ 518.   EASTERN STOCK PIGEON *Columba eversmanni*
☐ 519.   WOOD PIGEON *Columba palumbus*
☐ 520.   SPECKLED WOOD PIGEON *Columba hodgsonii*
☐ 521.   NILGIRI WOOD PIGEON *Columba elphinstonii*
☐ 522.   CEYLON WOOD PIGEON *Columba torringtoni*
☐ 523.   ASHY WOOD PIGEON *Columba pulchricollis*

☐ 524. PURPLE WOOD PIGEON *Columba punicea*
☐ 525. ANDAMAN WOOD PIGEON *Columba palumboides*
☐ 526. BARTAILED CUCKOO-DOVE *Macropygia unchall*
☐ 527. ANDAMAN CUCKOO-DOVE *Macropygia*
☐ *rufipennis*
☐ 529. TURTLE DOVE *Streptopelia turtur*
☐ 530. RUFOUS TURTLE DOVE *Streptopelia orientalis*
☐ 534. INDIAN RING DOVE *Streptopelia decaocto*
☐ 535. RED TURTLE DOVE *Streptopelia tranquebarica*
☐ 537. SPOTTED DOVE *Streptopelia chinensis*
☐ 541. LITTLE BROWN or SENEGAL DOVE *Streptopelia senegalensis*
☐ 542. EMERALD or BRONZEWINGED DOVE *Chalcophaps indica*
☐ 544b. NICOBAR PIGEON *Caloenas nicobarica*

## Family *PSITTACIDAE*: Parrots

☐ 546. ALEXANDRINE PARAKEET *Psittacula eupatria*
☐ 550. ROSERINGED PARAKEET *Psittacula krameri*
☐ 551. REDBREASTED PARAKEET *Psittacula alexandri*
☐ 553. NICOBAR PARAKEET *Psittacula caniceps*
☐ 554. LORD DERBY'S PARAKEET *Psittacula derbyana*
☐ 555. REDCHEEKED PARAKEET *Psittacula longicauda*
☐ 558. BLOSSOMHEADED PARAKEET *Psittacula cyanocephala*
☐ 562. SLATYHEADED PARAKEET *Psittacula himalayana*
☐ 563. EASTERN SLATYHEADED PARAKEET *Psittacula finschii*
☐ 564. BLUEWINGED PARAKEET *Psittacula columboides*
☐ 565. LAYARD'S PARAKEET *Psittacula calthropae*
☐ 566. INDIAN LORIKEET *Loriculus vernalis*
☐ 568. CEYLON LORIKEET *Loriculus beryllinus*

## Family *CUCULIDAE*: Cuckoos

☐ 569. REDWINGED CRESTED CUCKOO *Clamator coromandus*
☐ 571. PIED CRESTED CUCKOO *Clamator jacobinus*
☐ 572. LARGE HAWK-CUCKOO *Cuculus sparverioides*
☐ 573. COMMON HAWK-CUCKOO or BRAIN-FEVER BIRD *Cuculus varius*
☐ 575. HODGSON'S HAWK-CUCKOO *Cuculus fugax*
☐ 576. INDIAN CUCKOO *Cuculus micropterus*
☐ 578. THE CUCKOO *Cuculus canorus*
☐ 581. SMALL CUCKOO *Cuculus poliocephalus*
☐ 582. INDIAN BANDED BAY CUCKOO *Cacomantis sonneratii*
☐ 584. INDIAN PLAINTIVE CUCKOO *Cacomantis passerinus*
☐ 585. RUFOUSBELLIED PLAINTIVE CUCKOO *Cacomantis merulinus*

☐ 586. EMERALD CUCKOO *Chalcites maculatus*
☐ 587. VIOLET CUCKOO *Chalcites xanthorhynchus*
☐ 588. DRONGO-CUCKOO *Surniculus lugubris*
☐ 590. KOEL *Eudynamys scolopacea*
☐ 593. LARGE GREENBILLED MALKOHA *Rhopodytes tristis*
☐ 595. SMALL GREENBILLED MALKOHA *Rhopodytes viridirostris*
☐ 598. SIRKEER CUCKOO *Taccocua leschenaultii*
☐ 599. REDFACED MALKOHA *Phaenicophaeus pyrrhocephalus*
☐ 600. CROW-PHEASANT or COUCAL *Centropus sinensis*
☐ 603. ANDAMAN CROW-PHEASANT *Centropus (sinensis) andamanensis*
☐ 604. CEYLON COUCAL *Centropus chlorohynchus*
☐ 605. LESSER COUCAL *Centropus toulou*

## Family *STRIGIDAE*: Owls

☐ 606. BARN OWL *Tyto alba*
☐ 608. GRASS OWL *Tyto capensis*
☐ 609. BAY OWL *Phodilus badius*
☐ 612. SPOTTED SCOPS OWL *Otus spilocephalus*
☐ 614. STRIATED or PALLID SCOPS OWL *Otus brucei*
☐ 617. SCOPS OWL *Otus scops*
☐ 623. COLLARED SCOPS OWL *Otus bakkamoena*
☐ 627. EAGLE-OWL or GREAT HORNED OWL *Bubo bubo*
☐ 628. FOREST EAGLE-OWL *Bubo nipalensis*
☐ 630. DUSKY HORNED OWL *Bubo coromandus*
☐ 631. BROWN FISH OWL *Bubo zeylonensis*
☐ 633. TAWNY FISH OWL *Bubo flavipes*
☐ 635. COLLARED PIGMY OWLET *Glaucidium brodiei*
☐ 636. JUNGLE OWLET *Glaucidium radiatum*
☐ 639. BARRED OWLET *Glaucidium cuculoides*
☐ 642. BROWN HAWK-OWL *Ninox scutulata*
☐ 648,649. LITTLE OWL *Athene noctua*
☐ 652. SPOTTED OWLET *Athene brama*
☐ 653. FOREST SPOTTED OWLET *Athene blewitti*
☐ 654. HUME'S WOOD OWL *Strix butleri*
☐ 657. MOTTLED WOOD OWL *Strix ocellata*
☐ 659. BROWN WOOD OWL *Strix leptogrammica*
☐ 662. HIMALAYAN WOOD OWL *Strix aluco*
☐ 663. LONGEARED OWL *Asio otus*
☐ 664. SHORTEARED OWL *Asio flammeus*
☐ 665. TENGMALM'S or BOREAL OWL *Aegolius funereus*

## Family *PODARGIDAE*: Frogmouths

☐ 666. CEYLON FROGMOUTH *Batrachostomus moniliger*
☐ 667. HODGSON'S FROGMOUTH *Batrachostomus hodgsoni*

## Family *CAPRIMULGIDAE*: Nightjars, Goatsuckers

☐ 669. GREAT EARED NIGHTJAR *Eurostopodus macrotis*
☐ 671. INDIAN JUNGLE NIGHTJAR *Caprimulgus indicus*

☐ 673.  EUROPEAN NIGHTJAR *Caprimulgus europaeus*

☐ 673a. EGYPTIAN NIGHTJAR *Caprimulgus aegyptius*

☐ 674.  SYKES'S NIGHTJAR *Caprimulgus mahrattensis*

☐ 680.  COMMON INDIAN NIGHTJAR *Caprimulgus asiaticus*

☐ 682.  FRANKLIN'S or ALLIED NIGHTJAR *Caprimulgus affinis*

Family *APODIDAE*: Swifts

☐ 683.  HIMALAYAN SWIFTLET *Collocalia brevirostris*

☐ 685.  INDIAN EDIBLE-NEST SWIFTLET *Collocalia unicolor*

☐ 687.  WHITEBELLIED SWIFTLET *Collocalia esculenta*

☐ 688.  WHITETHROATED SPINETAIL SWIFT *Chaetura caudacuta*

☐ 690.  COCHINCHINA SPINETAIL SWIFT *Chaetura cochinchinensis*

☐ 691.  LARGE BROWNTHROATED SPINETAIL SWIFT *Chaetura gigantea*

☐ 692.  WHITERUMPED SPINETAIL *Chaetura sylvatica*

☐ 693.  ALPINE SWIFT *Apus melba*

☐ 696.  THE SWIFT *Apus apus*

☐ 697.  PALLID SWIFT *Apus pallidus*

☐ 698.  DARKBACKED SWIFT *Apus acuticauda*

☐ 699.  LARGE WHITERUMPED SWIFT *Apus pacificus*

☐ 703.  HOUSE SWIFT *Apus affinis*

☐ 707.  PALM SWIFT *Cypsiurus parvus*

☐ 709.  CRESTED TREE SWIFT *Hemiprocne longipennis*

Family *TROGONIDAE*: Trogons

☐ 712.  MALABAR TROGON *Harpactes fasciatus*

☐ 715.  REDHEADED TROGON *Harpactes erythrocephalus*

☐ 716.  WARD'S TROGON *Harpactes wardi*

Family *ALCEDINIDAE*: Kingfishers

☐ 717.  HIMALAYAN PIED KINGFISHER *Ceryle lugubris*

☐ 719.  LESSER PIED KINGFISHER *Ceryle rudis*

☐ 721.  BLYTH'S or GREAT BLUE KINGFISHER *Alcedo hercules*

☐ 722.  COMMON KINGFISHER *Alcedo atthis*

☐ 725.  BLUE-EARED KINGFISHER *Alcedo meninting*

☐ 727.  THREETOED KINGFISHER *Ceyx erithacus*

☐ 727a. THREETOED KINGFISHER *Ceyx erithacus rufidorsus*

☐ 729.  BROWWINGED KINGFISHER *Pelargopsis amauroptera*

☐ 730.  STORKBILLED KINGFISHER *Pelargopsis capensis*

☐ 733.  RUDDY KINGFISHER *Halcyon coromanda*

☐ 735.  WHITEBREASTED KINGFISHER *Halcyon smyrnensis*

☐ 739.  BLACKCAPPED KINGFISHER *Halcyon pileata*

☐ 740.  WHITECOLLARED KINGFISHER *Halcyon chloris*

Family *MEROPIDAE*: Bee-eaters

☐ 744.  CHESTNUTHEADED BEE-EATER *Merops leschenaulti*

☐ 746.  EUROPEAN BEE-EATER *Merops apiaster*

☐ 747.  BLUECHEEKED BEE-EATER *Merops superciliosus*

☐ 748.  BLUETAILED BEE-EATER *Merops philippinus*

☐ 750.  GREEN BEE-EATER *Merops orientalis*

☐ 753.  BLUEBEARDED BEE-EATER *Nyctyornic athertoni*

Family *CORACIIDAE*: Rollers

☐ 754.  EUROPEAN ROLLER *Coracias garrulus*

☐ 755.  INDIAN ROLLER *Coracias benghalensis*

☐ 759.  BROADBILLED ROLLER *Eurystomus orientalis*

Family *UPUPIDAE*: Hoopoes

☐ 763.  HOOPOE *Upupa epops*

Family *BUCEROTIDAE*: Hornbills

☐ 767.  COMMON GREY HORNBILL *Tockus birostris*

☐ 768.  MALABAR GREY HORNBILL *Tockus griseus*

☐ 770.  WHITETHROATED BROWN HORNBILL *Ptilolaemus tickelli*

☐ 771.  RUFOUSNECKED HORNBILL *Aceros nipalensis*

☐ 772.  WREATHED HORNBILL *Rhyticeros undulatus*

☐ 773.  NARCONDAM HORNBILL *Rhyticeros plicatus (narcondami)*

☐ 774.  INDIAN PIED HORNBILL *Anthracoceros malabaricus*

☐ 775.  MALABAR PIED HORNBILL *Anthracoceros coronatus*

☐ 776.  GREAT PIED HORNBILL *Buceros bicornis*

Family *CAPITONIDAE*: Barbets

☐ 778.  GREAT HILL BARBET *Megalaima virens*

☐ 782.  LARGE GREEN BARBET *Megalaima zeylanica*

☐ 784.  LINEATED BARBET *Megalaima lineata*

☐ 785.  SMALL GREEN BARBET *Megalaima viridis*

☐ 786.  YELLOWFRONTED BARBET *Megalaima flavifrons*

☐ 787.  GOLDENTHROATED BARBET *Megalaima franklinii*

☐ 788.  BLUETHROATED BARBET *Megalaima asiatica*

☐ 789.  BLUE-EARED BARBET *Megalaima australis*

☐ 790.  CRIMSONTHROATED BARBET *Megalaima rubricapilla malabarica*

☐ 791. CRIMSONTHROATED BARBET *Megalaima rubricapilla rubricapilla*
☐ 792. CRIMSONBREASTED BARBET, COPPER-SMITH *Megalaima haemacephala*

Family *INDICATORIDAE*: Honeyguides

☐ 794. HONEYGUIDE *Indicator xanthonotus*

Family *PICIDAE*: Woodpeckers

☐ 796. WRYNECK *Jynx torquilla*
☐ 798. SPECKLED PICULET *Picumnus innominatus*
☐ 800. RUFOUS PICULET *Sasia ochracea*
☐ 804. RUFOUS WOODPECKER *Micropternus brachyurus*
☐ 807. SCALYBELLIED GREEN WOODPECKER *Picus squamatus*
☐ 808. LITTLE SCALYBELLIED GREEN WOODPECKER *Picus myrmecorphoneus*
☐ 809. BLACKNAPED GREEN WOODPECKER *Picus canus*
☐ 813. LARGE YELLOWNAPED WOODPECKER *Picus flavinuicha*
☐ 815. SMALL YELLOWNAPED WOODPECKER *Picus chlorolophus*
☐ 819. LESSER GOLDENBACKED WOODPECKER *Dinopium benghalense*
☐ 824. HIMALAYAN GOLDENBACKED THREE-TOED WOODPECKER *Dinopium shorii*
☐ 825. INDIAN GOLDENBACKED THREETOED WOODPECKER *Dinopium javanense*
☐ 827. PALEHEADED WOODPECKER *Gecinulus grantia*
☐ 828. HIMALAYAN GREAT SLATY WOODPECKER *Mulleripicus pulverulentus*
☐ 830. INDIAN GREAT BLACK WOODPECKER *Dryocopus javensis*
☐ 833. RUFOUSBELLIED WOODPECKER or SAP-SUCKER *Hypopicus hyperythrus*
☐ 834. GREAT SPOTTED or REDCROWNED PIED WOODPECKER *Picoides major*
☐ 835. SIND PIED WOODPECKER *Picoides assimilis*
☐ 837. HIMALAYAN PIED WOODPECKER *Picoides himalayensis*
☐ 838. DARJEELING PIED WOODPECKER *Picoides cathpharius*
☐ 840. CRIMSONBREASTED PIED WOODPECKER *Picoides cathpharius*
☐ 842. BROWNFRONTED PIED WOODPECKER *Picoides auriceps*
☐ 844. STRIPEBREASTED PIED WOODPECKER *Picoides atratus*
☐ 845. FULVOUSBREASTED PIED WOODPECKER *Picoides macei*
☐ 847. YELLOWFRONTED PIED WOODPECKER *Picoides mahrattensis*
☐ 850. GREYCROWNED PYGMY WOODPECKER *Picoides canicapillus*
☐ 855. THREETOED WOODPECKER *Picoides tridactylus*
☐ 856. HEARTSPOTTED WOODPECKER *Hemicircus canente*

☐ 857. REDEARED BAY WOODPECKER *Blythipicus pyrrhotis*
☐ 858. BLACKBACKED WOODPECKER *Chrysocolaptes festivus*
☐ 861. LARGER GOLDENBACKED WOODPECKER *Chrysocolaptes lucidus*

Family *EURYLAIMIDAE*: Broadbills

☐ 864. COLLARED BROADBILL *Serilophus lunatus*
☐ 865. LONGTAILED BROADBILL *Psarisomus dalhousiae*

Family *PITTIDAE*: Pittas

☐ 866. BLUENAPED PITTA *Pitta nipalensis*
☐ 867. INDIAN PITTA *Pitta brachyura*
☐ 868. BLUEWINGED PITTA *Pitta moluccensis*
☐ 869. HOODED or GREENBREASTED PITTA *Pitta sordida*
☐ 871. BLUE PITTA *Pitta cyanea*

Family *ALAUDIDAE*: Larks

☐ 872. SINGING BUSH LARK *Mirafra javanica*
☐ 873. BUSH LARK *Mirafra assamica*
☐ 877. REDWINGED BUSH LARK *Mirafra erythroptera*
☐ 878. ASHYCROWNED FINCH-LARK *Eremopterix grisea*
☐ 879. BLACK CROWNED FINCH-LARK *Eremopterix nigriceps*
☐ 880. DESERT FINCH-LARK *Ammomanes deserti*
☐ 881. BARTAILED DESERT LARK *Ammomanes cinctures*
☐ 882. RUFOUSTAILED FINCH-LARK *Ammomanes phoenicurus*
☐ 884. BIFASCIATED or LARGE DESERT LARK *Alaemon alaudipes*
☐ 886. SHORT-TOED LARK *Calandrella cinerea*
☐ 888a. LESSER SHORT-TOED LARK *Calandrella rufescens*
☐ 891. SAND LARK *Calandrella raytal*
☐ 892. EASTERN CALANDRA LARK *Melanocorypha bimaculata*
☐ 894. LONGBILLED CALANDRA LARK *Melanocorypha maxima*
☐ 897. HORNED LARK *Eremophila alpestris*
☐ 899. CRESTED LARK *Galerida cristata*
☐ 901. MALABAR CRESTED LARK *Galerida malabarica*
☐ 902. SYKES'S CRESTED LARK *Galerida deva*
☐ 903. SKYLARK *Alauda arvensis*
☐ 907. EASTERN SKYLARK *Alauda gulgula*

Family *HIRUNDINIDAE:* Swallows

☐ 910. COLLARED SAND MARTIN *Riparia riparia*
☐ 912. PLAIN SAND MARTIN *Riparia paludicola*
☐ 913. CRAG MARTIN *Hirundo rupestris*
☐ 914. DUSKY CRAG MARTIN *Hirundo concolor*
☐ 915. PALE CRAG MARTIN *Hirundo obsoleta*
☐ 916. SWALLOW *Hirundo rustica*
☐ 919. HOUSE SWALLOW *Hirundo tahitica*
☐ 921. WIRETAILED SWALLOW *Hirundo smithii*

☐ 922.   INDIAN CLIFF SWALLOW *Hirundo fluvicola*
☐ 923.   STRIATED or REDRUMPED SWALLOW
         *Hinudo daurica*
☐ 930.   HOUSE MARTIN *Delichon urbica*
☐ 932.   NEPAL HOUSE MARTIN *Delichon nipalensis*

Family *LANIIDAE*: Shrikes

☐ 933.   GREY SHRIKE *Lanius exubitor*
☐ 937.   LESSER GREY SHRIKE *Lanius minor*
☐ 938.   BURMESE SHRIKE *Lanius collurioides*
☐ 940.   BAYBACKED SHRIKE *Lanius vittatus*
☐ 941.   REDBACKED SHRIKE *Lanius collurio*
☐ 945.   GREYBACKED or TIBETAN SHRIKE *Lanius
         tephronotus*
☐ 946.   RUFOUSBACKED SHRIKE *Lanius schach*
☐ 949.   BROWN SHRIKE *Lanius cristatus*
☐ 951.   WOODCHAT SHRIKE *Lanius senator*

Family *ORIOLIDAE*: Orioles

☐ 952.   GOLDEN ORIOLE *Oriolus oriolus*
☐ 954.   BLACKNAPED ORIOLE *Oriolus chinensis dif-
         fusus*
☐ 958.   BLACKHEADED ORIOLE *Oriolus xanthornus*
☐ 961.   MAROON ORIOLE *Oriolus traillii*

Family *DICRURIDAE*: Drongos

☐ 963.   BLACK DRONGO or KING-CROW *Dicrurus
         adsimilis*
☐ 965.   GREY or ASHY DRONGO *Dicrurus
         leucophaeus*
☐ 967.   WHITEBELLIED DRONGO *Dicrurus
         caerulescens*
☐ 970.   CROWBILLED DRONGO *Dicrurus annectans*
☐ 971.   BRONZED DRONGO *Dicrurus aeneus*
☐ 972.   LESSER RACKET-TAILED DRONGO
         *Dicrurus remifer*
☐ 973.   HAIRCRESTED or SPANGLED DRONGO
         *Dicrurus hottentottus*
☐ 975.   ANDAMAN DRONGO *Dicrurus andamanen-
         sis*
☐ 977.   GREATER RACKET-TAILED DRONGO
         *Dicrurus paradiseus*

Family *ARTAMIDAE*: Swallow-Shrikes or Wood
Swallows

☐ 982.   ASHY SWALLOW-SHRIKE *Artamus fuscus*
☐ 983.   WHITEBREASTED SWALLOW-SHRIKE
         *Artamus leucorhynchus*

Family *STURNIDAE*: Starlings, Mynas

☐ 984.   SPOTTEDWINGED STARE *Saroglossa
         spiloptera*
☐ 986.   GLOSSY STARE or STARLING *Aplonis
         panayensis*
☐ 987.   GREYHEADED MYNA *Sturnus malabaricus*
☐ 988.   WHITEHEADED MYNA *Sturnus malabaricus
         blythi*

☐ 991.   NICOBAR WHITEHEADED MYNA
         *Sturnus erythropygius*
☐ 993.   CEYLON WHITEHEADED MYNA *Sturnus
         senex*
☐ 994.   BLACKHEADED or BRAHMINY MYNA
         *Sturnus pagodarum*
☐ 995.   DAURIAN MYNA *Sturnus sturninus*
☐ 996.   ROSY PASTOR *Strnus roseus*
☐ 997.   STARLING *Sturnus vulgaris*
☐ 1002.  PIED MYNA *Sturnus contra*
☐ 1005.  CHINESE or GREYBACKED MYNA *Stur-
         nus sinensis*
☐ 1006.  COMMON MYNA *Acridotheres tristis*
☐ 1008.  BANK MYNA *Acridotheres ginginianus*
☐ 1009.  JUNGLE MYNA *Acridotheres fuscus*
☐ 1012.  ORANGEBILLED JUNGLE MYNA
         *Acridotheres javanicus*
☐ 1013.  COLLARED MYNA *Acridothers albocinctus*
☐ 1014.  GOLDCRESTED MYNA *Mino coronatus*
☐ 1015.  GRACKLE or HILL MYNA *Gracula relgiosa*
☐ 1019.  CEYLON HILL MYNA *Gracula ptilogenys*

Family *CORVIDAE*: Crows, Magpies, Jays, etc.

☐ 1020.  REDCROWNED JAY *Garrulus glandarius*
☐ 1022.  BLACKTHROATED JAY *Garrulus lan-
         ceolatus*
☐ 1023.  GREEN MAGPIE *Cissa chinensis*
☐ 1024.  CEYLON MAGPIE *Cissa ornata*
☐ 1025.  YELLOWBILLED BLUE MAGPIE *Cissa
         flavirostris*
☐ 1027.  REDBILLED BLUE MAGPIE *Cissa erythror-
         hyncha*
☐ 1029.  WHITERUMPED MAGPIE *Pica pica*
☐ 1032.  INDIAN TREE PIE *Dendrocitta vagabunda*
☐ 1035.  BLACKBROWED TREE PIE *Dendrocitta
         frontalis*
☐ 1036.  WHITEBELLIED TREE PIE *Dendrocitta
         leucogastra*
☐ 1038.  HIMALAYAN TREE PIE *Dendrocitta for-
         mosae*
☐ 1040.  ANDAMAN TREE PIE *Dendrocitta bayleyi*
☐ 1041.  HUME'S GROUND CHOUGH *Podoces
         humilis*
☐ 1042.  NUTCRACKER *Nucifraga caryocatactes*
☐ 1045.  YELLOWBILLED or ALPINE CHOUGH
         *Pyrrhocorax graculus*
☐ 1046.  REDBILLED CHOUGH *Pyrrhocorax pyr-
         rhocorax*
☐ 1049.  HOUSE CROW *Corvus splendens*
☐ 1052.  ROOK *Corvus frugilegus*
☐ 1053.  JACKDAW *Corvus monedula*
☐ 1054.  JUNGLE CROW *Corvus macrohynchos*
☐ 1058.  CARRION CROW *Corvus corone*
☐ 1059.  RAVEN *Corvus corax*
☐ 1061.  BROWN-NECKED RAVEN *Corvus ruficollis*

Family *BOMBYCILLIDAE*: Waxwings, Silky
Flycatchers

☐ 1062.  WAXWING *Bombycilla garrulus*
☐ 1063.  GREY HYPOCOLIUS *Hypocolius ampelinus*

Family *CAMPEPHAGIDAE*: Cuckoo-Shrikes and Minivets

☐ 1065. PIED FLYCATCHER-SHRIKE *Hemipus picatus*
☐ 1068. LARGE WOOD SHRIKE *Tephrodornis virgatus*
☐ 1070. COMMON WOOD SHRIKE *Tephrodornis pondicerianus*
☐ 1072. LARGE CUCKOO-SHRIKE *Coracina novaehollandiae*
☐ 1076. BARRED CUCKOO-SHRIKE *Coracina striata*
☐ 1077. SMALLER GREY CUCKOO-SHRIKE *Coracina melaschistos*
☐ 1078. BLACKHEADED CUCKOO-SHRIKE *Coracina melanoptera*
☐ 1079a. PIED CUCKOO SHRIKE *Coracina nigra*
☐ 1081. SCARLET MINIVET *Pericrocotus flammeus*
☐ 1084. SHORTBILLED MINIVET *Pericrocotus brevirostris*
☐ 1085. LONGTAILED MINIVET *Pericrocotus ethologus*
☐ 1088. YELLOWTHROATED MINIVET *Pericrocotus solaris*
☐ 1089. ROSY MINIVET *Pericrocotus roseus*
☐ 1089a. ASHY MINIVET *Pericrocotus divaricatus*
☐ 1093. SMALL MINIVET *Pericrocotus cinnamomeus*
☐ 1096. WHITEBELLIED MINIVET *Pericrocotus erythropygius*

Family *IRENIDAE*: Fairy Bluebird, Ioras and Leaf Birds

☐ 1098. COMMON IORA *Aegithina tiphia*
☐ 1102. MARSHALL'S IORA *Aegithina nigrolutea*
☐ 1103. GOLDENFRONTED CHLOROPSIS or LEAF BIRD *Chloropsis aurifrons*
☐ 1106. ORANGEBELLIED CHLOROPSIS or LEAF BIRD *Chloropsis hardwickii*
☐ 1108. GOLDMANTLED CHLOROPSIS or LEAF BIRD *Choloropsis chochinchinensis*
☐ 1109. FAIRY BLUEBIRD *Irena puella*

Family *PYCNONOTIDAE*: Bulbuls

☐ 1111. FINCHBILLED BULBUL *Spizixos canifrons*
☐ 1112. BLACKHEADED BULBUL *Pycnonotus atriceps*
☐ 1114. GREYHEADED BULBUL *Pycnonotus priocephalus*
☐ 1115. BLACKHEADED YELLOW BULBUL *Pycnonotus melanicterus flaviventris*
☐ 1116. RUBYTHROATED YELLOW BULBUL *Pycnonotus melanicterus gularis*
☐ 1117. BLACKCAPPED YELLOW BULBUL *Pycnonotus melanicterus melanicterus*
☐ 1120. REDWHISKERED BULBUL *Pycnonotus jocosus*
☐ 1123. WHITE-EARED BULBUL *Pyenonotus leucogenys leucotis*
☐ 1125. WHITECHEEKED BULBUL *Pycnonotus leucogenys*
☐ 1128. REDVENTED BULBUL *Pycnonotus cafer*

☐ 1133. STRIATED GREEN BULBUL *Pycnonotus striatus*
☐ 1135. YELLOWTHROATED BULBUL *Pycnonotus xantholaemus*
☐ 1137. BLYTH'S BULBUL *Pycnonotus flavescens*
☐ 1138. WHITEBROWED BULBUL *Pycnonotus luteolus*
☐ 1140. WHITETHROATED BULBUL *Cringer flaveolus*
☐ 1141. OLIVE BULBUL *Hypsipetes viridescens*
☐ 1142. NICOBAR BULBUL *Hypsipetes nicobariensis*
☐ 1144. YELLOWBROWED BULBUL *Hypsipetes indicus*
☐ 1146. RUFOUSBELLIED BULBUL *Hypsipetes mcclellandi*
☐ 1147. BROWNEARED BULBUL *Hypsipetes flavalus*
☐ 1148. BLACK BULBUL *Hypsipetes madagascariensis*

Family *MUSCICAPIDAE*: Babblers, Flycatchers, Warbles, Thrushes and Chats

Subfamily *TIMALINAE*: Babblers

☐ 1154. SPOTTED BABBLER *Pellorneum ruficeps*
☐ 1160. MARSH SPOTTED BABBLER *Pellorneum palustre*
☐ 1161. BROWNCAPPED BABBLER *Pellorneum fuscocapillum*
☐ 1164. BROWN BABBLER *Pellorneum albiventre*
☐ 1166. TICKELL'S BABBLER *Trichastoma tickelli*
☐ 1167. ABBOTT'S BABBLER *Trichastoma abbotti*
☐ 1173. SLATYHEADED SCIMITAR BABBLER *Pomatorhinus horsfieldii*
☐ 1178. RUFOUSNECKED SCIMITAR BABBLER *Pomatorhinus ruficollis*
☐ 1181. RUSTYCHEEKED SCIMITAR BABBLER *Pomatorhinus erythrogenys*
☐ 1185. LARGE SCIMITAR BABBLER *Pomatorhinus hypoleucos*
☐ 1186. CORALBILLED SCIMITAR BABBLER *Pomatorhinus ferruginosus*
☐ 1189. LLOYD'S SCIMITAR BABBLER *Pomatorhinus ochraceiceps*
☐ 1191. SLENDERBILLED SCIMITAR BABBLER *Xiphirhynchus superciliaris*
☐ 1193. LONGBILLED WREN BABBLER *Rimator malacoptilus*
☐ 1194. STREAKED or SHORT-TAILED WREN-BABBLER *Napothera brevicaudata*
☐ 1195. SMALL WREN-BABBLER *Napothera epilepidota*
☐ 1198. SCALYBREASTED WREN-BABBLER *Pnoepyga albiventer*
☐ 1199. BROWN or LESSER SCALYBREASTED WREN-BABBLER *Pnoepyga pusilla*
☐ 1200. TAILED WREN-BABBLER *Spelaeornis caudatus*
☐ 1201. MISHMI WREN-BABBLER *Spelaeornis badeigularis*
☐ 1202. LONGTAILED WREN-BABBLER *Spelaeornis longicaudatus*

- ☐ 1203. STREAKED LONGTAILED WREN-BAB-BLER *Spelaeornis chocolatinus*
- ☐ 1205. LONGTAILED SPOTTED WREN-BAB-BLER *Spelaeornis troglodytoides*
- ☐ 1206. SPOTTED WREN-BABBLER *Spelaeornis formosus*
- ☐ 1207. WEDGEBILLED WREN *Sphenocichla humei*
- ☐ 1209. REDFRONTED BABBLER *Stachyris rufifrons*
- ☐ 1210. REDHEADED BABBLER *Stachyris ruficeps*
- ☐ 1211. REDBILLED BABBLER *Stachyris pyrrhops*
- ☐ 1212. GOLDHEADED BABBLER *Stachyris chrysaea*
- ☐ 1214. BLACKTHROATED BABBLER *Stachyris nigriceps*
- ☐ 1218. AUSTEN'S SPOTTED BABBLER *Stachyris oglei*
- ☐ 1222. RUFOUSBELLIED BABBLER *Dumetia hyperythra*
- ☐ 1224. BLACKHEADED BABBLER *Rhopocichla atriceps*
- ☐ 1128. YELLOWBREASTED BABBLER *Macronous gularis*
- ☐ 1129. REDCAPPED BABBLER *Timalia pileata*
- ☐ 1231. YELLOWEYED BABBLER *Chrysomma sinense*
- ☐ 1233. JERDON'S BABBLER *Chrysomma altirostre*
- ☐ 1235. BEARDED TIT-BABBLER, or REED-LING *Panurus biarmicus*
- ☐ 1236. GREAT PARROTBILL *Conostoma aemodium*
- ☐ 1237. BROWN SUTHORA or PARROTBILL *Paradoxornis unicolor*
- ☐ 1238. FULVOUSFRONTED SUTHORA or PAR-ROTBILL *Paradoxornis fulvifrons*
- ☐ 1241. ORANGE SUTHORA or BLACKFRONTED PARROTBILL *Paradoxornis nipalensis humii*
- ☐ 1242. ORANGE SUTHORA or PARROTBILL *Paradoxornis nipalensis poliotis*
- ☐ 1246. LESSER REDHEADED SUTHORA or PAR-ROTBILL *Paradoxornis atrosuperciliaris*
- ☐ 1247. GREATER REDHEADED PARROTBILL *Paradoxornis ruficeps*
- ☐ 1249. GREYHEADED PARROTBILL *Paradoxornis gularis*
- ☐ 1251. GOULD'S PARROTBILL *Paradoxornis flavirostris*
- ☐ 1252. WHITETHROATED PARROTBILL *Paradoxornis guttaticollis*
- ☐ 1254. COMMON BABBLER *Turdoides caudatus*
- ☐ 1256. STRIATED BABBLER *Turdoides earlei*
- ☐ 1257. SLENDERBILLED BABBLER *Turdoides longirostris*
- ☐ 1258. LARGE GREY BABBLER *Turdoides malcolmi*
- ☐ 1259. RUFOUS BABBLER *Turdoides subrufus*
- ☐ 1265. JUNGLE BABBLER *Turdoides striatus*
- ☐ 1266. CEYLON RUFOUS BABBLER *Turdoides rufescens*
- ☐ 1267. WHITEHEADED BABBLER *Turdoides affinis*
- ☐ 1269. SPINY BABBLER *Turdoides nipalensis*
- ☐ 1270. CHINESE BABAX *Babax lanceolatus*
- ☐ 1271. GIANT TIBETAN BABAX *Babax waddelli*
- ☐ 1272. ASHYHEADED LAUGHING THRUSH *Garrulax cinereifrons*
- ☐ 1274. WHITETHROATED LAUGHING THRUSH *Garrulax albogularis*
- ☐ 1275. NECKLACED LAUGHING THRUSH *Garrulax moniligerus*
- ☐ 1277. BLACKGORGETED LAUGHING THRUSH *Garrulax pectoralis*
- ☐ 1279. STRIATED LAUGHING THRUSH *Garrulax striatus*
- ☐ 1283. WHITECRESTED LAUGHING THRUSH *Garrulax leucolophus*
- ☐ 1285. CHESTNUTBACKED LAUGHING THRUSH *Garrulax nuchalis*
- ☐ 1286. YELLOWTHROATED LAUGHING THRUSH *Garrulax galbanus*
- ☐ 1287. YELLOWBREASTED LAUGHING THRUSH *Garrulax delesserti*
- ☐ 1290. VARIEGATED LAUGHING THRUSH *Garrulax variegatus*
- ☐ 1291. ASHY LAUGHING THRUSH *Garrulax cineraceus*
- ☐ 1294. RUFOUSCHINNED LAUGHING THRUSH *Garrulax rufogularis*
- ☐ 1299. WHITESPOTTED LAUGHING THRUSH *Garrulax ocellatus*
- ☐ 1300. GREYSIDED LAUGHING THRUSH *Garrulax caerulatus*
- ☐ 1303. RUFOUSNECKED LAUGHING THRUSH *Garrulax ruficollis*
- ☐ 1304. SPOTTEDBREASTED LAUGHING THRUSH *Garrulax merulinus*
- ☐ 1306. WHITEBROWED LAUGHING THRUSH *Garrulax sannio*
- ☐ 1307. NILGIRI LAUGHING THRUSH *Garrulax cachinnans*
- ☐ 1309. WHITEBREASTED LAUGHING THRUSH *Garulax jerdoni*
- ☐ 1314. STREAKED LAUGHING THRUSH *Garrulax lineatus*
- ☐ 1317. MANIPUR STREAKED LAUGHING THRUSH *Garrulax virgatus*
- ☐ 1318. BROWNCAPPED LAUGHING THRUSH *Garrulax austeni*
- ☐ 1319. BLUEWINGED LAUGHING THRUSH *Garrulax squamatus*
- ☐ 1320. PLAINCOLOURED LAUGHING THRUSH *Garrulax subunicolor*
- ☐ 1321. PRINCE HENRI'S LAUGHING THRUSH *Garrulax henrici*
- ☐ 1322. BLACKFACED LAUGHING THRUSH *Garrulax affinis*
- ☐ 1324. REDHEADED LAUGHING THRUSH *Garrulax erythrocephalus*
- ☐ 1331. CRIMSONWINGED LAUGHING THRUSH *Garrulax phoeniceus*
- ☐ 1333. SILVEREARED MESIA *Leiothrix argentauris*
- ☐ 1336. REDBILLED LEIOTHRIX *Leiothrix lutea*
- ☐ 1338. FIRETAILED MYZORNIS *Myzornis pyrrhoura*
- ☐ 1339. NEPAL CUTIA *Cutia nipalensis*

☐ 1340. RUFOUSBELLIED SHRIKE-BABBLER *Pteruthius rufiventer*
☐ 1341. REDWINGED SHRIKE-BABBLER *Pteruthius flaviscapis*
☐ 1343. GREEN SHRIKE-BABBLER *Pteruthius xanthochlorus*
☐ 1345. CHESTNUT-THROATED SHRIKE-BABBLER *Pteruthius melanotis*
☐ 1346. CHESTNUTFRONTED SHRIKE-BABBLER *Pteruthius aenobarbus*
☐ 1347. WHITEHEADED SHRIKE-BABBLER *Gampsorhynchus rufulus*
☐ 1348. SPECTACLED BARWING *Actinodura egertoni*
☐ 1352. HOARY BARWING *Actinodura nipalensis*
☐ 1355. AUSTEN'S BARWING *Actinodura waldeni*
☐ 1357. REDTAILED MINLA *Minla ignotincta*
☐ 1359. BARTHROATED SIVA *Minla strigula*
☐ 1362. BLUEWINGED SIVA *Minla cyanouroptera*
☐ 1365. WHITEBROWED YUHINA *Yuhina castaniceps*
☐ 1366. WHITENAPED YUHINA *Yuhina bakeri*
☐ 1368. YELLOWNAPED YUHINA *Yuhina flavicollis*
☐ 1372. STRIPETHROATED YUHINA *Yuhina gularis*
☐ 1373. RUFOUSVENTED YUHINA *Yuhina occipitalis*
☐ 1374. BLACKCHINNED YUHINA *Yuhina nigrimenta*
☐ 1375. WHITEBELLIED YUHINA *Yuhina xantholeuca*
☐ 1376. GOLDENBREASTED TIT-BARBBLER *Alcippe chrysotis*
☐ 1378. DUSKY-GREEN or YELLOWTHROATED TIT-BABBLER *Alcippe cinerea*
☐ 1379. CHESTNUT-HEADED TIT-BABBLER *Alcippe castaneceps*
☐ 1381. WHITEBROWED TIT-BABBLER *Alcippe vinipectus*
☐ 1385. BROWNHEADED TIT-BABBLER *Alcippe cinereiceps*
☐ 1386. REDTHROATED TIT-BABBLER *Alcippe rufogularis*
☐ 1388. RUFOUSHEADED TIT-BABBLER *Alcippe brunnea*
☐ 1390. QUAKER BABBLER *Alcippe poioicephala*
☐ 1392. NEPAL BABBLER *Alcippe nepalensis*
☐ 1395. CHESTNUTBACKED SIBIA *Heterophasia annectens*
☐ 1396. BLACKCAPPED SIBIA *Heterophasia capistrata*
☐ 1399. GREY SIBIA *Heterophasia gracilis*
☐ 1400. BEAUTIFUL SIBIA *Heterophasia pulchella*
☐ 1401. LONGTAILED SIBIA *Heterophasia picaoides*

Subfamily ***MUSCICAPINAE***: Flycatchers

☐ 1402. OLIVE FLYCATCHER *Rhinomyias brunneata*
☐ 1403. SPOTTED FLYCATCHER *Muscicapa striata*
☐ 1406. SOOTY FLYCATCHER *Muscicapa sibirica*
☐ 1407. BROWN FLYCATCHER *Muscicapa latirostris*
☐ 1408. BROWNBREASTED FLYCATCHER *Muscicapa muttui*

☐ 1409. RUFOUSTAILED FLYCATCHER *Muscicapa ruficauda*
☐ 1410. FERRUGINOUS FLYCATCHER *Muscicapa ferruginea*
☐ 1411. REDBREASTED FLYCATCHER *Muscicapa parva*
☐ 1413. KASHMIR REDBREASTED FLYCATCHER *Muscicapa subrubra*
☐ 1414. ORANGEGORGETED FLYCATCHER *Muscicapa strophiata*
☐ 1415. WHITEGORGETED FLYCATCHER *Muscicapa monileger*
☐ 1417. RUFOUSBREASTED BLUE FLYCATCHER *Muscicapa hyperythra*
☐ 1418. RUSTYBREASTED BLUE FLYCATCHER *Muscicapa hodsonii*
☐ 1419. LITTLE PIED FLYCATCHER *Muscicapa westermanni*
☐ 1421. WHITEBROWED BLUE FLYCATCHER *Muscicapa superciliaris*
☐ 1423. SLATY BLUE FLYCATCHER *Muscicapa leucomelanura*
☐ 1426. SAPPHIREHEADED FLYCATCHER *Muscicapa sapphira*
☐ 1427. BLACK-AND-ORANGE FLYCATCHER *Muscicapa nigrorufa*
☐ 1428. LARGE NILTAVA *Muscicapa grandis*
☐ 1429. SMALL NILTAVA *Muscicapa macgrigoriae*
☐ 1432. RUFOUSBELLIED NILTAVA *Muscicapa sundara*
☐ 1433. RUFOUSBELLIED BLUE FLYCATCHER *Muscicapa vivida*
☐ 1434. WHITETAILED BLUE FLYCATCHER *Muscicapa conreta*
☐ 1435. WHITEBELLIED BLUE FLYCATCHER *Muscicapa pallipes*
☐ 1436. BROOKS'S FLYCATCHER *Muscicapa poliogenys*
☐ 1439. PALE BLUE FLYCATCHER *Muscicapa unicolor*
☐ 1440. BLUETHROATED FLYCATCHER *Muscicapa rubeculoides*
☐ 1441. LARGEBILLED BLUE FLYCATCHER *Muscicapa banyumas*
☐ 1442. TICKELL'S BLUE FLYCATCHER *Muscicapa tickelliae*
☐ 1444. DUSKY BLUE FLYCATCHER *Muscicapa sordida*
☐ 1445. VERDITER FLYCATCHER *Muscicapa thalassina*
☐ 1446. NILGIRI FLYCATCHER *Muscicapa albicaudata*
☐ 1447. PYGMY BLUE FLYCATCHER *Muscicapella hodgsoni*
☐ 1449. GREYHEADED FLYCATCHER *Culicicapa ceylonensis*
☐ 1450. YELLOWBELLIED FANTAIL FLYCATCHER *Rhipidura hypoxantha*
☐ 1451. WHITEBROWED FANTAIL FLYCATCHER *Rhipidura aureola*
☐ 1455. WHITETHROATED FANTAIL FLYCATCHER *Rhipidura albicollis*

☐ 1588. ORANGEBARRED LEAF WARBLER *Phylloscopus pulcher*
☐ 1592. PLAIN or YELLOWBROWED LEAF WARBLER *Phylloscopus inornatus*
☐ 1593. BROOKS'S LEAF WARBLER *Phylloscopus subviridis*
☐ 1594. PALLAS'S LEAF WARBLER *Phylloscopus proregulus*
☐ 1599. GREYFACED LEAF WARBLER *Phylloscopus maculipenis*
☐ 1601. LARGEBILLED LEAF WARBLER *Phylloscopus magnirostris*
☐ 1605. DULL GREEN LEAF WARBLER *Phylloscopus trochiloides*
☐ 1606. LARGE CROWNED LEAF WARBLER *Phylloscopus occipitalis*
☐ 1609. BLYTH'S LEAF WARBLER *Phylloscopus reguloides*
☐ 1612. BLACKBROWED LEAF WARBLER *Phylloscopus cantator*
☐ 1613. ALLIED FLYCATCHER-WARBLER *Seicercus affinis*
☐ 1615. BLACKBROWED FLYCATCHER-WARBLER *Seicercus burkii*
☐ 1617. GREYHEADED FLYCATCHER-WARBLER *Seicercus xeinthoschistos*
☐ 1620. GREYCHEEKED FLYCATCHER-WARBLER *Seicercus poliogenys*
☐ 1621. CHESTNUT-HEADED FLYCATCHER-WARBLER *Abroscopus castaniceps*
☐ 1622. YELLOWBELLIED FLYCATCHER-WARBLER *Abroscopus superciliaris*
☐ 1624. BLACKFACED FLYCATCHER-WARBLER *Abroscopus schisticeps*
☐ 1626. WHITETHROATED FLYCATCHER-WARBLER *Abroscopus albogularis*
☐ 1627. BROADBILLED FLYCATCHER-WARBLER *Abroscopus hodgsoni*
☐ 1629. GOLDCREST *Regulus regulus*
☐ 1632. CRESTED TIT-WARBLER *Leptopoecile elegans*
☐ 1633. STOLICZKA'S TIT-WARBLER *Leptopoecile sophiae*

Subfamily *TURDINAE:* Thrushes and Chats

☐ 1635. GOULD'S SHORTWING *Brachypteryx stellata*
☐ 1636. RUSTYBELLIED SHORTWING *Brachypteryx hyperythra*
☐ 1637. RUFOUSBELLIED SHORTWING *Brachypteryx major*
☐ 1639. LESSER SHORTWING *Brachypteryx leucophrys*
☐ 1640. WHITEBROWED SHORTWING *Brachypteryx montana*
☐ 1641. RUFOUS CHAT *Erythropygia galactotes*
☐ 1642. NIGHTINGALE *Erithacus megarhynchos*
☐ 1643. RUBYTHROAT *Erithacus calliope*
☐ 1644. BLUETHROAT *Erithacus svecicus*
☐ 1647. HIMALAYAN RUBYTHROAT *Erithacus pectoralis*
☐ 1650. BLUE CHAT *Erithacus brunneus*

☐ 1652. FIRETHROAT *Erithacus pectardens*
☐ 1653. SIBERIAN BLUE CHAT *Erithacus cyane*
☐ 1656. ORANGEFLANKED BUSH ROBIN *Erithacus cyanurus*
☐ 1658. GOLDEN BUSH ROBIN *Erithacus chrysaeus*
☐ 1659. WHITEBROWED BUSH ROBIN *Erithacus indicus*
☐ 1660. RUFOUSBELLIED BUSH ROBIN *Erithacus hyperythrus*
☐ 1661. MAGPIE-ROBIN or DHYAL *Copsychus saularis*
☐ 1665. SHAMA *Copsychus malabaricus malabaricus*
☐ 1668. ANDAMAN SHAMA *Copsychus malabaricus albiventris*
☐ 1669. EVERSMANN'S REDSTART *Phoenicurus erythronotus*
☐ 1670. BLUEHEADED REDSTART *Phoenicurus caeruleocephalus*
☐ 1671. KASHMIR BLACK REDSTART *Phoenicurus ochruros phoenicuroides*
☐ 1672. BLACK REDSTART *Phoenicurus ochruros rufiventris*
☐ 1673. REDSTART *Phoenicurus phoenicurus*
☐ 1674. HODGSON'S REDSTART *Phoenicurus hodgsoni*
☐ 1675. BLUEFRONTED REDSTART *Phoenicurus frontalis*
☐ 1676. WHITETHROATED REDSTART *Phoenicurus schisticeps*
☐ 1677. DAURIAN REDSTART *Phoenicurus auroreus*
☐ 1678. GULDENSTADT'S REDSTART *Phoenicurus erythrogaster*
☐ 1679. PLUMBEOUS REDSTART *Rhyacornis fuliginosus*
☐ 1680. HODGSON'S SHORTWING *Hodgsonius phoenicuroide*
☐ 1681. WHITETAILED BLUE ROBIN *Cinclidium leucurum*
☐ 1682. BLUEFRONTED ROBIN *Cinclidium frontale*
☐ 1683. HODGSON'S GRANDALA *Grandala coelicolor*
☐ 1684. LITTLE FORKTAIL *Enicurus scouleri*
☐ 1685. BLACKBACKED FORKTAIL *Enicurus immaculatus*
☐ 1686. SLATYBACKED FORKTAIL *Enicurus schistaceus*
☐ 1687. LESCHENAULT'S FORKTAIL *Enicurus leschenaulti*
☐ 1688. SPOTTED FORKTAIL *Enicurus maculatus*
☐ 1690. PURPLE COCHOA *Cochoa purpurea*
☐ 1691. GREEN COCHOA *Cochoa viridis*
☐ 1692. BROWN ROCK CHAT *Cercomela fusca*
☐ 1693. STOLICZKA'S BUSH CHAT *Saxicola macrorhyncha*
☐ 1694. HODGSON'S BUSH CHAT *Saxicola insignis*
☐ 1697. STONE CHAT *Saxicola torquata*
☐ 1699. WHITETAILED STONE CHAT *Saxicola leucura*
☐ 1700. PIED BUSH CHAT *Saxicola caprata*
☐ 1704. JERDON'S BUSH CHAT *Saxicola jerdoni*
☐ 1705. DARK-GREY BUSH CHAT *Saxicola ferrea*
☐ 1706. ISABELLINE CHAT *Oenanthe isabellina*

☐ 1707. REDTAILED CHAT *Oenanthe xanthoprymna*
☐ 1708. WHEATEAR *Oenanthe oenanthe*
☐ 1710. DESERT WHEATEAR *Oenanthe deserti*
☐ 1711. BARNES'S CHAT *Oenanthe finschi*
☐ 1712. PIED CHAT *Oenanthe picata*
☐ 1713. HOODED CHAT *Oenanthe monacha*
☐ 1714. HUME'S CHAT *Oenanthe alboniger*
☐ 1715. PLESCHANKA'S PIED CHAT or WHEATEAR *Oenanthe pleschanka*
☐ 1716. WHITECAPPED REDSTART or RIVER CHAT *Chaimarrornis leucocephalus*
☐ 1717. (BROWN BACKED) INDIAN ROBIN *Saxicoloides fulicata cambaiensis*
☐ 1720. INDIAN ROBIN *Saxicoloides fulicata*
☐ 1722. ROCK THRUSH *Monticola saxatilis*
☐ 1723. BLUEHEADED ROCK THRUSH *Monticola cinclorhynchus*
☐ 1724. CHESTNUTBELLIED ROCK THRUSH *Monticola rufiventris*
☐ 1726. BLUE ROCK THRUSH *Monticola solitarius*
☐ 1727. CEYLON WHISTLING THRUSH *Myiophonus blighi*
☐ 1728. MALABAR WHISTLING THRUSH *Myiophonus horsfieldii*
☐ 1729. BLUE WHISTLING THRUSH *Myiophonus caeruleus*
☐ 1731. PIED GROUND THRUSH *Zoothera wardii*
☐ 1732. SIBERIAN GROUND THRUSH *Zoothera sibirica*
☐ 1733. ORANGEHEADED GROUND THRUSH *Zoothera citrina*
☐ 1734. WHITETHROATED GROUND THRUSH *Zoothera citrina cyanotus*
☐ 1737. SPOTTEDWINGED GROUND THRUSH *Zoothera spiloptera*
☐ 1739. PLAINBACKED MOUNTAIN THRUSH *Zoothera mollissima*
☐ 1740. LONGTAILED MOUNTAIN THRUSH *Zoothera dixoni*
☐ 1741. GOLDEN or SMALLBILLED MOUNTAIN THRUSH *Zoothera dauma*
☐ 1745. LARGE BROWN THRUSH *Zoothera monticola*
☐ 1746. LESSER BROWN THRUSH *Zoothera marginata*
☐ 1747. BLACKBREASTED THRUSH *Turdus dissimilis*
☐ 1748. TICKELL'S THRUSH *Turdus unicolor*
☐ 1749. WHITECOLLARED BLACKBIRD *Turdus albocinctus*
☐ 1750. GREYWINGED BLACKBIRD *Turdus boulboul*
☐ 1752. BLACKBIRD *Turdus merula maximus*
☐ 1753. BLACKBIRD *Turdus merula nigropileus*
☐ 1755. BLACKBIRD *Turdus merula simillimus*
☐ 1757. BLACKBIRD *Turdus merula kinnisii*
☐ 1758. GREYHEADED THRUSH *Turdus rubrocanus*
☐ 1760. KESSLER'S THRUSH *Turdus kessleri*
☐ 1761. FEA'S THRUSH *Turdus feai*
☐ 1762. DARK THRUSH *Turdus obscurus*
☐ 1763. BLACKTHROATED THRUSH *Turdus ruficollis atrogularis*
☐ 1764. REDTHROATED THRUSH *Turuds ruficollis ruficollis*
☐ 1765. DUSKY THRUSH *Turdus naumanni*
☐ 1766. FIELDFARE *Turdus pilaris*
☐ 1767. REDWING *Turdus illiacus*
☐ 1768. MISTLE THRUSH *Turdus viscivorus*

Family ***TROGLODYTIDAE***: Wrens

☐ 1770. WREN *Troglodytes troglodytes*

Family ***CINCLIDAE***: Dippers

☐ 1773. WHITEBREASTED DIPPER *Cinclos cinclus*
☐ 1775. BROWN DIPPER *Cinclus pallasii*

Family ***PRUNELLIDAE***: Accentors or 'Hedge Sparrows'

☐ 1777. ALPINE ACCENTOR *Prunella collaris*
☐ 1780. ALTAI ACCENTOR *Prunella himalayana*
☐ 1781. ROBIN ACCENTOR *Prunella rubeculoides*
☐ 1783. RUFOUSBREASTED ACCENTOR *Prunella strophiata*
☐ 1784. BROWN ACCENTOR *Prunella fulvescens*
☐ 1785a. (RADDE'S) BROWN ACCENTOR *Prunella fulvescens ocularis*
☐ 1787. BLACKTHROATED ACCENTOR *Prunella atrogularis*
☐ 1787a. SIBERIAN ACCENTOR *Prunella montanella*
☐ 1788. MAROONBACKED ACCENTOR *Prunella immaculata*

Family ***PARIDAE***: Tits or Titmice

☐ 1789. SULTAN TIT *Melanochlora sultanea*
☐ 1794. GREY TIT *Parus major*
☐ 1798. WHITEWINGED BLACK TIT *Parus nuchalis*
☐ 1799. GREENBACKED TIT *Parus monticolus*
☐ 1800. YELLOWBREASTED BLUE TIT or AZURE TIT *Parus cyanus flavipectus*
☐ 1800a. (TIEN SHAN) YELLOWBREASTED BLUE TIT *Parus cyanus tianschanicus*
☐ 1802. CRESTED BLACK TIT *Parus melanolophus*
☐ 1803. COAL TIT *Parus ater*
☐ 1804. BLACK TIT *Parus rfonuchalis*
☐ 1805. RUFOUSBELLIED CRESTED TIT *Parus rubidiventris*
☐ 1808. BROWN CRESTED TIT *Parus dichrous*
☐ 1809. YELLOWCHEEKED TIT *Parus xanthogenys*
☐ 1812. BLACKSPOTTED YELLOW TIT *Parus spilonotus*
☐ 1814. YELLOWBROWED TIT *Sylviparus modestus*
☐ 1815. FIRECAPPED TIT *Cephalopyrus flammiceps*
☐ 1817. PENDULINE TIT *Remiz pendulinus*
☐ 1818, 1819, REDHEADED TIT *Aegithalos concinnus*
☐ 1821. WHITECHEEKED TIT *Aegithalos leucogenys*
☐ 1822. WHITETHROATED TIT *Aegithalos niveogularis*
☐ 1823. RUFOUSFRONTED TIT *Aegithalos iouschistos*

Family *SITTIDAE*: Nuthatches, Creepers

- [ ] 1824. KASHMIR NUTHATCH *Sitta europaea cashmirensis*
- [ ] 1826. EUROPEAN NUTHATCH *Sitta europaea nagaensis*
- [ ] 1830. CHESTNUTBELLIED NUTHATCH *Sitta castanea*
- [ ] 1832. WHITECHEEKED NUTHATCH *Sitta leucopsis*
- [ ] 1834. WHITETAILED NUTHATCH *Sitta himalayensis*
- [ ] 1836. ROCK NUTHATCH *Sitta tephronota*
- [ ] 1837. BEAUTIFUL NUTHATCH *Sitta formosa*
- [ ] 1838. VELVETFRONTED NUTHATCH *Sitta frontalis*
- [ ] 1839. WALL CREEPER *Tichodroma muraria*
- [ ] 1841. SPOTTED GREY CREEPER *Salpornis spilontos*

Family *CERTHIIDAE:* Tree Creepers

- [ ] 1842. TREE CREEPER *Certhia familiaris*
- [ ] 1847. HIMALAYAN TREE CREEPER *Certhia himalayana*
- [ ] 1849. SIKKIM TREE CREEPER *Certhia discolor*
- [ ] 1851. NEPAL TREE CREEPER *Certhia nipalensis*

Family *MOTACILLIDAE*: Pipits and Wagtails

- [ ] 1852. INDIAN TREE PIPIT *Anthus hodgsoni*
- [ ] 1854. TREE PIPIT *Anthus trivialis*
- [ ] 1856. MEADOW PIPIT *Anthus pratensis*
- [ ] 1858. PADDYFIELD PIPIT *Anthus novaeseelandiae*
- [ ] 1861. TAWNY PIPIT *Anthus campestris*
- [ ] 1864. REDTHROATED PIPIT *Anthus cervinus*
- [ ] 1865. VINACEOUSBREASTED PIPIT *Anthus roseatus*
- [ ] 1868. BROWN ROCK PIPIT *Anthus similis*
- [ ] 1870. NILGIRI PIPIT *Anthus nilghiriensis*
- [ ] 1871. WATER PIPIT or ALPINE PIPIT *Anthus spinoletta*
- [ ] 1873. UPLAND PIPIT *Anthus sylvanus*
- [ ] 1874. FOREST WAGTAIL *Motacilla indica*
- [ ] 1876. YELLOW WAGTAIL *Motacilla flava*
- [ ] 1883. YELLOWHEADED WAGTAIL *Motacilla citreola*
- [ ] 1884. GREY WAGTAIL *Motacilla cinerea*
- [ ] 1885,1886. PIED or WHITE WAGTAIL *Motacilla alba*
- [ ] 1891. LARGE PIED WAGTAIL *Motacilla maderaspatensis*

Family *DICAEIDAE:* Flowerpeckers

- [ ] 1892. THICKBILLED FLOWERPECKER *Dicaeum agile*
- [ ] 1895. YELLOWVENTED FLOWERPECKER *Dicaeum chrysorrheum*
- [ ] 1896. YELLOWBELLIED FLOWERPECKER *Dicaeum melanoxanthum*
- [ ] 1897. LEGGE'S FLOWERPECKER *Dicaeum vincens*
- [ ] 1898. ORANGBELLIED FLOWERPECKER *Dicaeum trigonostigma*
- [ ] 1899. TICKELL'S FLOWERPECKER *Dicaeum erythrohynchos*
- [ ] 1902. PLAINCOLOURED FLOWERPECKER *Dicaeum concolor*
- [ ] 1904. SCARLETBACKED FLOWERPECKER *Dicaeum cruentatum*
- [ ] 1905. FIREBREASTED FLOWERPECKER *Dicaeum ignipectus*

Family *NECTARINIIDAE*: Sunbirds, Spiderhunters

- [ ] 1906. RUBYCHEEK *Anthreptes singalensis*
- [ ] 1908. PURPLERUMPED SUNBIRD *Nectarinia zeylonica*
- [ ] 1909. SMALL SUNBIRD *Nectarinia minima*
- [ ] 1910. VAN HASSELT'S SUNBIRD *Nectarinia sperata*
- [ ] 1912. LOTEN'S SUNBIRD *Nectarinia lotenia*
- [ ] 1913. OLIVEBACKED SUNBIRD *Nectarinia jugularis*
- [ ] 1917. PURPLE SUNBIRD *Nectarinia asiatica*
- [ ] 1919. MRS GOULD'S SUNBIRD *Aethopyga gouldiae*
- [ ] 1923. NEPAL YELLOWBACKED SUNBRID *Aethopyga nipalensis*
- [ ] 1925. BLACKBREASTED SUNBIRD *Aethopyga saturata*
- [ ] 1927. YELLOWBACKED SUNBIRD *Aethopyga siparaja*
- [ ] 1930. FIRETAILED SUNBIRD *Aethopyga ignicauda*
- [ ] 1931. LITTLE SPIDERHUNTER *Arachnothera longirostris*
- [ ] 1932. STREAKED SPIDERHUNTER *Arachnothera magna*

Family *ZOSTEROPIDAE*: White-eyes

- [ ] 1933. WHITE-EYE *Zosterops palpebrosa*
- [ ] 1937. CEYLON WHITE-EYE *Zosterops ceylonensis*

Family *PLOCEIDAE*: Weaver Birds

Subfamily *PASSERINAE*: House and Rock Sparrows

- [ ] 1938. HOUSE SPARROW *Passer domesticus*
- [ ] 1940. SPANISH SPARROW *Passer hispaniolensis*
- [ ] 1942. TREE SPARROW *Passer montanus*
- [ ] 1945. SIND JUNGLE SPARROW *Passer pyrrhonotus*
- [ ] 1946. CINNAMON TREE SPARROW *Passer rutilans*
- [ ] 1947a. SCRUB SPARROW, DEAD SEA SPARROW *Passer moabiticus*
- [ ] 1949. YELLOWTHROATED SPARROW *Petronia xanthocollis*
- [ ] 1950. ROCK SPARROW *Petronia petronia*
- [ ] 1951. SNOW FINCH *Montifringilla nivalis*
- [ ] 1952. TIBET SNOW FINCH *Montifringilla adamsi*
- [ ] 1953. MANDELLI'S SNOW FINCH *Montifringilla taczanowskii*

☐ 1954. REDNECKED SNOW FINCH *Montifringilla ruficollis*
☐ 1955. BLANFORD'S SNOW FINCH *Montifringilla blanfordi*
☐ 1956. PERE DAVID'S SNOW FINCH *Montifringilla davidiana*

Subfamily **PLOCEINAE**: Weaver Birds, Bayas

☐ 1957. BAYA *Ploceus philippinus*
☐ 1960. FINN'S BAYA *Ploceus megarhunchus*
☐ 1961. BLACKTHROATED WEAVER BIRD *Ploceus benghalensis*
☐ 1962. STREAKED WEAVER BIRD *Ploceus manyar*

Subfamily **ESTRILDINAE**: Avadavat, Munias

☐ 1964. RED MUNIA, or AVADAVAT *Estrilda amandava*
☐ 1965. GREEN MUNIA *Estrilda formosa*
☐ 1966. COMMON SILVERBILL, WHITE-THROATED MUNIA *Lonchura malabarica*
☐ 1968. WHITEBACKED MUNIA *Lonchura striata*
☐ 1973. RUFOUSBELLIED MUNIA *Lonchura kelaarti*
☐ 1974. NUTMEG MANNIKIN, SPOTTED MUNIA *Lonchura punctulata*
☐ 1978. BLACKHEADED MUNIA *Lonchura malacca*
☐ 1978a. JAVA SPARROW *Padda oryzivora*

Family **FRINGILLIDAE**: Finches

Subfamily **FRINGILLINAE:** Chaffinch

☐ 1979. CHAFFINCH *Fringilla coelebs*
☐ 1980. BRAMBLING *Fringilla montifringilla*

Subfamily **CARDUELINAE**: Rosefinches and Allies

☐ 1981. HAWFINCH *Coccothraustes coccothraustes*
☐ 1982. BLACK-AND-YELLOW GROSBEAK *Coccothraustes icterioides*
☐ 1983. ALLIED GROSBEAK *Coccothraustes affinis*
☐ 1985. WHITEWINGED GROSBEAK *Coccothraustes carnipes*
☐ 1986. SPOTTEDWINGED GROSBEAK *Coccothraustes melanozanthos*
☐ 1989. GOLDFINCH *Carduelis carduelis*
☐ 1990. HIMALAYAN GREENFINCH *Carduelis spinoides*
☐ 1993. TIBETAN SISKIN *Serinus thibetanus*
☐ 1994. LINNET *Acanthis cannabina*
☐ 1995,1996. TWITE *Acanthis flavirostris*
☐ 1997. REDBROWED FINCH *Callacanthis burtoni*
☐ 1998. GOLDFRONTED FINCH *Serinus pusillus*
☐ 2000. HODGSON'S MOUNTAIN FINCH *Leucosticte nemoricola*
☐ 2003. BRANDT'S MOUNTAIN FINCH *Leucosticte brandti*
☐ 2006. TRUMPETER BULLFINCH *Rhodopechys githagineus*
☐ 2007. MONGOLIAN TRUMPETER BULLFINCH *Rhodopechys mongolicus*
☐ 2008. LICHTENSTEIN'S DESERT FINCH *Rhodopechys obsoleta*
☐ 2009. CRIMSONWINGED DESERT FINCH *Rhodopechys sanguinea*

☐ 2013. COMMON ROSEFINCH, SCARLET GROSBEAK *Carpodacus erythrinus*
☐ 2015. NEPAL ROSEFINCH *Carpodacus nipalensis*
☐ 2016. BLANFORD'S ROSEFINCH *Carpodacus rubescens*
☐ 2017. PINKBROWED ROSEFINCH *Carpodacus rhodochrous*
☐ 2017a. VINACEOUS ROSEFINCH *Carpodacus vinaceus*
☐ 2018. REDMANTLED ROSEFINCH *Carpodacus rhodochlamys*
☐ 2019. SPOTTEDWINGED ROSEFINCH *Carpodacus rhodopeplus*
☐ 2021. WHITEBROWED ROSEFINCH *Carpodacus thura*
☐ 2023. BEAUTIFUL ROSEFINCH *Carpodacus pulcherrimus*
☐ 2025. LARGE ROSEFINCH *Carpodacus edwardsii*
☐ 2026. THREEBANDED ROSEFINCH *Carpodacus trifasciatus*
☐ 2027. GREAT ROSEFINCH *Carpodacus rubicilla*
☐ 2028. EASTERN GREAT ROSEFINCH *Carpodacus rubicilloides*
☐ 2031. REDBREASTED ROSEFINCH *Carpodacus puniceus*
☐ 2032. CROSSBILL *Loxia curvirostra*
☐ 2033. REDHEADED ROSEFINCH *Propyrrhula subhimachala*
☐ 2034. SCARLET FINCH *Haematospiza sipahi*
☐ 2035. GOLDHEADED BLACK FINCH *Pyrrhoplectes epauletta*
☐ 2036. BROWN BULLFINCH *Pyrrhula nipalensis*
☐ 2038. BEAVAN'S BULLFINCH *Pyrrhula erythaca*
☐ 2039. REDHEADED BULLFINCH *Pyrrhula erythrocephala*
☐ 2040. ORANGE BULLFINCH *Pyrrhula aurantiaca*

Family **EMBERIZIDAE**: Buntings

☐ 2041. CORN BUNTING *Emberiza calandra*
☐ 2042. PINE BUNTING *Emberiza leucocephalos*
☐ 2043. BLACKHEADED BUNTING *Emberiza melanocephala*
☐ 2044. REDHEADED BUNTING *Emberiza bruniceps*
☐ 2045. CHESTNUT BUNTING *Emberiza rutila*
☐ 2046. YELLOWBREASTED BUNTING *Emberiza aureola*
☐ 2047. BLACKFACED BUNTING *Emberiza spodocephala*
☐ 2048. WHITECAPPED BUNTING *Emberiza stewarti*
☐ 2049. ORTOLAN BUNTING *Emberiza hortulana*
☐ 2050. GREYNECKED BUNTING *Emberiza buchanani*
☐ 2051. ROCK BUNTING *Emberiza cia*
☐ 2055. GREYHEADED BUNTING *Emberiza fucata*
☐ 2056. LITTLE BUNTING *Emberiza pusilla*
☐ 2057. STRIOLATED BUNTING *Emberiza striolata*
☐ 2058. REED BUNTING *Emberiza schoeniclus*
☐ 2060. CRESTED BUNTING *Melophus lathami*

# Picture Credits

Mohit Aggarwal, bird nos: 444, 782. Ravi Agarwal, bird no 484. Ashish Chandola, bird nos 28, 46, 401, 1322. RS Chundawat, bird no 1697. Ashok Dilwali, viii–ix, xxi, xxv, bird nos 42, 73, 90, 255, 506, 542, 776, 847, 1109, 1120, 1461. RK Gaur xxix, bird nos 20, 55, 62, 63, 67, 82, 93, 94, 105, 115, 214, 247, 294, 321, 326, 343, 347, 366, 545, 921, 952, 1002, 1274, 1283, 1525, 1671, 1710, 1883, 1962, 1990, 2027, 2052, 2060. Sharad Gaur, bird nos 360, 432, 1886. Bikram Grewal, bird nos 238, 396, 899, 977. Gulmohur Press, xii, xiv, xvi, xvii, xviii, xxiv (top), xxviii, xxxiv, xxxv.

R.Fotomedia, New Delhi: Ashish Chandola, bird no 173. Rupin Dang, bird nos 285, 774, 777, 1027, 1106, 1333, 1336, 1932. R Dev, bird nos 27, 37. Ashim Ghosh, xix, bird no 1692. Dr Katiyar, bird no 1538. BN Khazanchi, bird no 97. E Hanumantha Rao, bird nos 21, 29, 66, 100, 301, 311, 350, 397, 430, 437, 535, 550, 755, 940, 1254, 1899. Hashim Tyabji, bird no 744. Joanna Van Gruisen, bird nos 5, 88, 232, 788, 1115.

Porpoise Photostock bird no 763, 958, 1911; IA Babu, bird nos 44, 49, 52, 61, 463, 750. B Das Gupta, bird nos 50, 388, 455, 513, 600, 1128. MI Fernandes, bird no 1734. Karuna Karan x–xi. MK Kuppuraj, bird nos 161, 380, 440, 1098, 1138, 1858. Premendo Lad, bird no 867. Sunjoy Monga, bird nos 182, 252, 314, 963, 996, 1029, 1049, 1781, 1957. Rishad Naoroji, xxvii, bird nos 139, 163, 168, 219, 359, 492. AK Raju, bird nos 188, 573, 719, 735, 1032, 1511, 1517, 1700, 1876. H Satish, bird no 178. Krupakar Senani, bird nos 124, 370, 503, 537, 541, 623, 709, 722, 753, 798, 804, 808, 850, 861, 914, 967, 988, 1015, 1078, 1081 (both), 1093, 1154, 1222, 1231, 1389, 1442, 1442, 1458, 1498, 1661, 1665, 1809, 1830, 1838, 1884, 1909, 1917, 1931, 1933, 1949, 1964, 1966, 1974, 1978. Ravi Shekaran, bird no 357.

Sanctuary Magazine: EK Bharucha, bird no 1907. Gertrud Denzau, bird nos 196, 389, 606, 682, 767, 878, 1644. EP Eric D'Cunha, bird nos 973, 1103. MK Kuppuraj, bird no 318. Premendu Lad, bird no 627. TNA Perumal, bird nos 657, 1891. Trevor Price, bird nos 1411, 1650.

Kamal Sahai xxiv (bottom), xxxviii, bird nos 26, 157, 186, 222, 236, 323, 325, 339, 496, 590, 652, 739, 792, 933, 946, 1794. Sondeep Shankar, xv. Toby Sinclair, vi–vii, xix (bottom), xx, xxiii, bird nos 38, 60, 70, 72, 130, 133, 135, 174, 246, 558, 571, 578, 588, 675, 994, 1008, 1054, 1070, 1125, 1148, 1265, 1314, 1419, 1445, 1449, 1705, 1717, 1729, 1763, 1965. Joanna Van Gruisen, title page, xxii, xxx, bird nos 5, 36, 69, 188, 227, 282, 290, 299, 349, 354, 358, 393, 404, 429, 436, 458, 487, 727, 730, 877, 897, 1046, 1451, 1465, 1566, 1678, 1722, 1773, 1784, 1815, 1946, 1982, 1998, 2013.

# Nomenclature

Given below are some alternate names to those in current use throughout the Indian region.

| Common Name | Alternate Name | Common Name | Alternate Name |
|---|---|---|---|
| 27. Indian Shag | Indian Cormorant | 819. Lesser Goldenbacked Woodpecker | Black-rumped Flameback |
| 36. Little Green Heron | Striated Heron | 824. Himalayan Goldenbacked Threetoed Woodpecker | Himalayan Flameback |
| 46. Large Egret | Great Egret | | |
| 56. Chestnut Bittern | Cinnamon Bittern | 825. Indian Goldenbacked Threetoed Woodpecker | Common Flameback |
| 62. White-necked Stork | Woolly-necked Stork | 830. Indian Great Black Woodpecker | White-bellied Woodpecker |
| 62. Adjutant Stork | Greater Adjutant | | |
| 69. White Ibis | Black-headed Ibis | 847. Yellowfronted Pied Woodpecker | Yellow-crowned Woodpecker |
| 70. Black Ibis | Red-naped Ibis | | |
| 73. Flamingo | Greater Flamingo | 850. Grey crowned Pygmy Woodpecker | Grey-capped Woodpecker |
| 88. Lesser Whistling Teal | Lesser Whistling-Duck | | |
| 89. Large Whistling Teal | Fulvous Whistling-Duck | 852. Brown Crowned Pygmy Woodpecker | Brown-capped Woodpecker |
| 97. Spotbill | Spot-billed Duck | | |
| 114. Cotton Teal | Cotton Pygmy-Goose | 862. Large Goldenbacked Woodpecker | Greater Flameback |
| 127. Black-crested Baza | Black Baza | | |
| 133. Pariah Kite | Black Kite | 877. Redwinged Bush Lark | Indian Lark |
| 161. Crested Hawk-Eagle | Changeable Hawk-Eagle | 878. Ashycrowned Finch Lark | Ashy-crowned Sparrow-Lark |
| 164. Booted Hawk-Eagle | Booted Eagle | | |
| 173. Whitebellied Sea Eagle | White-bellied Fish-Eagle | 902. Syke's Crested Lark | Tawny Lark |
| 174. Pallas's Fishing Eagle | Pallas's Sea-Eagle | 916. Rufousbacked Shrike | Long-tailed Shrike |
| 177. Himalayan Greyheaded Fishing Eagle | Lesser Fish-Eagle | 958. Blackheaded Oriole | Black-hooded Oriole |
| | | 982. Ashy Swallow-Shrike | Ashy Wood-Swallow |
| 195. Short-toed Eagle | Short-toed Snake-Eagle | 987. Greyheaded Myna | Chestnut-tailed Starling |
| 219. Red headed Merlin | Red-necked Falcon | 994. Brahminy Myna | Brahminy Starling |
| 238. Black Partridge | Black Francolin | 996. Rosy Pastor | Rosy Starling |
| 241. Painted Partridge | Painted Francolin | 1022. Blackthroated Jay | Black-headed Jay |
| 246. Grey Partridge | Grey Francolin | 1025. Yellow-billed Blue Magpie | Gold-billed Magpie |
| 329. Bluebreasted Banded Rail | Slaty-breasted Rail | 1027. Redbilled Blue Magpie | Blue Magpie |
| | | 1029. Whiterumped Magpie | Black-billed Magpie |
| 349. Purple Moorhen | Purple Swamphen | 1032. Indian Tree Pie | Rufous Treepie |
| 369. Spurwinged Lapwing | River Lapwing | 1054. Indian Jungle Crow | Large-billed Crow |
| 437. Great Stone Plover | Great Thick-Knee | 1103. Goldenfronted Choloropsis | Golden-Fronted Leafbird |
| 487. Indian Sandgrouse | Chestnut-bellied Sandgrouse | | |
| | | 1106. Orangebellied Chloropsis | Orange-bellied Leafbird |
| 489. Imperial Sandgrouse | Black-bellied Sandgrouse | 1107. Goldmantled Chloropsis | Blue-winged Leafbird |
| 490. Grey Fronted Green Pigeon | Pompadour Green-Pigeon | 1125. Whitecheeked Bulbul | Himalayan Bulbul |
| | | 1154. Spotted Babbler | Puff-throated Babbler |
| 531. Rufous Turtle Dove | Oriental Turtle-Dove | 1222. Rufousbellied Babbler | Tawny-bellied Babbler |
| 534. Indian Ring Dove | Eurasian Collared-Dove | 1228. Yellowbreasted Babbler | Striped Tit-Babbler |
| 535. Red Turtle Dove | Red Collared-Dove | 1267. Whiteheaded Babbler | Yellow-billed Babbler |
| 541. Little Brown Dove | Laughing Dove | 1307. Nilgiri Laughing Thrush | Rufous-breasted Laughingthrush |
| 558. Blossomheaded Parakeet | Plum-headed Parakeet | | |
| 564. Bluewinged Parakeet | Malabar Parakeet | 1309. White Breasted Laughing Thrush | Grey-breasted Laughingthrush |
| 566. Indian Lorikeet | Vernal Hanging-Parrot | | |
| 584. Indian Plaintive Cuckoo | Grey-bellied Cuckoo | 1358. Barthroated Siva | Chestnut-tailed Minla |
| 598. Sirkeer Cuckoo | Sirkeer Malkoha | 1368. Yellownaped Yuhina | Whiskered Yuhina |
| 630. Dusky Horned Owl | Dusky Eagle-Owl | 1380. Whitebrowed Tit-Babbler | White-browed Fulvetta |
| 671. Indian Jungle Nightjar | Grey Nightjar | 1389. Quaker Babbler | Brown-cheeked Fulvetta |
| 682. Franklin's Nightjar | Savanna Nightjar | 1398. Blackcapped Sibia | Rufous Sibia |
| 685. Indian Edible-Nest Swiftlet | Indian Swiftlet | 1409. Rufoustailed Flycatcher | Rusty-tailed Flycatcher |
| | | 1421. White browed Blue Flycatcher | Ultramarine Flycatcher |
| 699. Large Whiterumped Swift | Fork-tailed Swift | | |
| 703. House Swift | Little Swift | 1433. Rufousbellied Blue Flycatcher | Snowy-browed Flycatcher |
| 717. Himalayan Pied Kingfisher | Crested Kingfisher | | |
| 727. Indian Threetoed Kingfisher | Black-backed Kingfisher | 1448. Greyheaded Flycatcher | Grey-headed Canary-Flycatcher |
| | | 1465. Blacknaped Flycatcher | Black-naped Monarch |
| 735. Whitebreasted Kingfisher | White-Throated Kingfisher | 1478. Strongfooted Bush Warbler | Brownish-flanked Bush-Warbler |
| | | | |
| 777. Great Himalayan Barbet | Great Barbet | 1498. Streaked Fantail Warbler | Zitting Cisticola |
| 782. Large Green Barbet | Brown-headed Barbet | 1503. Franklin's Wren-Warbler | Grey-breasted Prinia |
| 785. Small Green Barbet | White-cheeked Barbet | 1506. Rufousfronted Wren-Warbler | Rufous-fronted Prinia |
| 790. Crimsonthroated Barbet | Crimson-Breasted Barbet | | |
| | | 1508. Streaked Wren-Warbler | Graceful Prinia |
| 794. Orangerumped Honeyguide | Yellow-rumped Honeyguide | 1511. Plain Wren-Warbler | Plain Prinia |
| | | 1517. Ashy Wren-Warbler | Ashy Prinia |
| 808. Little Scalybellied Green Woodpecker | Streak-throated Woodpecker | 1523. Yellowbellied Wren-Warbler | Yellow-bellied Prinia |
| | | 1527. Brown Hill Warbler | Striated Prinia |
| 807. Blacknaped Green Woodpecker | Grey Faced Woodpecker | 1531. Longtailed Grass Warbler | Rufous-vented Prinia |

| Common Name | Alternate Name | Common Name | Alternate Name |
|---|---|---|---|
| 1548.Striated Marsh Warbler | Striated Grassbird | 1848 Sikkim Tree Creeper | Brown-throated Tree-Creeper |
| 1550.Indian Great Reed Warbler | Clamorous Reed-Warbler | 1851.Nepal Tree Creeper | Rusty-flanked Tree-Creeper |
| 1614.Blackbrowed Flycatcher-Warbler | Golden-spectacled Warbler | 1852.Indian Tree Pipit | Olive-backed Pipit |
| 1616.Greyheaded Flycatcher-Warbler | Grey-hooded Warbler | 1881.Yellowheaded Wagtail | Citrine Wagtail |
| 1620.Greycheeked Flycatcher-Warbler | Grey-cheeked Warbler | 1891.Large Pied Wagtail | White-browed Wagtail |
| 1637.Rufousbellied Shortwing | White-bellied Shortwing | 1899.Tickell's Flowerpecker | Pale-billed Flowerpecker |
| 1650.Blue Chat | Indian Blue Robin | 1901.Plaincoloured Flowerpecker | Plain Flowerpecker |
| 1665.Shama | White-rumped Shama | 1906.Rubycheek | Ruby-cheeked Sunbird |
| 1678.Guldenstadt's Redstart | White-winged Redstart | 1909.Small Sunbird | Crimson-backed Sunbird |
| 1692.Brown Rock Chat | Indian Chat | 1911.Loten's Sunbird | Long-billed Sunbird |
| 1700.Dark-Grey Bush Chat | Grey Bushchat | 1927.Yellowbacked Sunbird | Crimson Sunbird |
| 1706.Isabelline Chat | Isabelline Wheatear | 1946.Cinnamon Tree Sparrow | Russet Sparrow |
| 1712.Pied Chat | Variable Wheatear | 1949.Yellowthroated Sparrow | Chestnut-shouldered Petronia |
| 1716.Whitecapped Redstart | White-capped Water-Redstart | 1966.Whitethroated Munia | White-throated Silverbill |
| 1723.Blueheaded Rockthrush | Blue-capped Rock-Thrush | 1968.Whitebacked Munia | White-rumped Munia |
| 1794.Grey Tit | Great Tit | 1974.Spotted Munia | Scaly-breasted Munia |
| 1798.Whitewinged Black Tit | White-naped Tit | 1983.Allied Grosbeak | Collared Grosbeak |
| 1802.Crested Black Tit | Black-crested Tit | 1990.Himalayan Greenfinch | Yellow-breasted Greenfinch |
| 1804.Simla Black Tit | Dark-grey Tit | 1998.Goldfronted Finch | Fire-fronted Serin |
| 1809.Yellowcheeked Tit | Black-lored Tit | 2003.Brandt's Mountain Finch | Black-headed Mountain-Finch |
| 1812.Blackspotted Yellow Tit | Yellow-cheeked Tit | 2028.Eastern Great Rosefinch | Streaked Rosefinch |
| 1818.Redheaded Tit | Black-throated Tit | 2032.Crossbill | Red Crossbill |
| 1841.Spotted Grey Creeper | Spotted Creeper | 2035.Goldheaded Black Finch | Gold-naped Finch |
| 1847.Himalayan Tree Creeper | Bar-tailed Tree-Creeper | 2048.Whitecapped Bunting | Chestnut-breasted Bunting |
| | | 2055.Greyheaded Bunting | Chestnut-eared Bunting |
| | | 2057.Striolated Bunting | House Bunting |

# Index of Scientific Names

# Index of Common Names